Following the Gospel Through the Year

Raymond Chapman is Emeritus Professor of English in the University of London and a non-stipendiary priest in the Diocese of Southwark. A Deputy Chairman of the Prayer Book Society, he is the author of numerous literary and religious titles, including the bestselling *Leading Intercessions – Prayers for Sundays, Holy Days and Festivals.* He lives in Barnes, London.

Following the Gospel Through the Year

*Reflections on the Gospels
for Sundays and Holy Days
Years A, B and C*

Raymond Chapman

CANTERBURY
PRESS

Norwich

First published in 2001 by The Canterbury Press Norwich
(a publishing imprint of Hymns Ancient & Modern Limited
a registered charity)
St Mary's Works, St Mary's Plain
Norwich, Norfolk NR3 3BH

British Library Cataloguing in Publication data

A catalogue record of this book is available
from the British Library

ISBN 1-85311-436-7

Typeset by Rowland Phototypesetting Ltd,
Bury St Edmunds, Suffolk
Printed and bound in Great Britain by
Biddles Ltd, Guildford and King's Lynn

Contents

Introduction

The adoption of the Revised Common Lectionary by many churches has brought a new pattern to the readings at Sunday services.

For the principal service on Sundays, which is usually but need not be eucharistic, there are three readings: one is from the Old Testament or Apocrypha and is followed by a psalm; one is from the New Testament; and one is the Gospel for the day. The readings are in a three-year cycle, with continuous reading from one of the Synoptic Gospels in a year, and additional readings from the Fourth Gospel.

The Sundays after Trinity give a choice of two tracks. Track 1 has continuous reading through certain Old Testament books; track 2 has selective Old Testament readings to link with the Gospel. The Psalm is linked with Old Testament readings in both tracks. The New Testament reading is continuous through the Epistles.

The Revised Common Lectionary thus ensures that there will be an Old Testament reading, which has so often been omitted in recent eucharistic lectionaries, and restores the Early Church principle of *lectio continua* – continuous reading through an Epistle or Gospel instead of moving weekly from one book to another. The sequence emphasizes the ongoing rhythm of the Christian year from Advent to Trinity, an understanding much needed today when there is a social anticipation of the feasts of Christmas and Easter and little attention is paid to others. Further, the continuous reading of a Gospel allows the narrative to unfold in sequence and brings understanding of the distinctive style and approach of the different Evangelists. More meaning is given to the Sundays of 'Ordinary Time' outside the special seasons.

To assist with the reading of a Gospel through each year, a short introduction to the work of the Evangelists is included in this book. Reflections on the principal seasons of the Church offer a devotional introduction to the specific passages for each year.

Introduction

A section has been given to every Sunday over the three-year cycle and to the principal holy days. In some cases, the Church of England provision has been followed when it is different from that of the Revised Common Lectionary. Each section is introduced by a sentence or two that may suggest a link between the Old Testament reading – following track 2 in the Trinity season – and the Gospel.

The passage for the day is throughout based on a verse or two from its Gospel, short enough to focus attention and to aid subsequent memory. However, it is recommended that the whole Gospel passage should be read in connection with it. For further reflection, the original meditation is followed by a quotation from another author, mostly chosen from writers who have formed the classic tradition of Christian devotion but also including a few living authors. I have modernized spelling and punctuation where necessary but have retained the usage of the original authors in such matters as capital letters for the divine pronouns and the generic use of masculine forms. Authors are cited using the names by which they are best known, without titles or other ascriptions. A short prayer follows, with a penitential and petitionary reference to the Gospel theme, in a form designed primarily for private devotion but which can readily be adapted for collective use.

It is hoped that this book will be helpful to those charged with public preaching or the preparation of written devotional material based on the yearly readings. They may find something here to start their own response and to be rendered in their individual styles. Those who lead the intercessions in the service may also find ideas to incorporate in their prayers.

But this book is not only for the leaders of worship. It goes out with the desire that private devotions may be more enriched by the guidance and rhythm of the Church lectionary and that it may open some ways into a deeper relationship with Jesus Christ whose gospel is proclaimed when Christians gather for worship.

The Four Gospels

The first three Gospels are known as the Synoptic Gospels; *synoptic* means 'seen together', and the Gospels have much in common which makes it easy to compare them. Each in turn provides the principal readings for a year of the three-year cycle, and this gives an opportunity to become familiar with their distinctive qualities and the way in which they portray Jesus and his teaching. It is generally accepted that Mark was the first Gospel to be written and that Matthew and Luke are based on it. There was probably a source of other sayings of Jesus which they both used, and each of them has material found only in his own record. Certainly oral accounts of the life of Jesus were being used as a basis for preaching before the first written versions were made.

Matthew was the Gospel most highly regarded in the Early Church, and was believed to be the earliest. It stands first in the New Testament and is the Gospel of Year A. Tradition identifies the author with Matthew the tax collector who was called to be one of the disciples (Matthew 9:9), though it was more likely written by an unknown author in Syrian Antioch. The Gospel begins with an account of the Nativity different from that in Luke, which gives emphasis to the role of Joseph and includes the story of the Magi. Matthew follows the ministry of Jesus from his baptism to his Passion, the sections of narrative being set around five main collections of the teaching. Its special value is the fullness of its account of the teaching which Jesus gave, including the long discourse known as the Sermon on the Mount. Matthew makes a strong point of how Jesus fulfils the Jewish expectations and gives the New Law to replace the Old. He seems to have been writing for both Jewish and Gentile Christians, assuring the former that Jesus is the Messiah and the latter that all nations are included in the Kingdom. He makes provision for some of the problems that were already occurring in the new community, such

as litigation between believers and questions about divorce (18:15–
18; 19:9). The Passion narrative is notable for the repentance and
suicide of Judas, and the dream of Pilate's wife. The Resurrection
appearances are preceded by a great earthquake and an angel opening
the tomb, to the terror of the guard set to watch it. The disciples are
told to return to Galilee to meet their risen Lord. There is no account
of the Ascension, though it is implied in the final commission to the
disciples to preach and baptize throughout the world and the promise
that their Lord will be always with them. Matthew has much to say
of the cost and obligations of discipleship, and the universal blessing
of the gospel.

Mark, read in Year B, is the shortest of the Gospels. An early
tradition assigns it to John Mark, the companion of St Paul. He is
said to have been with St Peter in Rome and to have set down his
memories of Jesus. Certainly Mark, followed by the other synoptic
writers, does not spare the faults of the Twelve, especially Peter. He
may have been the young man who fled naked from Gethsemane
(14:51–52), leaving a kind of personal signature in the narrative.
Mark has no Nativity story, but begins with a proclamation of the
gospel, the good news of Jesus Christ, and the preaching of John the
Baptist. There is less of the direct teaching of Jesus than in Matthew.
This Gospel moves quickly from one episode to another – 'immediately' is one of Mark's favourite words – but it is not loose and
unstructured. It makes much of the growing conflict between Jesus
and the authorities and his greater conflict with the powers of evil.
Jesus is presented as a hidden Messiah, ordering those whom he heals
to keep silent and warning the disciples not to reveal his true identity
(8.30).The account of the Passion is particularly stark and sombre
and the Resurrection appearances are not described in the earliest
manuscripts, which end with the words that the women at the tomb
said nothing to anyone because they were afraid. Mark seems to have
writing for Gentile readers, for he often explains Jewish customs. He
occasionally gives the exact words that Jesus used in Aramaic (e.g.
5:41; 7:34), translating them into the Greek which was the inter-
national tongue of the time. In Year B we are drawn close to the
humanity of Jesus before his divinity is revealed, and to the fallibility
of his followers who are yet sustained in faith.

Luke, the author of the Gospel for Year C, was with St Paul on
some of his missionary journeys and wrote the Acts of the Apostles,
which tells the story of the beginning of the Christian Church. He is

described as a physician (Colossians 4:14) and he is often precise about some of the diseases which are miraculously healed. He is clearly a man of some culture, acquainted with both Jewish and Gentile society, who writes elegant Greek and is a skilful narrator. At the beginning of his Gospel he declares his intention of writing 'an orderly account' of the life of Jesus (1:4). He knew Mark (Colossians 4:10; Philemon 24) and used much of his material. He gives the fullest account of the Nativity, including the devotional songs attributed to Zechariah, Mary and Simeon, and the only record of the Ascension. He tells of Pilate sending Jesus to Herod, and the Resurrection appearance on the road to Emmaus. He also adds an extended account of the journey of Jesus from Galilee to Jerusalem after the Transfiguration. He relates some of the longest and best-known parables of Jesus, such as those that are popularly known as the Good Samaritan and the Prodigal Son. He gives us the fullest account of the life of Jesus, emphasizing his compassion for the afflicted and for the outcasts of society, a tenderness shown on Calvary in the promise to the penitent thief. Luke has much to say of the power of the Spirit in the ministry of Jesus, which leads towards the account of Pentecost in Acts.

John raises even more questions than the Synoptic Gospels. His account stands apart from them in not following the same common sources and having a different chronology of the events in the life of Jesus. There are no Nativity stories, and the Gospel begins with a prologue, which declares Jesus to be the eternal Word of God from the beginning, made incarnate for human salvation. The writer refers to himself as 'the disciple whom Jesus loved' and claims to be a reliable eye-witness of the events he records. Traditionally he has been identified as John son of Zebedee, one of the twelve disciples, though others may have edited his work. Whoever wrote the Gospel, his method is different from that of the Synoptics. He includes no parables but records at length the sayings of Jesus, particularly those supposed to have been given after the Last Supper before the Passion. He is a sophisticated writer, marking the narrative with specific 'signs' in some of the miracles and giving to Jesus significant utterances beginning with 'I am'. He makes much of the image of light, from the prologue onwards, and of the necessity of faith in Jesus as Son of God, one with the Father. He says little of Galilee and sets most of his account in Jerusalem, but places the last of the Resurrection appearances by the Sea of Galilee. John has sometimes been called the 'spiritual Gospel', but this should not make the reader neglect the importance of his relation of facts and the specific settings which he gives to many events. In the cycle of the current lectionary, passages from this Gospel are sometimes included in order to give additional emphasis to certain elements in the teaching of Jesus.

The Seasons of the Year

Advent

Waiting is something that we regard at best as a waste of time that could be well employed, and at worst as an experience of growing impatience, anger or anxiety. Buses come along on every route except the one we want; the doctor takes excessive time over every patient before us in the waiting-room; post after post does not bring a decision on the job application. Waiting is a bitter word, waiting is a curse in an age when we live by the clock and there always seems to be too much to do.

Waiting is a holy word. It is a Bible word. The Old Testament is a 1000-year record of waiting for the coming of the Messiah, for the Day of the Lord when his power and glory would be revealed to all nations. The New Testament tells of the coming of Jesus Christ, the true Messiah for all people, whose followers must in their turn learn to wait. The Twelve had to wait for the coming of the Holy Spirit before they began the work on the new Church, and those who came to faith through their word, then and in the ages that followed, wait for the return of their Lord to judge the world and make all things new. Waiting is God's word.

Advent is a celebration of waiting. It looks both back and forward – back to the old prophecies of the Messiah, forward to the Second Coming. Its human images are the prophets: Isaiah; John the Baptist – the forerunner, the messenger of the Lord, the prophetic voice in the wilderness; the Blessed Virgin Mary, waiting for the promised son who was the Son of God. We honour their witness, we try to share their patient trust.

A candle is lit on each of the Sundays in Advent. Week by week, the Light is coming into the world. A few days stand for the centuries of waiting, as the light grows stronger until it reaches its climax with the fifth candle of Christmas.

Advent is a bridge time, a threshold time. It is for the whole Church what certain times are in individual lives as they move from one phase to another. It is the time of movement from a world that did not know Christ to one on which Incarnate God had walked.

It is a time to look forward, not only to the celebration of the Nativity, but farther to the last things, to death, judgement, heaven and hell. It is to the threshold between life in this world and death that we direct our thoughts. We look back to what has been, and forward to what must be, the unfashionable contemplation of our own death and its meaning for a Christian. In the Advent candles we see the light coming into the world. In meditation on death we see also the end of all things when the divine purpose is accomplished. Advent is a strange time, a time of paradox and creative tension.

How are we to think of these things at one of the busiest times of the year, when Christmas presses upon us in our families, at work, in every shop, every newspaper? This is a time to find the still centre of devotion, the time, short enough though it may be, to keep still and contemplative, to think on these mysteries of past and future. It is almost impossible to avoid completely the social anticipation of Christmas, and we need not be too hard on ourselves or our friends in this matter. But it is still possible to keep a kind of little Lent, to forego some little indulgence and above all to make some extra devotion, particularly reflection on those last things. Advent is so much neglected, so often wasted.

The great cycle of the Christian year begins again, as we wait for the Lord whose incarnate life we shall follow from birth to death and beyond. It is the new year of the Church, a solemn beginning, a happy beginning.

They that wait upon the Lord shall renew their strength. They shall mount up with wings like eagles. They shall run and not be weary. They shall walk and not faint.

Isaiah 40:31

The best is at the end – the patient walking, the waiting that does not lose heart.

Christmas

The high point of the year for children, and for many adults who will not openly admit that there is more to it than eating and drinking. The season of goodwill – but does that mean that the rest of the year is a long season of ill will? What does that say of our usual feelings towards our fellow men and women? What is it that calls us to make even such lip-service to God's demand of love?

It is the hallowing of pagan mysteries, the search for hope when the night is long and the sun seems to be fading away. A time to shut the doors, light the fire and keep out the powers of darkness. It is not the anniversary of a birth, for God left no record of the moment of his human birth. We do not know at what time of the year the great miracle happened in Bethlehem. Not a birthday, and yet a beginning, though what was begun had been from the beginning, before the beginning of human knowledge. It was a beginning that has been made new in every trusting soul from then until now and beyond.

Images of the stable throng around us on cards and pictures and church windows. There must be an ox, an ass – not too many or the proportions will be spoiled – and a more generous allowance of sheep following their shepherds. There must be angels, suspended above the thatched roof or under it. The Wise Men, three in number and elevated to kings with their attendants, must be fitted in, though their visit was not on that first night of wonder. The piety of the Middle Ages still creates the images for eyes little accustomed to stable life. The nineteenth century, heartily pioneered by Charles Dickens, sets up a rival scene, bustling with stage coaches in the snow and lighted inn windows, with perhaps a church in the distance to give a blessing to all this unaccustomed goodwill. And if there is snow, the picture can be simplified to a winsome robin.

Houses lit and decorated pay their homage to the great act of divine love. Inside, is there deeper human love in return, or the strain of extra spending, enforced idleness and the coming of the unwelcome ones seldom seen? Do the dark powers sometimes gain their entry through the door that should be ready to welcome the Christ Child?

It is a great muddle, a confused attempt to give expression to the inexpressible, and surely the Christ Child enters if there is even the least articulate sense that this is something more than another Bank

7

Holiday. If we tell them that this is the fulfilment of the Messianic promises, the incarnation of the Son of God, the confusion will seem more confused. Look through the tinsel gaiety and the alcoholic haze to see the basic, the simple, the incredible, the true. Perhaps we can understand and give our neighbours the understanding that the time of waiting is over, God has come to his people not as a remote king but as one of them. It is indeed a high time of the year, for those who will receive it as little children.

Epiphany

The end of the Christmas festivities, when the dusty decorations are taken down and the dry needles are swept up where the Christmas tree stood. A reluctant return to the routine of work in a cold month with half the winter still to come. A time to pick up the bills and worry about the abused digestion.

So it seems to many people but our pattern of worship has rediscovered the celebration of the Incarnation for a longer time. Forty days from Christmas to the Feast of the Presentation, forty days to make a pattern of faith with the forty days of Lent and the forty days of Easter. The Epiphany season is a time of continuing glory, when the light that shone around the shepherds in the fields near Bethlehem is shown in the wonderful life that began that night. Epiphany means a showing forth, a revelation and we follow the life of Jesus through his baptism, his first miracle at Cana, the calling of his disciples and the beginning of his ministry. Light shines in a cold season and the people of God sing his praises and worship him in the beauty of holiness.

Lent

After the pleasure, we count the cost: a pessimistic assumption that a good time has to be paid for in some material way. After Christmas and Epiphany, joy in the light that has come into the world, we count the cost. Not a cost that we can ever pay, not one that brings any regret for the time of rejoicing. The price was paid, once for all, by the Child of the manger who grew to be the Man of the Cross.

Lent is not a time for putting self at the centre. It is a time to focus more acutely on the life of Christ, his Passion and death, before we turn again to the unqualified joy of his Resurrection. The result is inevitable; the gulf between the reality of our lives and the sacrificial love of Christ is seen in its full extent. If we start from him, and not from the self, penitence is less likely to be marred by the false humility that can end in self-importance.

Now shall life be committed more deeply, more thoughtfully, more prayerfully, to the faith that has already been embraced. Forty days to be joined with the great forties of the Bible, where days and years are all one in the divine purpose. Moses communes with God on the mountain for forty days, and leads his people through the wilderness for forty years. Elijah goes forty days in the strength of divine feeding, to reach his own encounter with God. There are times of wandering and uncertainty, times of growth and discernment. Jesus, forty days in the wilderness, hungry, weary and tempted, draws them into the example of the yearly time of Lent. There are journeys that lead to the place where God's will must be done and his presence more fully known. Jesus, walking from Galilee, through Samaria to Jerusalem, walking the last steps to Calvary, draws them into a meaning for the human journeys of every human life.

Forty days of sorrow for our sins, and deep sorrow for the reality of sin itself, the alienation from God, the rebellion that stirs sometimes even in the faithful heart. There are those who would deny the seriousness of sin, even those in our churches who hope to please society and make more converts by playing down its dreadful reality. It is a hope that is well meaning, but wrong in seeming to undercut the cost which we should pay if Jesus had not paid it for us. It is sadly true that too many Christians have suffered, in Lent and at other times, from a burden of guilt. Repentance that does not bring release from guilt is not complete; it is a failure to accept the fullness of God's pardoning grace. It is not that the Church has been too obsessed with sin, but rather that she has not always freed her members from the burden of guilt. Sinners who know the reality of their pardoned sin are those who best know what St Paul calls the glorious liberty of the children of God (Romans 8:21).

As repentance is not the same as guilt, sorrow need not be the same as misery. It is by equating the two that Christians sometimes give a false impression of the meaning of Lent, and of every expression of penitence at any time. A miserable Christian is a poor advertisement, indeed an unwilling work of the devil. Counting the cost means joy that this great work of forgiveness has been done and that we can, however inadequately, know of its mystery and take part in its commemoration.

Forty days to journey between joy and joy, to walk with Jesus from glory to glory. When the journey is done, forty days to celebrate the time when he appeared to his disciples after his Resurrection and taught them many things until the time came for his glorious Ascension.

Have a happy Lent.

Easter

Easter is the crown of the Christian year. It is the day for telling the good news that is told every day. It is a season that contains every season. It is the joy lightening the darker times of penitence and sorrow. It is the focus of truth filling all the universe. It is the proof and the promise that Jesus, called the Christ, was not just an inspired teacher or a righteous man, but a man in whom was all the fullness of the Godhead, the incarnate Son who lived a fully human life even to death, who overcame death and rose in glory. His Resurrection is our present strength and our future hope, the guarantee of our own resurrection, a future in which our present already shares.

The signs of resurrection are all around us. In the yearly renewal of nature, in recovery from illness, in reconciliation after estrangement, in the knowledge of God's pardon, in all new hopes and fresh starts, its power is there. These are meaningful for us because they draw their power from the one great moment, the centre of history when Christ rose again.

The contraries and paradoxes of the whole Christian story are drawn together at this time. The twelve disciples, learners who often failed to understand, who deserted their Lord in his time of need, are now Apostles, messengers of the good news, transformed from fear to courage, from despair to hope. The change in them is a major piece of evidence for the historical Resurrection.

As we pray in adoration, in penitence, in thanksgiving, in petition and intercession, our prayers are gathered up in the Resurrection faith. For the Christian every day is Resurrection day, but at Easter above all times we have pure rejoicing. Do we always come to our worship with equal joy and assurance?

But this is a time of triumph. Let us not fear triumphalism – not the old triumphalism that sometimes asserted power and claimed authority above compassion – but the triumph of the Cross and the empty tomb. Christianity is a triumphant faith, the triumph of joy over sorrow, life over death; the conquest of sin.

With all Christian people, we greet the greatest of the good news: Christ is risen, alleluia. He is risen indeed, alleluia, alleluia.

Pentecost

Fifty days after the Resurrection, at the time of the Jewish Feast of Weeks, the promise that the Apostles would not be left without power and guidance is fulfilled. They have known the apparent defeat of all their hopes, the shame of desertion, the wonder of the Resurrection, the days of further teaching, the second parting at the Ascension. Now the Holy Spirit comes in tongues of fire, giving them the grace to preach the gospel to many people.

This is sometimes seen as the 'birthday of the Church'. The Holy Spirit is for evermore present with all Christian believers, bringing them strength and encouragement and leading them to the truth. The Holy Spirit is a gift to the Church, to uphold and inspire her for ever until the final consummation of God's purpose. We call on the power of the Holy Spirit in the sacraments, the blessing of baptism, the wonderful celebration of the Eucharist. It is a good time for individual churches within the universal Church to take stock, give praise for past mercies and look prayerfully to the future.

The Holy Spirit is a gift to the world, which is a good world, God's world, though marred by human sin. The power of the Apostles to speak in many tongues shows that divine grace is not confined to one nation or race. The Holy Spirit is at work in the world, often silently and unknown, but mighty in power.

The Holy Spirit is a gift to the individual who will receive the gift in faith and love. The mystical union of God and humanity, restored by the redemption brought by Christ, means that we live in the Spirit and the Spirit lives in us. The Holy Spirit who descended as a dove at the baptism of Jesus comes, silent and unseen, at every baptism when a new member is received into the Church. There is no need to seek for special gifts or great signs. Anything that makes some Christians claim superiority over others in knowledge or favour is wrong. The power of the Holy Spirit appears in quiet lives, in the acceptance of the routine prescribed for us, as much as in any spectacular events in the history of the Church.

As he died, Jesus said, 'It is finished' – *tetelestai* – 'it has been accomplished' (John 19:30). This is fulfilled at Pentecost; the total triumph of the Son, crucified, risen, ascended, glorified, brings the human race into the new relationship to receive the full power of the Spirit.

The Holy Spirit is from the beginning, in the Church, in the world and in the individual soul, sustaining through time and leading to the consummation of the divine purpose.

Trinity Sunday

On the Sunday after Pentecost we praise the Holy Trinity: Father, Son and Holy Spirit. This is the greatest of Christian mysteries, which many have tried to explain by analogies but which we can never fully understand in this world. It is enough to know that it has been the distinctive belief of Christians through the centuries. It is a defence against the corruption of faith and the errors of those who claim new revelations previously unknown to the Church. It is associated with highest praise and adoration, acknowledgement of the divine majesty, greatness and power. The word 'glory' best expresses our worship, and gives us joy which stays with us through the long season following this day.

Ordinary Time

The short period between the Presentation and Ash Wednesday, and the much longer period between Pentecost and Advent, are known as 'Ordinary Time'. They carry no special seasonal emphasis connected with the great events of the Christian story. The Sundays in Ordinary Time are named as 'Propers', their number and dating dependent on the secular calendar, although the Collects are described as being for Sundays after Trinity. It all sounds rather complicated, but the publishers of annual church calendars put it all together neatly every year.

The word 'Ordinary' may at first suggest something not very important or interesting, a dull season with no character of its own, but this is far from being the case. The first period of Ordinary Time follows the cycle from Advent to the Presentation when we have celebrated the coming of Christ and the signs of his revelation to the world. Now we turn towards the solemnity of Lent and the Passion, and the subsequent joy of Easter and all that follows, and the Sundays mark the transition. After Pentecost, the birthday of the Church, comes the time for reflection on all that has been revealed and for growth in faith, and Christian living. Ordinary time reminds us that we cannot live for ever on the heights. The work of God on earth is done mainly through faithful obedience in daily life, in the routine of work and recreation, of family and strangers, upheld by the times of shared worship and private prayer.

There is more. These are the periods when the Gospel for the year is read in sequence on Sunday. We hear of the development of the early ministry of Jesus Christ, leading to the climax of his atoning death and mighty resurrection. In his words of mercy and healing, in his words of comfort and exhortation, we find the pattern for which to strive in our own lives.

The liturgical colour for Ordinary Time is green, the colour of nature, of the world created and sustained by God, a reminder that the environment which we too often take for granted is itself holy. And perhaps one way of thinking about Christianity is that the 'ordinary' things have been sanctified by the presence of God Incarnate.

Christ the King

The Sunday next before Advent is celebrated as the festival of Christ the King, a commemoration of his reign over all. The great events of his incarnate life have their festivals during the year, from the Nativity to the Ascension. Now, at the end of the Church year, we honour his triumph and glory. The Lord whom we know through the record of his human years as Jesus of Nazareth is the cosmic Christ, the Son eternally begotten of the Father, the living Word, the Light of the world. We can only grasp at the mystery of his being by words that must be inadequate but draw us a little closer to him.

The idea of 'triumphalism' is often rejected by Christians today, and rightly so if it is associated with ecclesiastical power seeking to dominate the minds and wills of people, or with the special privileges granted to a particular branch of the Church. But here is another sense in which we must be truly triumphalist, affirming the victory of Christ over sin and death and joining our worship with the perpetual worship of heaven, the worship of the blessed who are the Church Triumphant.

At the end of Ordinary Time we celebrate the timeless, the everlasting. All things find their focus in Christ, who lifts up into glory all that is sincerely done in his name, however slight it may seem in terms of this world.

On this Sunday we look back over the year and try to see in the light of Christ all that is past. We look forward to the new year, beginning with Advent when we recall the promises of the Messiah, the one who came in a more wonderful way than even the great prophets could have dreamed. It is also the season when we think much about judgement, both here and now and at the end. Christ the King is Christ the Judge, a reality never to be forgotten. He is also Christ the Saviour who meets repentance with infinite mercy.

He is Lord of lords and King of kings, and those with him are called and chosen and faithful.

Revelation 17:14

Festivals

There are two cycles of worship in the Christian year. That which follows the events of our Lord's incarnate life from Advent to Pentecost, and then keeps Ordinary Time for the rest of the year, is technically known as the *Temporale*. This is the scheme followed in Sunday worship week by week, but there is also the *Sanctorale*, which commemorates the same calendar dates every year as Festivals. The services on these days are in honour of the Apostles and other people of the New Testament, or to recall particular events such as the Annunciation and the Transfiguration. Yearly worship thus has a double rhythm, the two systems continually working together.

On the saints' days we think of the particular virtues and achievements of these heroes of faith, but the principal object of worship is to praise God for the grace that gives such power to ordinary people who are chosen to do his work, and the gifts granted to enable them in his service. It is appropriate to reflect also on the wonderful way in which such gifts have been given through the ages and are still given. For example, St Andrew is associated with missions, and St Luke with doctors and the work of healing. Even the fallibility which the Bible so often reveals is drawn into praise. St Peter fell into disgrace many times, but still had a powerful role in the beginning of the Church. The fact that we are commemorating real human beings and not plaster images is a continual source of encouragement for ordinary, very fallible, Christians. There are also lesser commemorations which are often observed, which reveal the whole history of the Church from New Testament times until now, drawing many women and men to serve people in the name of God.

The spirit of the Festivals is one of rejoicing, even though many of those whom we are remembering suffered grievously for their faith, even to the martyr's death. The triumph of their faith is the triumph of God who brings good out of evil, joy out of suffering, life out of death. The Cross which was the image of hope for the saints still carries its message of assurance.

These are holy days – the origin of the holiday – and in the past they were marked by rest from all but essential work and by attendance at the service of the day. In our more secular world, they can still touch with their holiness the daily life that we must follow between Sunday and Sunday.

Gospel Reflections

Year A

First Sunday of Advent

Advent teaches us to wait, but also to be prepared. In our busy lives we can too easily fail to think about the purpose of life and the certainty of death, not morbidly but seeking to follow the will of God.

Matthew 24:36–44
You also must be ready, for the Son of Man comes at an unexpected hour (v.44).

Although Christ has told us that no one knows when his second coming will be, people have been predicting the end of the world at various times over the last 2000 years. When the state of things seems bad – and it usually does – there are sure to be proclamations that the end is near. Few of us take these prophecies seriously but prefer to go on with the business of living here and now. But if the danger of speculating about the end is neglect of present reality, there is also danger in setting aside all that the Bible says about it. Those who are like the servant who says, 'My master is delayed' (Matthew 24:48), can too easily become indifferent to their duty, and take comfort in the thought that there is plenty of time to repent and do better. We do not know when Christ will come again, but we do know that he comes for each one of us at the time of our death. This is the season to reflect deeply on the truth that should never be forgotten: that death is the one certainty in human life. We must be ready, not with morbid anxiety but acknowledging our natural fear and trusting in the love of God who made us for this end and this new beginning.

Hosanna! Welcome to our hearts! Lord, here
Thou hast a temple too; and full as dear
As that of Sion, and as full of sin:
Nothing but thieves and robbers dwell therein:
Enter, and chase them forth, and cleanse the floor:
Crucify them! that they may never more
    Profane that holy place
Where thou hast chose to set thy face!
And then if our stiff tongues shall be
    Mute in the praises of thy deity,
The stones out of the temple wall
    Shall cry aloud and call
Hosanna! And thy glorious footsteps greet!

Jeremy Taylor

Lord who created me, who knew the depths of my being before I was born, as you have guided and held me through life until this hour, enable me still to serve you in this world, keep me alert and watchful against temptation and come when you will to call me through death into eternal life.

Second Sunday of Advent

We do well sometimes to withdraw from the comforts and activities of daily life, and find time for quiet reflection. Even a few minutes of waiting in stillness upon God can give much strength.

Matthew 3:1–12
John the Baptist appeared in the wilderness (v.1).

Not in the quiet pools of Jerusalem, where Jesus would work miracles of healing; not in the fertile lake where he would call his disciples and feed the hungry crowd, but in the wilderness on the other side of the River Jordan. It was the river of promise, the river that the Israelites had crossed long ago to bring them into the land prepared for them. But Jesus came to it as they had come, from the desert of wandering and privation, the place between old slavery and new freedom. Here John, a strange, wild figure like a prophet out of the Old Testament, proclaimed the good news and called people to repentance; here he baptized all who came in faith, and prepared the way of the Lord who was coming to baptize with the Holy Spirit. The Gospel begins in a barren place, the place where men and women can be alone with God because there is no distraction, no beguiling comfort; the place where they are challenged and tested, the place where they understand more deeply their total dependence upon God. We begin our lives naked and helpless; in the years of strength, we may remember our weakness, cross back to the wilderness where we can begin again.

> The last and greatest herald of heaven's King,
> Girt with rough skins, hies to the deserts wild,
> Among that savage brood the woods forth bring,
> Which he than man more harmless found and mild.
> His food was locusts, and what young doth spring
> With honey that from virgin hives distilled;
> Parched body, hollow eyes, some uncouth thing
> Made him appear, long since from earth exiled.
> There burst he forth: 'All ye, whose hopes rely
> On God, with me amidst these deserts mourn;
> Repent, repent, and from old errors turn!'
> Who listened to his voice, obeyed his cry?
> Only the echoes, which he made relent,
> Rung from their marble caves 'Repent! Repent!'

William Drummond of Hawthornden

Lord, when I am too full of the cares and pleasures of the world, call me back to the wilderness where I can be free from all that stands between me and obedience to your will. Let me begin every day as a new journey, not trusting in what I have achieved but newly washed in the water of life.

Third Sunday of Advent

God works quietly but with complete constancy. When doubt and anxiety come close, we remember how his promises have been fulfilled in all ages.

Matthew 11:2–11
'Are you the one who is to come, or are we to wait for another?' (v.3).

Did I get it wrong? Was this not after all the promised Messiah whom I proclaimed? Are we still to wait as Israel has waited for centuries past? When I spoke the words of the great prophet Isaiah I thought they were about to be fulfilled, that there was a road in the desert for the coming of the Lord. Where now is the fulfilment of the promise? Imprisoned, soon to face death, the Baptist was troubled and uncertain. Life seemed to be going on as it was before he came from the wilderness with his strident call for repentance. The Day of the Lord, the vindication of Israel, was as far away as ever. The answer is the same then as now. Yes, life goes on, there is still oppression, injustice, personal and national calamities. But the Kingdom is already among you, as God's love heals, forgives, makes free. This was indeed the one who was to come, the one who has come. Today when the signs of his coming are less spectacular, they are still at work in lives that have been touched by the presence of the Lord. In Advent we wait for the one who has already come. Our prayers call him into hearts that have already received him. Life goes on, the same as ever but totally different.

The Holy Baptist was separated from the world. He was a Nazarite. He went out from the world, and placed himself over against it, and spoke to it from his vantage ground, and called it to repentance. Then went out all Jerusalem to him into the desert, and he confronted it face to face. But in his teaching he spoke of One who should come to them and speak to them in a far different way. He should not separate Himself from them. He should not display Himself as some higher being, but as their brother, as of their flesh and of their bones, as one among many brethren, as one of the multitude and amidst them; nay, He was among them already.

J.H. Newman

Lord, guide me to seek you and to find you in the little things of life. Lead me though what is familiar and understood into the mystery of the Incarnation which passes understanding but is the source of my hope. Keep my feet from following other ways, my mind from seeking other mysteries, my heart from desiring any other assurance but faith in Jesus the true Messiah.

Fourth Sunday of Advent

The Bible tells of many battles and conflicts, some hard to reconcile with the divine call to love. But Christ's conquest of evil is our assurance that we need fear no assaults upon the soul.

Matthew 1:18–25
'You are to name him Jesus, for he will save his people from their sins' (v.21).

The name that Joseph would hear was *Jeshua,* a name to herald a saviour and also to recall the successor of Moses who had led the people into the Promised Land. For a Jew under the oppression of Roman occupation, it was a double sign of hope. For Christians today, the book of Joshua is one of the more embarrassing and indeed distasteful parts of the Bible. Joshua was a hard man and the story of his victories is one of bloodshed and the destruction of those who already lived in Canaan. But he did save his people from their wilderness wandering, their homelessness and constant anxiety about the future.

The new Jeshua would save his people, not only the Jews but also the whole human race that had become alienated from God by sin. His conquest shed no blood but his own, brought death to none except his own death on the Cross. He destroyed none but the powers of sin and evil. With the power not of the sword but of sacrificial love, he led his people from their desert wandering and brought them home. As Advent moves into Christmas the name of Jesus tells of how the promise to Joseph was fulfilled in a way beyond his imagining.

Thou hidden Source of calm repose,
Thou all-sufficient Love Divine;
My help and refuge from my foes,
Secure I am if Thou art mine;
And lo! from sin, and grief, and shame,
I hide me, Jesus, in Thy name.

Thy mighty name salvation is,
And keeps my happy soul above;
Comfort it brings, and power, and peace,
And joy, and everlasting love;
To me, with Thy dear name, are given
Pardon, and holiness, and heaven.

Charles Wesley

Blessed Jesus, Saviour, be close to me as I come again to worship your wonderful birth. Make me worthy to share in your conquest where none shall perish but all shall be given life, and at the last lead me into the good land of the promise that is to all eternity.

Christmas Day

God, who is beyond our understanding, is revealed in Jesus Christ. All that we can know or need to know in this world of divinity is made known to us in the record of his humanity.

John 1:1–14
The Word became flesh and lived among us, and we have seen his glory, the glory as of the father's only son, full of grace and truth (v.14).

The story of the birth of Jesus at Bethlehem is so well known, so often told, sung, acted and depicted, that it seems to become a routine part of the Christmas holiday, a passing reminder of what the season is about. A birth is easy to understand, easy to depict imaginatively without knowledge of the details. But how can we depict the heart of the mystery? No picture, no narrative, can make the coming of God into the world of human beings a part of our annual pageant. Only the inspired words of the Evangelist can tell of the eternal God, perfect in power and majesty, entering into human life with all its limitations. We have seen his glory – but *who* saw it? The few who were privileged to be of his human family, to be his close friends, to hear him preach, to be the enemies who planned his death? Not for thirty years, but for all time, those who would receive him could share in the divine light, see with the inner eye of faith the glory that had come into the world. It could be seen in a precious relationship, a father and his son in all the suffering and the joy. The mutual love gives its blessing to the happy families of this day, heals the wounds of past estrangement, and draws us into one as children of the eternal Father.

The incorporeal, incorruptible and immaterial Word of God entered into our own situation, even though he previously was not far distant. No part of creation was deprived of him and he always filled all things since he existed together with his Father. But he came down to us on account of his benevolence and appeared among us. Seeing how all were liable to death, he had mercy on our race and compassion on our weakness. He came to the aid of our corruption and did not stand for the domination of death, in order that what had been created might not perish and that the Father's work on behalf of man might not be in vain. He took a body to himself which was in no way different from our own. For he did not wish simply to dwell in a body nor did he want only to seem to be a man. Had he only wanted to appear to be a man he could have appeared by means of a better body. But he took our own.

St Athanasius

Heavenly Father, with all your Church I praise you this day for the coming of the Son to take our nature and live a human life, even to suffering and death. I pray that the vision of glory will not fade, but will enlighten and guide me all my life, until I come to perfect knowledge in your heavenly kingdom.

First Sunday of Christmas

J oy and sorrow are mingled in every human life. In the season of
rejoicing, we remember the sufferings of the innocent, shared even
by the Holy Family.

Matthew 2:13–23
'Take the child and his mother, and flee to Egypt' (v.13).

Another dream, another command, the promise fulfilled yet turned
to desperate peril. Go away, leave this place where the humble and
the wise have knelt in wonder, before the feet of cruel men trample
over dreams of love. Go away, go to Egypt, the place of slavery from
which God brought his people into this land of promise which has
become a land of new oppression. It is God himself who goes into
exile, God made human to become the refugee, the homeless, the
hungry. Through the wilderness where he carried them for forty years,
he is carried back in a mother's arms. Today we sing our Christmas
hymns again, rejoicing in the Word made flesh, sorrowing for what
the Word suffered in the flesh. If we have shut ourselves away from
the reality of human pain and loss, if our festivity has become selfish,
let the cry of the children from Bethlehem long ago pierce our defens-
ive walls and mingle with the cry of children all around us every
day. In the faith of God incarnate, joy and sadness, acceptance and
accusation, are never far apart.

> Christ, I see thy crown of thorns in every eye, thy bleeding,
> wounded, naked body in every soul; thy death liveth in every
> memory; thy wounded body is embalmed in every affection; thy
> pierced feet are bathed in everyone's tears; and it is my privilege
> to enter with thee into every soul.
>
> Thomas Traherne

*God of joy, God of sorrow, God of our hearts, turn our stony hearts
into hearts of flesh so that we may share the divine compassion,
restore our lost innocence so that we may protect the innocent, guide
our wandering feet so that we may guide others to your protection.*

Second Sunday of Christmas

The promise of redemption and new life made known through the Old Testament prophets was fulfilled in Christ. Those who believe in him are saved not by merit but by the absolute love of God.

John 1:1–9, 10–18
Grace and truth came through Jesus Christ (v.17).

'Amazing grace', says the hymn, and it truly is amazing. Grace is the free love of God, granted to those who do not merit it, reaching out to those who do not seek it. Grace is the absolute, unconditional gift of God which saves, heals and brings eternal life. For centuries he loved his people although they were often unfaithful, but the supreme act of grace was his taking our human nature. With the coming of Jesus Christ in the flesh, grace was let loose into the world, lighting the dark places, making all things new. There was no more room for error, for failing to understand the true nature of God, for it was revealed in human life. Christ revealed the truth that had been from the beginning: that God is love. No deceit, no holding back, no concealment, but absolute certainty. It has been said that mercy is God not giving us what we deserve, and grace is his giving us what we do not deserve. Angels, shepherds, wise men, the Holy Family themselves, are agents of the undeserved love that appeared at Bethlehem and fills all things.

> But that unsearchable Love which showed itself in our original creation, rested not content with a frustrated work, but brought Him down again from His Father's bosom to do His will, and repair the evil which sin had caused. And with a wonderful condescension He came, not as before in power, but in weakness, in the form of a servant, in the likeness of that fallen creature whom He purposed to restore.
>
> J.H. Newman

Lord, whose truth is revealed in holy scripture and whose grace is known to every sinner who turns back in sorrow and love, teach me to respond to that amazing gift. Now in the time of Christmas joy, always while life shall last, draw me so deeply into the love of Christ that I may help others to know its meaning.

Epiphany

The Wise Men were the first Gentiles to see and acknowledge Christ. Their homage was a sign that the whole of the human race would be included in the salvation that he brought.

Matthew 2:1–12
On entering the house, they saw the child with Mary his mother; and they knelt down and paid him homage. Then, opening their treasure-chests, they offered him gifts of gold, frankincense and myrrh (v.11).

Tradition made them into kings with a splendid retinue, a gift to generations of artists. Modern scholars conjecture about the place from which they came and the cult to which they belonged. Piety sees in their gifts the role of Jesus as king, priestly mediator and sacrificial victim. What the commemoration brings to all is the understanding that the newborn Saviour was hidden from the mighty ones who would have destroyed him and revealed to those who came in faith, not knowing exactly whom they sought but following a light that could not be ignored. Adoration proves itself in giving, whether the precious treasures of a distant land or the giving of a little money, a little time, a little word that acknowledges the Christ Child in one of his own children. The star stood still at the end of their journey but it still beckons to the believers of many races who have come after them. It is a time for each one to have an epiphany, a new realization of God's love to confirm and strengthen faith.

> They gave to thee
> Myrrh, frankincense and gold
> But, Lord, with what shall we
> Present ourselves before thy majesty,
> Whom thou redeemedst when we were sold?
> We've nothing but ourselves, and scarce that neither;

Vile dirt and clay;
Yet it is soft and may
Impression take.
Accept it, Lord, and say, this thou hadst rather;
Stamp it, and on this sordid metal make
Thy holy image, and it shall outshine
The beauty of the golden mine.

Jeremy Taylor

Heavenly Father, give me the wisdom of simplicity that brings the faithful to kneel and adore. Open my heart so that I may open my gifts and offer them in your service. Lead me on day by day in the light of Christ until the end of the journey and the fullness of revelation.

Baptism of Christ

By receiving baptism, Jesus showed his total identification with the human race and gave an example of witness for his followers to continue.

Matthew 3:13–17
'I need to be baptized by you, and do you come to me?' (v.14).

John the Baptist had been forceful, positively insulting, in his reception of many of the notable Jews who came for baptism. They were a brood of vipers, fleeing from the wrath to come – not the terms in which present-day applicants for infant or adult baptism expect to be received. He was not a man to be easily impressed by rank and title. When Jesus came, unknown and without social prestige, John recognized that here was something more than worldly authority. Here was cleansing and pardon, the grace of new life that only God could bestow. 'I can give you nothing, I need what you can give me.' Jesus accepts the token of obedience, receives the symbolic washing away of sins that he has not committed. In the years of ministry that lay before him, and in the centuries of his risen presence in believers, he comes to people where they are. The maker and ruler of all that is, seen and unseen, asks for the gifts which he himself has given: for faith and hope and love, for following the pattern of obedience which he has shown. Sinners who come for the healing water of baptism are met not with the wrath of the Baptist but with the grace of the Holy Spirit, the giver of new life.

Today let us honour Christ's baptism and celebrate this feast in holiness. Be cleansed entirely and continue to be cleansed. Nothing gives such pleasure to God as the conversion and salvation of human beings, for whom his every word and every revelation exist. He wants you to become a living force for all humanity, lights shining in the world. You are to be radiant lights as you stand beside Christ, the great light, bathed in the glory of him who is the light of heaven. You are to enjoy more and more the pure and dazzling light of the Trinity, as now you have received – though not in its fullness – a ray of its splendour.

Gregory of Nazianzus

Jesus, Lord, when you come to me with your pardoning love, let me respond with the love of one who has nothing to give but love, nothing to offer but repentance. I need to be baptized by you, once in the sacred mystery of the Church, daily in the renewal of my life in you and for you, the Son beloved of the Father.

Second Sunday of Epiphany

C hrist is the light who gives spiritual sight and guides his followers to be faithful to the end.

John 1:29–42
Jesus said to them, 'Come and see' (v.39).

'Seeing is believing': that well-worn truism could be a popular title for the Fourth Gospel. From the first announcement of Christ as the light of the world, the Evangelist tells of those who in the time of his earthly ministry saw and believed. The disciples beheld his glory, sight was restored to the blind, on the eve of the Passion he told his friends that soon they would not see him but soon again they would see him in a new way. On the Resurrection morning the Beloved Disciple saw the empty tomb and believed. Thomas would not believe until he had seen, but blessing was promised to those in the future who would believe without seeing. The act of physical seeing of course stands for spiritual insight, the faith that is the opposite of spiritual blindness. Come and see: do not stand far off wondering if this is indeed the Christ, the Son of God, but draw near with faith and feel his presence. In prayer and praise, in the sacrament of his body and blood, the eyes of faith discern him. We do not learn about the Christian gospel as a study in philosophy or approach it as a club to join if we like it. It calls to us, and its witness is all around us.

Does the fish soar to find the ocean,
The eagle plunge to find the air –
That we ask of the stars in motion
If they have rumour of thee there?

Not where the wheeling systems darken,
And our benumbed conceiving soars!
The drift of pinions, would we hearken,
Beats at our own clay-shuttered doors.

The angels keep their ancient places;
Turn but a stone, and start a wing!
'Tis ye, 'tis your estranged faces,
That miss the many-splendoured thing.

Francis Thompson

Saviour, open my eyes to behold your glory and guide my feet to follow where you lead. As you brought the first disciples to see your earthly home, bring me to know your dwelling in me; as their doubt and questioning was turned to certainty, so turn my hesitant faith to assurance, that in looking I shall find and in finding I shall be blessed.

Third Sunday of Epiphany

The Christian duty is to bear witness to Christ. We can do it only if we are faithful to our calling and at peace with other believers.

Matthew 4:12–23
'Follow me, and I will make you fish for people' (v.19).

Perhaps it sounded like a joke, a passing remark to men preparing for their next fishing expedition. Jesus was not always sombre with his friends. He could play on words and give hidden meanings to apparently light remarks. There was something about this saying that commanded obedience so that two pairs of brothers left their occupation and their families to go with him. They were good at fishing, so they could turn their skill to the work of the gospel. There were fish in the lake to be caught, but much more importantly there were people to be saved, people in Galilee and Judaea and Samaria and in all the world. The great commission was yet to come, but they could make a start where they were and among those they knew. The nets that they had been preparing for work became symbols of the preaching and ministering that would draw people into the Kingdom of God. In all ages, the disciples of Jesus have been called to exercise their special skills, to find new opportunities in what had been taken for granted as routine. He wants us as we are, each with something to contribute, however humble it may seem, which only we can do.

> Thou art the Way
> Hadst thou been nothing but the goal
>   I cannot say
> If thou hadst ever met my soul.
>
> I cannot see –
> I, child of process – if there lies
>   An end for me
> Full of repose, full of replies.

I'll not reproach
The road that winds, my feet that err,
   Access, Approach
Art thou, Time, Way, and Wayfarer.

Alice Meynell

Lord Jesus, let me hear your call and be ready to obey. Let my ears never be closed by the demands of the moment or my expectations of the future. Show me the skill which I may not yet recognize and make it ready for your service. Just as I am, Lord, use me – just as I am.

Fourth Sunday of Epiphany

There is no limit to the love of God, and it is often shown in unexpected ways, given to simple people in homely situations.

John 2:1–11
'You have kept the good wine until now' (v.10).

Not only the best wine, but a huge amount of it: between 600 and 900 litres by modern measure. When we remember in the marriage service that Jesus was a wedding guest at Cana, we are not expecting such a volume of wine at the reception to follow! God had shown love and mercy to his people for centuries before, bearing with their sins and helping them in their troubles, but the fullness came only when he took flesh and dwelt among them. This was the first miracle of the Incarnation, the first sign that a new day had dawned for the world. It was done on a deeply human and personal occasion, the new life revealed when a young couple were beginning their own new life together. The generosity was itself a sign that the divine bounty has no limit and goes far beyond what we need or deserve. Perhaps it is also a reminder that when we ask for a particular grace we may receive more than we had expected, and the opportunity to use it. A prayer for patience may be answered by something that tests patience to the limit. But the wine of God's love is always good wine, even if we have to wait for it to be known.

Late have I loved you, O beauty so ancient and so new; late have I loved you! For you were within me and I was in the external world and sought you there, and in my unlovely state I plunged into those lovely created things which you made. You were with me, and I was not with you. The lovely things kept me from you though if they did not have their existence in you, they would have had no existence at all. You called and cried out loud to me and shattered my deafness. You were radiant and resplendent, you put to flight my blindness. You were fragrant, and I drew in my breath and now I pant after you. I tasted you and now I feel nothing but hunger and thirst for you. You touched me, and now I burn for your peace.

St Augustine

As you made the marriage feast holy by your presence, and enriched it by your gift, come, Lord Jesus, into the special days and the ordinary days of my life. Teach me to wait for the time when it is your will to grant what I desire, and give me a thankful heart to know that what you will to give is the most plentiful and the best.

The Presentation of Christ

When the promise of the Messiah was fulfilled, few could recognize him in a human child. The vision of one man was the beginning of the revelation to come.

Luke 2:22–40
'Master, now you are dismissing your servant in peace, according to your word; for my eyes have seen your salvation' (vv.29–30).

All that the Law required after the birth of a male child was fulfilled. Mary and Joseph did not try to use their angelic messages as a way of escaping their religious duty. But this time the routine ceremony was marked by strange happenings. Simeon and Anna saw that this was no ordinary child and gave their testimony to the glory of God. They were not clergy or religious leaders, just two devout old people who found new wonder in the familiar setting of the Temple. Simeon asked no more from life. He was ready to go, leaving the world to a greater act of divine love than his people had ever dreamed of even through their inspired prophets. For forty days we have celebrated the Incarnation. Now the time is fulfilled, the duty is performed, and we turn to look towards the Cross. The curtain falls on the infancy of Jesus, except for a brief glimpse of his boyhood when he was lost and found in the Temple. The vision of Simeon remains, to be recalled at evening services, often spoken at the end of a funeral, an assurance that it is never too late to see the glory of the Lord.

The old man who took the child in his arms, had upon him the gifts of the Holy Ghost, had been promised the blessed sight of his Lord before his death, came into the Temple by heavenly guidance, and now had within him thoughts unutterable, of joy, thankfulness, and hope, strangely mixed with awe, fear, painful wonder, and 'bitterness of spirit'. Anna too, the woman of fourscore and four years, was a prophetess; and the bystanders, to whom she spoke, were the true Israel, who were looking out in faith for the predicted redemption of mankind, those who (in the words of the prophecy) 'sought' and in prospect 'delighted' in the 'Messenger' of God's covenant of mercy.

J.H. Newman

Lord, as your glory was revealed to Simeon, give me the faith and hope that he knew. Let me remember that your time is not as our time, and that your message may come at any stage in human life. Keep me ready to hear your voice and to know the strength of the salvation that has been opened to all people.

Fifth Sunday of Epiphany

Those who have received the grace given through Christ have a duty to the world. Faith is proved not by pious words but by acts of love and integrity of life.

Matthew 5:13–20
'You are the light of the world' (v.14).

God said, 'Let there be light', and Christ is our light that the darkness cannot withstand. However, now we are told that *we* are the light of the world. A murky light, a feeble light, a light that is easily swallowed up in the darkness of sin and evil, scarcely a flicker in the gloom? No, the disciples of Jesus are light – not just those who heard him on the hill in Galilee, but men and women through every century, in every moment, who have longed to follow him in love. Let their light shine, because it shows not their glory but the glory of the Kingdom. Prayerful lives, deeds of mercy, gentle listening to the needs of others: these are God's beacons, a chain of light across the world which human eyes may see and as a result be lifted above the doubt and despair of life without faith. Filled with the Holy Spirit, we can be bearers of the light that comes from above. But why does God, who needs nothing outside himself, desire that we share in his light and be his agents of light to the world? The mystery of his love is unfathomable. He created us, sustains us, empowers us to be his children. It is enough to know his love, and to shine for him.

> How I wish I might deserve to have my lantern always burning at night in the temple of my Lord, to give light to all who enter the house of my God. Give me, I pray you, Lord, in the name of Jesus Christ, your Son and my God, that love that does not fail so that my lantern, burning within me and giving light to others, may be always lighted and never extinguished. Jesus, our most loving Saviour, be pleased to light our lanterns, that they may burn for ever in your temple, receiving eternal light from you, the eternal light, to lighten our darkness and to ward off from us the darkness of the world.
>
> Columbanus

Lord Jesus Christ, light of the world, give me my portion of the light that is your will for me. Keep me humble and secret in all things that might bring me the admiration of others, but clear and shining in all that shows your glory and your power to make even such a weak and sinful one your witness to the world.

Sixth Sunday of Epiphany

The commandments of God remain strong and binding, but they require not formal obedience to rules but the harder way of self-denial and love. We must grow up and leave our natural inclinations behind so that we may be faithful in his service.

Matthew 5:21–37
'If you are angry with a brother or sister, you will be liable to judgement' (v.22).

This is one of the 'uncomfortable words' of the Gospel. Who has not been angry at some time? Who indeed can say that objective anger – at injustice, cruelty or exploitation – is not sometimes justified? The line between anger on behalf of another and resentment about a real or fancied personal wrong is too easily crossed. Jesus gives this warning as part of a deeper understanding of the commandment not to commit murder. Then as now, highly 'religious' people could get caught up in the literal meaning of the Law and ignore its deeper message. To acquit oneself of murder is easy enough for most people. To come closer to the whole problem of violence, abuse and bitterness is less welcome. Look down the long road that begins with a burst of impatience and ends with the killing of another human being. There are many stages on it – how far has any one of us reached? How confident is any one of us that the road does not suddenly drop into a steep slope that carries the traveller inescapably along to the end? 'Be careful,' says Jesus, 'you who rely on the letter of a law that you have no temptation to break. My new law of love makes you free from legalistic fear, but it lays a new obligation on you, a true gentleness that does not hide behind pious words.'

> In the season of enmity, when wrath is inflamed and the soul kindled, even the least thing appears great, and what is not very reproachful is counted intolerable. And often these little things have given birth even to murder, and overthrown whole cities. For just as where friendship is, even grievous things are light, so when enmity lies beneath, very trifles appear intolerable. And however simply a word is spoken, it is surmised to have been spoken with an evil meaning.
>
> St John Chrysostom

Shield me, dear Lord, from the tempests of anger, the hostility that makes strangers into enemies, the resentment that corrupts friendship, the bitterness that isolates the soul from its humanity. Teach me to understand more clearly the beginnings of this peril, so that I may never stray from the path of love which is the way for all who would follow you.

Seventh Sunday of Epiphany

Since Christ has made us his own, we must so follow the example of his humanity that we grow closer to his divinity. It would be a frightening thought if we did not have the aid of the Holy Spirit dwelling within us. God calls us to share in his holiness.

Matthew 5:38–48
'Be perfect, therefore, as your heavenly Father is perfect' (v.48).

After the strong demands already made in the Sermon on the Mount, this seems too much! We often excuse others, or more often ourselves, by saying, 'Well, no one is perfect.' Christians acknowledge Jesus Christ as perfect God and perfect Man, but no other has achieved that perfection and at first it may seem almost irreverent to suggest that anyone could. But what do we mean when we speak of our fallen state and our imperfection? From what height have we fallen? From the perfection with which God created the human race and saw that all he had created was very good. We were made to be perfect images of himself. Christ lived and died as man to restore that image in us. We can seek no less than perfection, not taking refuge in excuses and half-finished duties. Yes, we shall continue to fail. Yes there has been no human life save one that has been free from sin. But no, we must not despair at our failures and think that it is not worth trying. No, we must not be satisfied with imperfection. To feel the divine discontent within oneself and yet not to be anxious – that is not easy, but when was the Christian way ever promised to be easy? Lent is not far away, when we try yet again to make ourselves fit for the name that we bear.

Love bade me welcome: yet my soul drew back,
    Guilty of dust and sin.
But quick-eyed Love, observing me grow slack
    From my first entrance in,
Drew nearer to me, sweetly questioning,
    If I lacked any thing.

'A guest', I answered, 'worthy to be here':
    Love said, 'You shall be he'.
'I, the unkind, the ungrateful? Ah my dear,
    I cannot look on thee'.
Love took my hand, and smiling did reply,
    'Who made the eyes but I?'

'Truth, Lord, but I have marred them: let my shame
    Go where it doth deserve'.
'And know you not', says Love, 'who bore the blame?'
    'My dear, then I will serve.'
'You must sit down', says Love, 'and taste my meat'.
    So I did sit and eat.

George Herbert

God, challenging and enabling, break through the excuses and the half-truths, the complacency. Break through with a strength beyond my own. Lead me back to the perfection that I have spoiled and hidden: restore your image in me.

Second Sunday before Lent

We are not to run ahead of God. His time is not our time and his design will be made known when he chooses, not when we think it should be. Worrying about what now seems uncertain is a denial of his loving purpose for all that he has made.

Matthew 6:25–34
'Today's trouble is enough for today' (v.34).

'Live for the moment' is the motto of the seeker after continual pleasure, the cry of irresponsibility that can lead to personal and collective disaster. Yet living under the shadow of the next day, being never fully occupied in what is known and immediate, is the most wasteful way of living. Jesus was not telling his disciples to cast aside all planning and prudence. His followers, then and now, must always try to do better each day than on the day before. They are to remember that their lives are limited in time and that the end must come for each one. Can we live in that knowledge, without losing present opportunities through future fears? There is no marvellous time-machine by which we can undo the past or forestall the future. Anxiety is a part of our human condition and few totally avoid it, but to accept it without resisting and trying to overcome it is a fault which, with the help of prayer, can be rejected. No false optimism, no refusal to be realistic about whatever makes life fall behind desire. Even in the darkness, the moment is precious and it is all we have for obedience or rejection of God's will. For the promise that goes with this command is that if we seek his Kingdom all our needs will be provided.

> Lead, kindly light, amid the encircling gloom,
>   Lead Thou me on;
> The night is dark and I am far from home,
>   Lead thou me on.
> Keep Thou my feet, I do not ask to see
> The distant scene, one step enough for me.
>
> J.H. Newman

Dear Lord, my trust really is in you alone, but it is so fragile, so easily forgotten. Tomorrow creeps into my life before this day is over. Help me to look to the future as it stands in your great purpose, to ask the questions that will make me a part of it, and to find the answers in the present time.

Sunday Next before Lent

God has never left the human race without knowledge of himself. The signs of his glory have appeared in all ages, but only in Jesus Christ were they fully revealed. In him we know all that we can know in this world about the inexpressible wonder of the divine.

Matthew 17:1–9
When they looked up, they saw no one except Jesus himself alone (v.8).

It was a moment out of time. The importunate crowds, demanding miracles of healing and signs of power, were left behind. To be alone with their Master was enough joy for the most favoured disciples. A greater wonder than they could have conceived was about to break upon them. Moses and Elijah, the Law and the Prophets, speaking with the one they knew and loved in the flesh. The Old and the New Covenants came together and the glory of God shone upon them. Surely this was the triumphant conclusion of his ministry, the final revelation to the unbelieving world. No: there was still the road to Jerusalem and to Calvary, the Passion, the death of the Cross, before the morning of Resurrection could dawn. There is much still to be travelled for all who follow Christ. Before Easter, the testing journey through Lent. There are dark roads to walk, a wilderness experience perhaps to know. We are not alone; Moses and Elijah withdraw and only Jesus remains with his disciples; he now is the sole hope of humanity. We go down the mountain with him; on the plain there are needs to be met, troubles to endure; but the glory of the Transfiguration remains wherever the faithful confess his name.

> See then in the Church is exhibited to us the Kingdom of God. Here is the Lord, here is the Law and the Prophets; but the Lord as the Lord; the Law in Moses, Prophecy in Elias; only they as servants and as ministers. They as vessels; he as the fountain; Moses and prophets spake and wrote; but when they poured out, they were filled from Him.

> St Augustine

Thanks be to God for the moments of wonder, the glimpses of glory in quiet devotion and in the little things that shine with his presence and then are gone. Keep that glory alight in me on the difficult days when belief is hard and duty is a burden. Strengthen me to accept with joy the discipline of this Lent.

Ash Wednesday

Repentance for sin is commanded throughout the Bible. It must be proved by suitable words and acts of contrition, but the pardon which it brings is absolute and leaves no burden of unresolved guilt.

Matthew 6:1–6, 16–21
'Where your treasure is, there your heart will be also' (v.21).

A day of mixed feelings, like all times of transition when we cross the threshold of change. The devotions of the day humble the spirit and lift the heart. But how shall we manage through the next forty days? The resolutions, the rule of life that seemed so well tuned in preparation – will it all prove too hard to keep? Is it too little, not a worthy offering of ourselves? Beneath it all, we hear the insidious little voice that questions the value of anything we do. Can we please God by a few little adjustments to our way of life? Is there any point in a few acts of self-denial, a little extra devotion, when it is seen in the great totality of the Christian life? Let these acts of the will, weak and feeble in themselves, serve to test where our true values lie. Pleasures that are innocent, even desirable as proceeding from God's bountiful love, can grow too big. They are the cuckoo pleasures that begin to fill our life and crowd out more important things. Let a short time of abstinence test whether they are creating a habit of dependence. The ashes on the forehead this day mark out those who desire to live fully in this world but never to be enslaved by its values. The depth of Lenten meaning is this search for the true treasures of the heart.

It is the sign of the cross that is marked on the forehead. It is not, of course, the first time that the cross has been traced there. For, when new Christians come to baptism, they are signed with the cross, the sign that inspires them to confess the faith of Christ crucified. The cross on Ash Wednesday is a reminder of our baptism. In the innocency of our childhood or in the ardour of adult commitment, we received in baptism God's grace for our Christian pilgrimage. That pilgrimage goes on being a struggle, so often an upward climb, but we are engaged in it still, thankful for that grace without which the struggling would have been long since lost. Symbolically, on Ash Wednesday, we put the cross back, in ash this time as we recognise our failure, but the cross nevertheless.

Michael Perham

Lord, teach me to know myself. In the searching light of your love, show me the things that really matter to me, and the things that matter too much. Lead me through this Lent to the true treasure that comes from you alone. Let it fill my heart until there is no room for any desire that does not follow your will.

First Sunday of Lent

Yielding to temptation has been the failure of men and women since the beginning. In Christ we find the human example of resistance and the divine guidance which enable us to rise above our bad inclinations.

Matthew 4:1–11
Jesus was led up by the Spirit into the wilderness to be tempted by the devil (v.1).

What a mean and misused word 'temptation' has come to be. Tempted to give a smart answer, tempted to a bit of extravagance, tempted even to the indulgence of a chocolate cake. We debase the great words of the Bible and so push away their demands. Temptation is a serious business, the testing of integrity and purpose, the very sifting of the soul to find how much of the truth remains. It is serious, but it is not itself sin. Look at Jesus, tempted in the perfection of his humanity, experiencing this particular burden of the common lot. Sin starts only when the presentation of what is forbidden is considered, found attractive and accepted. To know temptation is to know the possibility of right and wrong, and without that understanding we are less than human. It is well to begin Lent with this story. Jesus knew temptation after forty days of physical privation and spiritual pilgrimage. Our miniature attempt at forty days in the wilderness will certainly bring temptation, for it is at times of spiritual growth, perhaps when we feel strongest, that there is most danger. There is only one response – 'Away with you, Satan!'

> Lord, without thee I can do nothing; with thee I can do all. Help me by thy grace, that I fall not; help me by thy strength, to resist mightily the very first beginnings of evil, before it takes hold of me; help me to cast myself at once at thy sacred feet, and lie still there, until the storm be overpast; and, if I lose sight of thee, bring me back quickly to thee, and grant me to love thee better, for thy tender mercy's sake.

E.B. Pusey

Be with me, Lord Jesus, at this time of new resolve and fresh desire, because I know that temptation will come when I am seeking to be free from sin. Knowing my weakness and the power of evil, give me your strength to resist the wrong and follow the right, at this time and for all time to come.

Second Sunday of Lent

God is constant in his promises, unchanging in his nature. It is only his love that sets mercy between us and his judgement.

John 3:1–17
God did not send the Son into the world to condemn the world, but in order that the world might be saved through him (v.17).

There are Christians, individually and collectively, who seem to treat the Incarnation of Jesus as a repetition of the story of the Flood. The Genesis story tells how God, angry at the wicked state of the human race, decided to destroy it all except a few members of a righteous family. There are those who see Jesus as primarily a judge, condemning us all by the reality of his perfection. The wrath of God is not to be dismissed with the casual optimism of the Persian poet, 'He's a good fellow and 'twill all be well.' God's nature does not change and there will always be judgement for evil consciously and deliberately chosen. But the story of Jesus is the story of love, freely offered even to the ultimate price of divine suffering. In Lent we try more than ever to face our sins, to look at them honestly and seek the better way. Does the impetus come mostly from fear of judgement or from sorrow for having offended against the one who loves us enough to save us? Think about the feeling that draws to repentance. Is it most like the fear of having broken a law or like the sadness of having hurt a person who is truly loved? Noah took refuge from the waters of judgement. Christians leap into the living water of God incarnate in Christ.

It is not requisite for a man to worry himself about every detail of his life; but it is requisite that he should find out whether he truly repents of what he has done wrong, and whether he wants to be better: it is not necessary that he should be 'converted', or believe all that is written in the Bible, but it is necessary that he should have a living active trust in the mercy of God as revealed in the life and self-sacrifice of Jesus Christ: it is not necessary that he should like everyone equally, have no favourites and no enemies; but it is necessary that he should not be carrying about with him malice and spite, that he should recognize that in his enemy and in all men there is some part of God's spirit, and therefore something to love.

Stewart Headlam

Dear Christ, renew me with your life-giving spirit and open my eyes to see you as the Lord of salvation and not of condemnation. Grant that I shall never despair because of my sins, never accept them as of no account, but always come to you in the love that seeks to match the infinite love of your coming into the world.

Third Sunday of Lent

We too often try to conceal our sins, or to justify them by pleading special circumstances. True repentance that brings pardon requires complete honesty with ourselves and with God.

John 4:5–42
'Come and see a man who told me everything I have ever done!' (v.29).

'People don't understand me.' Not to be understood seems to be undervalued, unappreciated, another wound in the painful feeling of alienation. To be understood rather too well can also be uncomfortable. There is a secret core in each of us which we would like to keep from even our dearest. God knows it all. The Old Testament tells of many whose attempt to hide from God was in vain: Adam and Eve, Cain, Jonah, David after his sin over Bathsheba. The Samaritan woman was convinced on fairly slight evidence that here was no ordinary man; marriage and extramarital affairs are important but not everything that has been done in any life. But she was right: this is one of the times when Jesus, showing an attribute of God, reveals that he is very God incarnate. Confession of sins, whether silent and private or through another person, is not giving God any information previously unknown to him. It is the repentant one who is being informed, bringing to the surface what it would be more comfortable to repress. Nothing that is said or done this Lent will surprise God, but it may surprise us if we can open the conscience to the clear light that is the light of heaven where, as St Paul says, 'I will know fully, even as I have been fully known' (1 Corinthians 13:12).

So spake the false dissembler unperceived;
For neither Man nor Angel can discern
Hypocrisy, the only evil that walks
Invisible, except to God alone,
By his permissive will, through Heav'n and Earth:
And oft though wisdom wake, suspicion sleeps
At wisdom's gate, and to simplicity
Resigns her charge, while goodness thinks no ill
Where no ill seems.

John Milton

O God, knowing the secrets of the hearts and the shadows of the soul, guide me to know myself more fully and, without pride and without shame, to open myself before your judgement and your mercy.

Fourth Sunday of Lent

S elf-respect is necessary for a full life but self-regard leads to hypocrisy and dishonesty. Only if we understand that God sees us as we really are can we hope to do his will.

John 9:1–41
'Now that you say, "We see", your sin remains' (v.41).

A good short story is one that leads up to a strong ending which the reader remembers. Here, in a Gospel with much to say about seeing and believing and spiritual blindness, is an unusually long account of a healing miracle. It seems to become a story in its own right, with much human interest. It tells of healing, incredulity, fear, confrontation, gratitude, belief and disbelief – a summary of many events and responses in the ministry of Jesus. The exciting narrative ends with a simple, blunt rebuke. The sceptical Pharisees are told, 'You are so self-assured, so confident that you know everything about religion. You say that you can see it all, but you lack the true sight, the insight which confesses your need of forgiveness.' The man who has been healed, rejected by the religious authorities can only blurt out a simple profession of faith. Busy with the Lenten rule of abstention and extra devotions earnestly seeking spiritual growth, is there just a little danger of satisfaction in what is being done? Could we begin to think we are better than others whose faith is less articulate and active than ours?

> Behold the prodigal! To thee I come
> To hail my Father and to seek my home.
> Nor refuge could I find, nor friend abroad,
> Straying in vice and destitute of God.

O let thy terrors and my anguish end!
Be thou my refuge and be thou my friend.
Receive the son thou didst so long reprove,
Thou that art the God of love!

Matthew Prior

Dear Jesus, who opened the eyes of the blind, grant me the clear vision of you, my Lord and Healer. Free me from all false confidence in my own works, and make me trust in you alone. Let this be for me a time of true humility untainted by self-approval.

Mothering Sunday

No one is so loving or so vulnerable as a mother. The Bible tells of many mothers who bore heavy burdens: the mother of Moses hiding him from peril, Hannah dedicating Samuel to the Lord, Sara and Elizabeth bearing babies in old age, the mothers of the Innocents, and above all the Virgin Mary, mother of the Lord.

Luke 2:33–35
A sword will pierce your own soul too (v.35).

After the message of the angel, after the salutation of Elizabeth, after the pain and the joy of the birth, after the adoration of the shepherds, the shadow falls. The sword would strike many times, piercing that most loving mother: when he was lost and found in the Temple, when he wandered about with his group of friends and angry men threatened his life, when he set out on his last walk to Jerusalem, and at last at the foot of the Cross when life was ending. It was her hands and feet, her aching side, that were pierced as sharply as his. Did she remember the words of Simeon? Did she know that they were for all mothers in all ages? Their hopes and joys, their fears and sorrows, find their centre in that woman highly favoured, deeply afflicted. They find their image also in Mother Church, loving her children, often wounded by the hostility of the world and the unfaithfulness of those she has nurtured, sorrowing yet always joyful, servant of the Kingdom of God. Now, at the middle point of Lent, we stand in awe between joy and sorrow.

> At the Cross her station keeping,
> Stood the mournful Mother weeping,
> Close to Jesus at the last.
> Through her soul, of joy bereaved,
> Bowed with anguish, deeply grieved,
> Now at length the sword hath passed.

Stabat Mater

Heavenly Father, who made motherhood holy in the birth of your Son, look mercifully upon the joys and sorrows of all mothers, shield them and give them the strength of your love. Keep me and all your children faithful in the ways of your Church, to love her as Christ himself loved her, gave her life and being, and will hold her fast until the end.

Fifth Sunday of Lent

Death is a mystery which even the most devout cannot face without some anxiety. Natural fear of the unknown is overcome only by faith in the new and eternal life given by God in Christ.

John 11:1–45
Jesus said to her, I am the resurrection and the life' (v.25).

Like the prologue to a play, the coming Passion is foreshadowed in an ordinary family. The Lord whom they love will suffer death, will be wrapped in graveclothes and laid in a tomb. Women will mourn him, inconsolable at the loss of one so dear to them. Death strikes impartially at the greatest saint and the greatest sinner, at deeply loved youth and neglected age. Even the Son of God is not to be spared the common lot of the human nature that he has taken upon himself. But the one who must die is the Lord of life. He who can raise the dead will himself be raised, and death shall no longer be the final conqueror. Lazarus is not just the subject of an act of compassionate love. He is the forerunner, the pledge not of one miracle but of miracles without end. Lazarus would die again, not to return on earth but to enter a new and greater world. Passion Sunday leads us towards Calvary, to focus the devotions and offerings of Lent on the suffering and death of our Lord. Wonderfully, the Gospel tells of death breaking out into new life. Faith draws together the opposites of experience, harmonizes what cold reason sets at enmity. May that faith grow stronger in the two weeks of Passiontide.

> The Lord allowed death to enter this world so that sin might come to an end. But he gave us the resurrection of the dead so that our nature might not end once more in death; death was to bring guilt to an end, and the resurrection was to enable our nature to continue for ever. 'Death' in this context is a Passover to be made by everyone. You must keep facing it with perseverance. It is a Passover from corruption, from mortality to immortality, from rough seas to a calm harbour. The word 'death' must not trouble us; the blessings that come from a safe journey should bring us joy. What is death but the burial of sin and the resurrection of goodness?
>
> Ambrose of Milan

Lord, make me strong in the face of death. I know that it is the opening of the only way to your full presence, but I am still afraid. When I think of my death, comfort me with the assurance that it is in your risen self that I trust and in your resurrection that I shall know my own.

Palm Sunday

Jesus, already accepting complete humility in his Incarnation, comes into Jerusalem for the last days before his Passion. He will not draw back from any aspect of human suffering and death.

Matthew 27:11–54
All of them said, 'Let him be crucified' (v.22).

How many of those who bayed for blood in the presence of Pilate had
been among the crowd that had hailed the entry of Jesus into Jerusalem
six days before? Probably not many: this was a 'rent-a-crowd' response,
worked up by those who wanted Jesus out of the way and had to resort
to the Roman power. Yet there is a strange link between the shouts of
Palm Sunday and those of Good Friday. The Messiah was hailed with
'Hosanna!' – 'Save now!' Some of them hoped that there would a great
liberation, a spectacular vindication of the power of God working
through his chosen people. Now the call for crucifixion seems the end
of all hope, the prophetic voice silenced, the miracles of compassion
ended, the people left to walk in darkness. Neither friend nor enemy
knows that this death will be the beginning of life. To save them now,
and to save humankind for ever, the Messiah has to pass through
the death of the Cross. The raging mob is unwittingly calling for the
means of salvation. The Palm Sunday procession signifies not just the
one triumphal entry, but the endless line of the redeemed in all ages.
So many times, but never more wonderfully than in this, God brings
love out of malice and hatred, a good end from an evil motive.

It was but now their sounding clamours sung,
   'Blessed is he that comes from the Most High.'
And all the mountains with Hosanna rung;
And now, 'Away with him – away!' they cry,
And nothing can be heard but 'Crucify!'
   It was but now the crown itself they gave,
   And golden name of King unto him gave;
And now, no king but only Caesar they will have.

Giles Fletcher

*God of love, saving through suffering and death, hear the cries of
those who do not know for what they ask. By the power of the Cross,
save now, save ever, the confused and the angry among your children
as well as the assured and the loving. Lead me now into this Holy
Week, to walk with my Saviour through triumph and trial, to the
end and the beginning.*

Maundy Thursday

For many centuries the Passover meal has celebrated for the Jewish people their release from Egypt. On the night before Good Friday, Christians share in a meal that commemorates release not from material slavery but from the slavery of sin, release sealed not in the blood of a lamb but in the blood of him who is called the Lamb of God.

John 13:1–17, 31–35
'Now the Son of Man has been glorified, and God has been glorified in him' (v.31).

As T. S. Eliot's Thomas Becket says in a Christmas sermon, speaking of the Eucharist, 'Who in the world would both mourn and rejoice at the same time and for the same reason?' What is true through all the year is brought most deeply to us when we come to the communion of Maundy Thursday. Perhaps we never feel closer to our Lord than on this night. The disciples meet as they so often have for a meal of fellowship, but the fellowship is soon to be broken up in fear, desertion and betrayal. The meal follows the normal course of this season, but it culminates in strange words and promises not yet understood. Though they did not yet know it, the faithful eleven were to be united more strongly than ever with each other, and with those who would follow them in the ages to come. Their Master's glory is shown now not in transfiguration but in lowly service and the words of love. But outside the door there is darkness, the lonely garden, the agony and the Cross. The highest grace of the divine appears in the deepest suffering of the human. It is the end, and it is the beginning.

Jesus is in a garden, not of delights like the first Adam, where he ruined himself and the whole human race; but of pains in which he was saved and the whole human race. He suffers this pain and desertion in the horror of the night. I believe that Jesus never complained but this once only; but then he complains as if he could no longer contain his excessive pain: My soul is sorrowful even unto death. Jesus seeks companionship and consolation from men. This was the only time in his life, as it seems to me.

But he does not receive it, for his disciples were asleep. Jesus will be in agony to the end of the world: we must not sleep all the while.

Blaise Pascal

Lord Jesus Christ, as you come to me in the communion of bread and wine made holy for the life of the world, may it give me strength to follow in humility and love the pattern of that evening, and courage to face the darkness of death whenever it shall come. You can be glorified in the weak and the vulnerable of this world: let me trust in that alone.

Good Friday

The unique heart of the Christian faith is the sacrificial death of God incarnate in a human being. Though some of the prophets had a vision of a suffering Messiah, none came near to the awful and wonderful truth of the mystery.

John 18:1–19:42
They crucified him, and with him two others, one on either side, with Jesus between them (19:18).

What more can we say after the stark words of the Evangelist? It was not simply an innocent human victim of injustice, not a man misunderstood because his teaching was ahead of his time. Many such have died, before and since, but it was the Son of God who suffered the extreme and most shameful Roman penalty and was numbered with the transgressors. Even though we know the end of the story, the triumph of life over death, we must mourn in silence on this day as we contemplate the terrible price of our salvation. No other death could draw the whole world into the agonized love of outstretched arms. Redemption flashed through the hour of total darkness. Blood cleansed the vile deeds of those who caused blood to be shed: the betrayal, the denial, the false accusations, the cruelty, the judgement that feared the power of Caesar above mercy. It is finished, and we can only wonder and adore, and share the time with other believers who have tried to make our sorrow articulate.

Am I a stone, and not a sheep,
    That I can stand, O Christ, beneath Thy cross,
    To number drop by drop Thy Blood's slow loss,
And yet not weep?

Not so those women loved
    Who with exceeding grief lamented Thee;
    Not so fallen Peter weeping bitterly;
Not so the thief was moved;

Not so the Sun and Moon
    Which hid their faces in a starless sky,
    A horror of great darkness at broad noon –
I, only I.

Yet give not o'er,
    But seek Thy sheep, true Shepherd of the flock;
    Greater than Moses, turn and look once more
And smite a rock.

Christina Rossetti

Hear us, O merciful Lord Jesus Christ, and remember now the hour in which thou didst commend thy blessed spirit into the bands of thy heavenly Father; and so assist us by this thy most precious death, that, being dead unto the world, we may live only unto thee, and that, at the hour of our departing from this mortal life, we may be received into thine everlasting kingdom, there to reign with thee, world without end.

Bishop John Cosin

Easter Eve

The reality of Christ's humanity is never more apparent than when his body is laid in the tomb. The mourning of every generation before and after finds its consummation there.

John 19:38–42
There was a garden in the place where he was crucified, and in the garden there was a new tomb in which no one had ever been laid. And so, because it was the Jewish day of Preparation, and the tomb was nearby, they laid Jesus there (vv.41–42).

It is finished. The sacred body that was born in a stable is laid in a hastily borrowed tomb. Of the gifts that were brought to the newborn child, it seems as if the gold of kingship and the incense of priesthood have gone, and only the embalming myrrh remains. Those who feared to acknowledge Jesus in life now bring their last service to him in death. Between the agony and the triumph, there is rest. The Church rests and waits, sharing the seventh day of God's rest from creation, before the first day of the new creation dawns. Neither the cry of dereliction nor the shout of triumph, only the silence of repose. It is a day to be quiet, to be still mournful because we are counting the great cost of our salvation, to be moving towards rejoicing because we know the end of the story. It is a threshold day, between mortal death and resurrection to eternal life. Lent is over, and all its failures, all its advances, are offered through the mercy of the Son who died. If we have opened ourselves to hear his word and to do his will, he fills our emptiness.

> All night had shout of men and cry
> Of woeful women filled his way;
> Until that noon of sombre sky
> On Friday, clamour and display
> Smote him; no solitude had he,
> No silence, since Gethsemane.
>
> Public was Death; but Power, but Might,
> But Life again, but Victory,
> Were hushed within the dead of night,

The shuttered dark, the secrecy.
And all alone, alone, alone,
He rose again behind the stone.

Alice Meynell

Gracious Saviour, you have guided and strengthened me through the days of penitence. Grant me now the gift of calm and assurance, as I prepare for the days of rejoicing. Confirm in me all that has been achieved, pardon what has been left undone, and bring me day by day nearer to the eternal life which you have promised to all who trust in you.

Easter Day

We share in the Resurrection of Christ. We do not need to seek him in secret places: he comes to meet us as soon as we turn to him.

Matthew 28:1–10
Jesus met them and said, 'Greetings!' And they came to him, took hold of his feet, and worshipped him (v.9).

The word of greeting, which appears several times in the different accounts of the Resurrection, is the one which Luke gives to the angel Gabriel in the story of the Annunciation, the salutation to Mary, highly favoured among women. Now the whole purpose has been fulfilled, the tale unfolded. It is given to the faithful women to be the first witnesses, they who had come to give the last office of respect to the broken body, while the men who had deserted him were still shut up in their remorse and fear. They knew at once that the greeting came from one they knew and yet had not fully known. They had seen their friend and master die. Now they saw him again as one to be worshipped as well as loved. Still he meets us, as we come to make our Easter offering of worship, to obey his command to remember him as we take the bread and the wine, his Body and his Blood. As the words on the eve of his Passion are spoken again, it is the risen

Christ who is present among us. We fall at his feet so that he may raise us up to be with himself.

> Most glorious Lord of life! that, on this day,
> Didst make thy triumph over death and sin;
> And, having harrowed hell, didst bring away
> Captivity thence captive, us to win:
> This joyous day, dear Lord, with joy begin;
> And grant that we, for whom thou didest die,
> Being with thy dear blood clean washed from sin,
> May live for ever in felicity!
> And that thy love we weighing worthily,
> May likewise love thee for the same again;
> And for thy sake, that all like dear didst buy,
> With love may one another entertain:
> So let us love, dear Love, like as we ought;
> Love is the lesson which the Lord us taught.

Edmund Spenser

Almighty Father, as your blessed Son rose from the dead and appeared in his risen body to those who believed in him, give me grace to see him with the eyes of faith, to make his Resurrection known wherever I may, and to be united with him in the eternal life where he lives and reigns with you and the Holy Spirit, one God, world without end.

Second Sunday of Easter

The Christian faith has been spread through all lands and in all ages by those who have not seen Christ in the flesh but have experienced his risen presence. God depends on us to be his witnesses in our time.

Year A

John 20:19–31

'Blessed are those who have not seen and yet have come to believe' (v.29).

Words were not enough, even the words of trusted friends. The evidence of joy on their faces, the change from mourning to delight – none of it was enough. Thomas was always the pessimist, loyal but sceptical. He was the first to propose to go with Jesus to the raising of Lazarus, believing that it meant death for them all. He was one of those who never believe that anything can come out right, that promises will be fulfilled. Physical evidence, cruel evidence of pain and death, drew from him the confession of divinity. When faith came, it was as wholehearted as his doubt had been. He was restored to the company of the faithful, but there was a greater blessing for those who come after and know by faith and not by sight that Jesus is Lord and God. Still there are many who would like to believe, but hold back because it seems too good to be true, a fairy story, a wish fulfilment. Only those who have tried to suffer in spirit with Jesus, who have followed him with devotion from the manger to the Cross, can know the Resurrection joy and tell the world, 'We have seen the Lord.'

> What conclusion, dear sisters and brothers, do you draw from this? Do you think it was by chance that this chosen disciple was absent? Or that on his return he heard, that hearing he doubted, that doubting he touched, and touching he believed? This did not happen by chance, but by the providence of God. Divine mercy brought it about most wonderfully, so that when that doubting disciple touched his Master's wounded flesh he healed the wound of our unbelief as well as his own. Thomas's scepticism was more advantageous to us than was the faith of the other disciples who believed. When he was led to faith by actually touching Jesus, our hearts were relieved of all doubt, for our faith is made whole.
>
> Gregory the Great

Lord, give me the faith to look upon the mystery of the wounded body that heals, the death that brings life. Make me a witness to the silent, unseen grace that I have known, to reveal day by day the living presence of my Lord and my God.

Third Sunday of Easter

The promises of God, declared in many ways and confirmed by his mighty acts, have been fulfilled in the Passion and Resurrection of his Son. What was partially understood has become perfect knowledge for all who will draw near to him.

Luke 24:13–35
Then their eyes were opened, and they recognized Jesus (v.31).

It was at the evening meal that the memories came flooding back. A day of rumours that had aroused hope they had dared not allow to blossom was near its end. The stranger, who did not know what all the city knew, did not seem to be one with whom they could share their trouble, until he began to speak of things long known but never fully discerned. The words on the road had moved them, stirred something in their hearts, but it was the familiar actions of the table-fellowship that revealed the truth. This was he who had opened the eyes of the blind, a sign of his divine power as God's Messiah and of his human compassion. Now the eyes of faith, blinded by doubt and sorrow and despair, could see again. As the night drew in, a new day was dawning and the darkness in which they had walked for three days rolled away. Lift up your eyes, all you of little faith. Lift up your eyes above the ground-mists of fear and anxiety, and see the Lord. He who feeds the soul with the communion of his body and blood is the guest at every meal, the companion on every road.

> Thus Christ is seen to be changed, but none the less He is also seen to be essentially the same. Nothing has been left in the grave though all has been transfigured. He is the same, so that the marks of the passion can become sensibly present to the doubting Thomas: the same, so that He can eat of the broiled fish which the disciples had prepared: the same, so that one word spoken with the old accent makes Him known to the weeping Magdalene: the same, so that above all expectation and against the evidence of death the apostles could proclaim to the world that He who suffered upon the cross had indeed redeemed Israel: the same in patience, in tenderness, in chastening reproof, in watchful sympathy, in quickening love. In each narrative the marvellous contrast

is written – Christ changed and yet the same – without effort, without premeditation, without consciousness, as it appears, on the part of the Evangelists.

B.F. Westcott

Risen Lord, open my eyes to see you when I kneel at your holy table, and when I walk on my daily journey through this world. Give me the vision to see your holiness in other people, your beauty in all that you have made. Guide me, teach me, enlighten me, until the night is at hand, and as this life darkens let me see you in a greater light.

Fourth Sunday of Easter

The best Christian witness is now, as it has always been, the evidence of lives patient in adversity and thankfully joyful in prosperity. Those who are close to Jesus show that life in him is different and continually blessed.

John 10:1–10
I came that they may have life, and have it abundantly (v.10).

The good shepherd is not content only to protect his flock and lead in the right direction. He seeks out the finest pasture so that the sheep may flourish in the safety to which he has brought them. Psalm 23, most loved of the Old Testament images of God as shepherd, goes from comparing his people to sheep into a description of a banquet where they will be honoured guests. When he walked among men and women, Jesus shared their rejoicing as well as their sorrow, until the over-righteous accused him of being too fond of pleasure. He leads us still into pleasant pastures, if we accept his grace. We pass through this world as a pilgrimage to eternal life in the perfect pastures of heaven, but we do not turn away from its good things. There is a rabbinical saying that at the time of judgement people are called to account for the permissible pleasures that they have neglected. If life abundant is the will of Christ for his people, to refuse the opportunities for happiness is to spurn some of God's bounty. A serious concern for right living is one thing, but a miserable Christian is a work of the devil.

> He ate and drank the precious Word
> His Spirit grew robust –
> He knew no more that he was poor,
> Nor that his frame was Dust.
>
> He danced along the dingy Days
> And this Bequest of Wings
> Was but a Book – What Liberty
> A loosened spirit brings.

Emily Dickinson

Loving Shepherd of the sheep, lead me through this world so that I shall neither turn aside into false paths nor miss the delights that have been prepared for me to enjoy. Grant to me the grace that shows the life of faith as a life of joy, so that I may help others to find the life abundant that is your gift and your will.

Fifth Sunday of Easter

The deep heart of the Christian faith is not in a book, though we reverence and seek to obey the words of the Bible. It is not in formulas of belief, though we value the wisdom of the creeds. It is in a person, the Son of God who has opened the way between the human and the divine.

John 14:1–14
'Do you not believe that I am in the Father and the Father is in me?' (v.10).

There have been, and still are, many disputes about the exact nature of Jesus as God and man. Little words such as *of*, *from* and *by* have been tossed around in attempts to define the Incarnation. Theologians have rightly sought to guard the faith from errors that would diminish it. But the deep truth that has made people wonder, argue and sometimes even fight for its preservation lies in the words of the Lord on the evening before his Passion. He who has walked, talked, eaten, with men and women as one of them, who has shared their human needs and will soon endure the death of the body, tells his friends that they are in the presence of God. Human hands have just washed their feet and given them a lasting example of the love that they must share. A human voice speaks to human ears, revealing the mystery of God. To have known him was to have known God, the finite linked with the infinite. To know him still is to know God, in prayer and sacrament and silent presence. People have spoken *of* God and tried to follow his will by their example. Only one has spoken *as* God and embodied the living will of the Father. Sometimes the little words can be very meaningful.

> My song shall bless the Lord of all,
> My praise shall climb to His abode;
> Thee, Saviour, by that name I call,
> The great Supreme, the mighty God.
>
> Without beginning or decline,
> Object of faith and not of sense;
> Eternal ages saw Him shine,
> He shines eternal ages hence.
>
> As much, when in the manger laid,
> Almighty Ruler of the sky,
> As when the six days' work He made
> Filled all the morning stars with joy.
>
> Of all the crowns Jehovah bears,
> Salvation is His dearest claim;
> That gracious sound well pleased He hears,
> And owns Emmanuel for His name.

William Cowper

Thank you, dear Lord, for the love that has used human words and human experience to bring us to the truth. Keep me always in the sure faith that all I need to know of the Father has been shown in

Jesus Christ, and that by grace he has made himself known to me and made me his own.

Sixth Sunday of Easter

People have always sought for the meaning of life and an answer to the problem of suffering. The message of Christianity is that the Resurrection of Christ made new life and final confidence open to all who will receive it.

John 14:15–21
Because I live, you also will live (v.19).

Can I live any life but my own? Can anyone else live it for me? The cry of the modern world is for independence, individual choice, refusal of traditional models. Sometimes it is said that a couple live for one another, that a person lives for a job or a cause, but there is always the secret centre, the private place where even the dearest are not admitted. There is no substitute for personal identity. Only one person, one event, can combine complete individuality with universally shared being. The first Easter morning brought restoration of a beloved friend and master, pardon and a new chance for those who had failed him. For forty days he walked and talked with them again, a presence that was familiar yet wonderfully new. Soon the Apostles, and then the generations that followed, came to know that this was more than a happy return: it was the most mighty act of God since Creation, life not for a few but for all. Now men and women would know that life is not just being in an animated body, but being drawn into the divine purpose and knowing the love that made all things from the beginning and has made all things new.

> 'Give Me thy youth.' 'I yield it to Thy rod,
> As Thou didst yield Thy prime of youth for me.'
> 'Give Me thy life.' 'I give it breath by breath;
> As Thou didst give Thy life so give I Thee.'
> 'Give Me thy love.' 'So be it, my God, my God
> As Thou hast loved me, even to bitter death.'

> Christina Rossetti

Risen Lord, since I live in you and you live in me, make my life a true following of your own. May I love life in this world to the full as your gracious gift, but never love it so much that I forget it is only a beginning of the eternal life of glory. Because you live, I live, and I shall live for ever.

Ascension Day

The work of Christ on earth, incarnate in the person of Jesus of Nazareth, is ended. Now it is for those who believe in him, from the Apostles to the end of time, to continue that work in his name. Exalted to heaven, he gives the strength that we do not have in ourselves.

Luke 24:44–53
They worshipped him, and returned to Jerusalem with great joy (v.52).

Walking away happily from parting with a very dear friend – this is strange behaviour indeed. How different from the evening before his Passion when he spoke to them of his departure, and sorrow filled their hearts. They had learned so much since them – that in God's plan, the end is often the beginning. They had learned also that the good news of their risen Lord was now entrusted to them. His voice of promise was now their voices, his healing hands their hands, his feet of journeying mission their feet. What had they seen on the hill, that spring morning? Perhaps exactly what the Gospel tells that they saw, for how better could they understand that Jesus had left this world, not by a second death, not by a magical disappearance, but by the powerful symbol of rising to a higher place? Or was it the picture-language by which they tried to express the inexpressible? However the event took place, he left them in the human body they had known, still wounded but gloriously transformed. It was the pledge that humanity was lifted up from the depths of sin and despair, restored to its place in the Kingdom of God. It has been said that henceforth the human race is like a person standing in water up to the neck, safely living because the head is above the surface. It is a good thought, Christ the Head giving life to those who remain below.

We need not fear the shadow of false triumphalism that in the past has sometimes exalted the worldly power and glory of the Church. This is the real triumph, Christ the Lord at the right hand of the Father – another bit of picture-language but the traditional image of his glory.

> Christ is now raised above the heavens; but he still experiences on earth whatever sufferings we his members feel. He showed that this is true when he called out from heaven. 'Saul, Saul, why do you persecute me?' And: 'I was thirsty and you gave me drink.' Why then do we not exert ourselves on earth so as to be happy with him already in heaven through the faith, hope and charity which unite us with him? Christ, while in heaven, is also with us; and we, while on earth, are also with him. He is with us in his godhead and his power and his love; and we, though we cannot be with him in godhead as he is with us, can be with him in our love, our love for him. He did not leave heaven when he came down to us from heaven; and he did not leave us when he ascended to heaven again.

St Augustine

Lord Jesus Christ, I lift my eyes to your heavenly triumph, I am held in the mystery of awe and wonder. Let me praise you for your glory, but then turn my eyes to look back into the world around me, to see where your way leads me, and guide my feet to follow, and open my lips to tell the good news that you are Lord of all.

Seventh Sunday of Easter

No one can be a Christian in isolation. We need the support of shared worship and the knowledge of fellowship with those many, known or unknown to us, who are seeking to do his will and perhaps are suffering for his sake.

John 17:1–11

All mine are yours, and yours are mine; and I have been glorified in them (v.10).

We talk a great deal today about Christian unity, of seeking agreement, mutual respect and shared worship – and these are goals to be earnestly sought. What Jesus affirms in his great prayer to his Father before his Passion is not merely a state that is the reconciliation of differences but rather what may best be called 'oneness'. He and the Father are one, and all who believe in him are one in more than human terms: they are one in and with God. This is a great mystery, not to be analysed but to be accepted into the heart. But there is more: Jesus is glorified in his own people, a thought that would be wild, presumptuous, almost blasphemous if it were of human devising. But it is he who is God who has said it. Glory, the radiance of the divine presence, can shine in us. It is a wonderful and also terrifying realization for the Christian individually and for the Church collectively. Nothing but the grace of God can make us able to bear it. Between the triumph of the Ascension and the power of Pentecost, there is a time of silence to ponder and accept the inexpressible.

Look upon us, O Lord, and let all the darkness of our souls vanish before the beams of thy brightness. Fill us with holy love, and open to us the treasures of thy wisdom. All our desire is known unto thee, therefore perfect what thou hast begun, and what thy Spirit has awakened us to ask in prayer. We seek thy face, turn thy face unto us and show us thy glory. Then shall our longing be satisfied, and our peace shall be perfect.

St Augustine

Blessed Lord, Christ within me, make me able to bear the wonder of that presence which I dare not seek by my own desire. Grant that your glory may shine in me. Let the mutual love of Father and Son fill me with love, so that all my life, all my being, shall be worthy of the divinity made human for humanity's sake.

Pentecost

Whatever power for good we may have comes from the grace of the Holy Spirit in us. All God's people can share in this great gift.

John 20:19–23
He breathed on them and said to them, 'Receive the Holy Spirit' (v.22).

How does this gift of the Holy Spirit on the day of the Resurrection relate to the outpouring of divine power which came on the feast of Pentecost fifty days later? To enquire too anxiously is to misunderstand the eternal presence of God, Father, Son and Holy Spirit, and to set limits on the infinite. In our human condition we must learn and experience everything through the boundaries of time and location, but this is the condescension of God to our weakness and not an indication of how he is working in the world only from time to time or in particular places. The risen Christ empowers those who are to follow him, from the evening in the Upper Room through the generations until our time. They will receive the power from on high, a strength not their own, so that they may be workers in the unfolding of his purpose. Not only in the sacraments of the Church but at every moment when a human soul is open to God, the Holy Spirit comes in fullness of power and enabling love.

> May we, one and all, set forward with this season, when the Spirit descended, that so we may grow in grace, and in the knowledge of our Lord and Saviour. Let those who have had seasons of seriousness, lengthen them into a life; and let those who have made good resolves in Lent, not forget them in Eastertide; and let those who have hitherto lived religiously, learn devotion; and let those who have lived in good conscience, learn to live by faith; and let those who have made a good profession, aim at consistency; and let those who take pleasure in religious worship, aim at inward sanctity; and let those who have knowledge, learn to love; and let those who meditate, forget not mortification. Let not this sacred season leave us as it found us, let it leave us not as children, but as heirs and as citizens of the kingdom of heaven.
>
> J.H. Newman

Almighty God, fill my emptiness with the presence of the Holy Spirit, replace my weakness with the strength of the Holy Spirit, banish my darkness with the light of the Holy Spirit. As the risen Lord empowered his disciples for new tasks in his service, may I be empowered for whatever work, great or small, is your will for me.

Trinity Sunday

Wherever the gospel has been proclaimed, believers have been taught to acknowledge the power of the Holy Trinity in whose name they were baptized.

Matthew 28:16–20
Go therefore and make disciples of all nations, baptizing them in the name of the Father and of the Son and of the Holy Spirit (v.19).

In St Matthew's account it was the last command of Jesus to his disciples. It was one that they carried out as they went to spread the good news and to begin the work of the Christian Church. It has been obeyed ever since, in cathedrals and tiny mission stations, for children surrounded by their loving family and for lonely people at the point of death. A new beginning always seems to require an outward sign, a shared ceremony, and this is especially true for entrance into a religious faith. For Christians the words that seal the ceremony are unique, a declaration of the faith in God, Three in One and One in Three. The words will be repeated many times in the life that follows baptism, in blessing and absolution, at the beginning of sermons, in graces and private prayers. There have been and still are differences about the nature of baptism, the proper age and the method, but increasingly we have come to recognize the fellowship of the Church in all who have obeyed that great command and accepted faith in the Holy Trinity.

That in some real sense the Father, and the Son, and the Holy Ghost are They whom we are bound to serve and worship, from whom comes the Gospel of grace, and in whom the profession of Christianity centres, surely is shown, most satisfactorily and indisputably, by the words of this text. When Christ was departing,

He gave commission to His Apostles, and taught them what to teach and preach; and first of all they were to introduce their converts into His profession, or into His Church, and that by a solemn rite, which, as He had told Nicodemus at an earlier time, was to convey a high spiritual grace.

J.H. Newman

Almighty God, Father, Son and Holy Spirit, I give thanks for the grace of baptism and for all the powerful love that is the gift of the Holy Trinity. Fulfil in me the promises that were made at my baptism, increase in me the faith that I have professed, and keep me in that faith until this life is past and the mystery of which I have learned in human words shall be revealed in its fullness.

Proper 4

The practice of the Christian faith is not a hobby or a weekend activity. If it means anything, it is the groundwork of our lives, called to mind throughout the day to remind us that in our own strength we fall short and cannot stand firm.

Matthew 7:21–29
'Everyone who hears these words of mine and acts on them will be like a wise man who built his house on rock' (v.24).

Palestine is bordered by desert on one side and sea on the other. Water is soothing, sand is soft and yielding, rock is hard under the feet. Water swallows us, sand makes us stumble, on the hard rock we can stand upright. Here we can build, make for our own a little space of the earth, create a refuge that will not fall. Christ is the foundation, the refuge, the cornerstone. Some of his words are easy to hear, hard to follow. There are so many reasons for not acting on them. It is a busy time and some things, however right in themselves, must be postponed. To follow the conscience now might mean conflict, embarrassment or material loss. These are commandments for the exceptionally pious, not for ordinary Christians. So lives are built

69

on a foundation that has no strength when troubles and temptations come. A few minutes with the Bible, an hour in church, and soon all may be forgotten, fading like ripples on the water, footprints in the sand. From hour to hour and year to year, only the firm pressure of the rock keeps our feet firm, our spirits faithful.

> He calls the steadfastness of His doctrine a rock; because in truth His commands are stronger than any rock, setting one above all the waves of human affairs. For he who keeps these things strictly, will not have the advantage of men only when they are vexing him, but even of the very devils plotting against him. And that it is not vain boasting so to speak, Job is our witness, who received all the assaults of the devil, and stood unmoveable; and the Apostles too are our witnesses, for that when the waves of the whole world were beating against them, when both nations and princes, both their own people and strangers, both the evil spirits, and the devil, and every engine was set in motion, they stood firmer than a rock, and dispersed it all.

St John Chrysostom

Give me, O Lord, the wisdom that is grounded on your words. Keep me firm in faith and practice when I begin to slip into the softer path and the easier way, and draw me back to rest on the rock of my salvation.

Proper 5

The compassion of God breaks through all problems that seem insoluble and all human frailty that seems to bar the way. He comes to the aid of the weak and vulnerable in their greatest need.

Matthew 9:9–13, 18–26

'Those who are well have no need of a physician, but those who are sick' (v.12).

We who think we are living under pressure, are even 'stressed out', may yet find a little time to meditate on this Gospel passage. Jesus calls a new disciple, a most unlikely candidate in the opinion of the religious elite. His meal, crowded out by others who are similarly in bad repute, is harassed by hostile questions and then interrupted by a plea to visit a bereaved family and restore life to the dead. He leaves the table at once, only to have his walk to the house halted by yet another person in need. He responds at once to her silent approach, made in desperation and faith. His greatest act of compassion is greeted at first with mocking scepticism. Those corrupted by their way of life, equally with the chronically sick, the bereaved and the dead, all receive his healing touch. He does not complain that he is stressed out. His own comfort, his need for rest and food, do not come into question. The infinite love of God is not diminished by the demands of a human body. Just a thought for the times when everything seems too much.

> He that can apprehend and consider vice with all her baits and seeming pleasures, and yet abstain, and yet distinguish, and yet prefer that which is truly better, he is the true wayfaring Christian. I cannot praise a fugitive and cloistered virtue, unexercised and unbreathed, that never sallies out and sees her adversary, but slinks out of the race, where that immortal garland is to be run for not without dust and heat. Assuredly we bring not innocence into the world, we bring impurity much rather: that which purifies us is trial, and trial is by what is contrary.
>
> John Milton

Lord, you have called me to your service as you called Matthew. Heal the long sickness that keeps me from following you completely, and bring new life if my faith begins to die. When I am forgiven and restored, give me grace to be a channel of your healing power.

Proper 6

The mercy of God is not allocated by merit or achievement. It is absolute and unconditional, but those who are called to be his people are called also to share with others what they have been given.

Matthew 9:35–10:8
'You received without payment; give without payment' (10:8).

No 'missionary box', no retiring collection, no central fund, no private benevolence. They went on their journey without material support, poor as the poorest to whom they would preach. Tired, hungry, sore-footed, they went on speaking the words of truth and performing the works of mercy. One thing only was their sustenance: authority from their Master, appointment to do the work of God, and it was enough. So far they had given nothing, for what they had received was not to be bought with money, influence or good deeds. Now it was their turn to give, as freely as they had been given. Without that grace they were nothing, with it their poverty became wealth. He gives all – life that no human power can create, preservation so that his will may be done in us, pardon through the life of his own Son. Clothed, fed, with money in our purses – whether much or little – we can give only because he has given us the desire and the authority of his word beyond our deserving.

Is not all the world God's family? Are not we His creatures? Do we not live upon His meat, and move by His strength, and do our work by His light? And shall there be a mutiny among the flocks and herds, because their lord or their shepherd chooses their pastures, and suffers them not to wander into deserts and unknown ways? If we choose, we do it so foolishly that we cannot like it long, and most commonly not at all; but God is wise, affectionate to our needs, and powerful. Here, therefore, is the wisdom of the contented man, to let God choose for him; for when we have given up our wills to Him our spirits must needs rest, while our conditions have for their security the power, the wisdom, and the charity of God. Let us prepare our minds against changes, always expecting them, that we be not surprised when they come.

Jeremy Taylor

Thanks be to God for my creation, preservation and redemption. Strong in his love, may I never forget my weakness, busy about my affairs, may I always remember that he alone enables me day by day. I have received so much: may I have grace to give as freely as I have received.

Proper 7

No one can be a true follower of Christ without giving up the self-will that desires only comfort and pleasure. He has shown that the way to life is through death and that every death-point in our lives brings us closer to him.

Matthew 10:24–39
'Whoever does not take up his cross and follow me is not worthy of me' (v.38).

What a cross it is to bear a boring relative, a difficult colleague, an inconvenient journey. Or so people say, perhaps adding that they are keeping their fingers crossed. How attractive a gold or jewelled cross looks when worn as an ornament. In the world where Jesus walked among his people, 'cross' was a word of dread. It raised the spectre of the most shameful, the most painful death. He was not using a figure of speech when he called on his disciples to take up the cross. He was not offering a pretty decoration. He was saying, 'Follow me to the gallows, to the firing squad, to the gas chamber. Follow me to a place of execution and die there, mocked and in agony.' For some, the cost of discipleship has been as great as that, a tormented life, a martyr's death. For most it has mercifully been lighter, but without some cost there is no commitment. Perhaps all that is demanded is to turn from some besetting sin, to give up some indulgence that is causing damage, to give time to others that we would willingly give to our own pleasure. It will become a following of our Lord if it is offered as seriously as if it were the ultimate price.

St Francis and his companions, being called by God to carry the cross of Christ in their hearts, to practise it in their lives, and to preach it by their words, were truly crucified men both in their actions and in their works. They sought after shame and contempt, out of love for Christ, rather than the honours of the world, the respect and praise of men. They rejoiced to be despised, and were grieved when honoured. Thus they went about the world as pilgrims and strangers, carrying nothing with them but Christ crucified; and because they were of the true Vine, which is Christ, they produced great and good fruits in many souls which they gained to God.

The Little Flowers of St Francis

Lord Jesus, I dare not compare my trials and troubles with your suffering on the Cross, but in the strength of the Cross I may offer them as a token of faith. Grant that I may follow you with whatever burden is your will for me and bear it to the end.

Proper 8

God has spoken through many people: the Old Testament prophets, supremely in Jesus Christ, and for centuries through those who proclaimed the gospel. His word is open and never fails; whether to accept or reject it is left to human choice.

Matthew 10:40–42
'Whoever welcomes you welcomes me, and whoever welcomes me welcomes the one who sent me' (v.40).

The story of the stranger who is welcomed – or rejected – and turns out to be a divine visitor in disguise is found in many countries. In the Old Testament there are several of these encounters, such as the angelic figures who foretell the births of Isaac and of Samson; stories that prompt the writer of the letter to the Hebrews to say, 'Do not neglect to show hospitality to strangers, for by doing that some have entertained angels without knowing it' (Hebrews 13:2). Like many traditions, these stories contain a truth that is fulfilled in Christ. The mysterious link between the human and the divine is revealed and laid open for ever in his Incarnation. Those who speak his words are his emissaries, standing for him as an ambassador stands for a head of state. Because the fullness of the godhead is in Christ, they have the authority of God himself. Who are these ambassadors? They are not found only as the preacher in the pulpit, the evangelist at the door, or the vicar coming in for a quiet chat. They may be people whom we do not at first regard as messengers of the gospel. They may be people, known or unknown, who have a word of truth, or a need by which the command of love can be fulfilled.

O God, fountain of love, pour thy love into our souls, that we may love those whom thou lovest with the love thou givest us, and think and speak with the love thou givest us, and think and speak of them tenderly, meekly, lovingly; and so loving our brethren and sisters for thy sake, may grow in thy love, and dwelling in thy love may dwell in thee, for Jesus Christ's sake.

E.B. Pusey

Lord, open my eyes to see your presence in others, open my heart to receive you in them, open my door to welcome you in them. Open my ears to hear your word in the proclamation of scripture, in the teaching of the Church, and in the daily encounters when even casual talk may suddenly speak of you.

Proper 9

Only as we turn to God and are open to his liberating power can we find true freedom. Constraints that come from outside may be overcome, but the inner conflicts can be resolved only by grace.

Matthew 11:16–19, 25–30
'Come to me, all you that are weary and are carrying heavy burdens, and I will give you rest' (v.28).

A vision of humanity over the centuries rises in the imagination. Wanderers in the wilderness carrying all their possessions with them, slaves working to build the monuments of kings, women with their children fleeing from danger, labourers in the fields, the daily trek to fetch water. God sees them with the eyes of his compassion and brings them at last to the peace of his heavenly Kingdom. Human eyes are often indifferent but sometimes compassion is aroused by his Spirit and we try to relieve the burdens of others. Then there is another vision: the rich, the successful, the powerful in the ranks of this world. They have their burdens of stress and anxiety, the fragility of status, the inward emptiness of solitude. The invisible burdens lie heavy on the shoulders of all who pass through this human journey. Whether known and repented, unrealized or arrogantly ignored, the burden of sin lies heaviest of all. The love of Christ takes the load, soothes the aching shoulders and brings blessed rest to give strength for the next stage of the journey.

Now I saw in my dream that the highway, up which Christian was to go, was fenced on either side with a wall, and that wall was called Salvation. (Isaiah 36:1). Up this way, therefore, did burdened Christian run, but not without great difficulty, because of the load on his back. He ran thus till he came to a place somewhat ascending; and upon that place stood a Cross, and a little below, in the bottom, a Sepulchre. So I saw in my dream, that just as Christian came up with the Cross, his burden loosed from off his shoulders, and fell from off his back, and began to tumble, and so continued to do, till it came to the mouth of the Sepulchre, where it fell in, and I saw it no more. Then was Christian glad and lightsome, and said with a merry heart, 'He hath given me rest by his sorrow, and life by his death.'

John Bunyan

Loving Jesus Christ, your grace alone can take away the burden that holds me back from fullness of life. Teach me to cast my cares upon you because you care for me, so that I may be free to share the burdens of those who do not yet know your love.

Proper 10

The evidence of faith is shown not in words but in lives. It is as we respond or fail to respond to what God has given that we reveal or conceal his goodness and hasten or hinder his purpose.

Matthew 13:1–9, 18–23
Other seeds fell on good soil and brought forth grain, some a hundredfold, some sixty, some thirty (v.8).

Warning and encouragement are the twin poles of Bible teaching. The perils that surround us are never to be forgotten: the Lord tells us constantly to watch and pray. But to dwell on the negative can be as harmful as to ignore it. Eyes raised to the positive hope, to the goal set before us, are more likely to avoid the temptations that can cause us to stumble. Good works done in the name of Christ do not buy our salvation, for he paid the price that no human virtue could ever pay. They honour what he has done for our human condition and they make visible the praise that is owed to him. Having avoided despair about the dangers of life, let us not fall into despair about the heroic virtues of the saints. God our Maker knows our limitations. God our Redeemer makes the allowances that we dare not make for ourselves. He knows that even the good ground is far from perfect, and he who gives so freely receives in love that which is offered in love. Thirty, sixty or a hundred – all are accepted by the great Sower.

> Having therefore spoken of the ways of destruction, afterwards He mentions the good ground, not suffering them to despair, but giving a hope of repentance, and indicating that it is possible to change from the things before mentioned into this. And yet if both the land be good, and the Sower one, and the seed the same, wherefore did one bear a hundred, one sixty, one thirty? Here again the difference is from the nature of the ground, for even where the ground is good, great even therein is the difference. Seest thou, that not the husbandman is to be blamed, nor the seed, but the land that receives it? Not for its nature, but for its disposition. And herein too, great is His mercy to man, that He doth not require one measure of virtue, but while He receives the

first, and casts not out the second, He gives also a place to the third.

St John Chrysostom

Lord, the good seed of your word has come to me by your grace alone. Give me now the response of a life lived in the light of your glory. Let the measure of all I do be according to your will for me.

Proper 11

We live in the assurance of the ultimate triumph of God's loving purpose. There is much sorrow and suffering in the world as well as much goodness. Our faith tells us that all is moving towards the final glory.

Matthew 13:24–30, 36–43
'"Let both of them grow together until the harvest"' (v.30).

'How do you explain all the evil in the world?' asks the agnostic. 'How do you explain all the good in the world?' counters the believer. 'Why do the media only give us the bad news?' everyone wants to know. The Old Testament writers challenged God about the way in which the wicked seemed to flourish. It is a mixed world certainly, one in which for centuries theologians and philosophers have tired to discern the good and the bad, and have found large grey areas of uncertainty. St Paul warns, 'Do not pronounce judgement before the time, before the Lord comes' (1 Corinthians 4:5). The best way to counter wrong is by strengthening right. Slums are removed when there is better housing; disease is prevented when there is plenty of clean water. The wise gardener tends and feeds the desired plants and does not stand despairingly looking at the weeds. One person will delight in the beauty of the roses, another will curse them for being scratched by their thorns. Life in this world will never be perfect until the end of time as we know it, but the tender shoots of perfection are there to be cultivated.

This parable of our Blessed Lord will bear the very closest inspection, because it shows us exactly what happens in everyday life; whether it be in the brightness of the morning, in the splendour of the noonday, or in the gloaming of the evening, it is all the same, this parable is the experience of everyday life. It is the experience of anyone who tries to do good in any way whatever, whether it be educational, whether it be patriotic, whether it be philanthropic, or whether it be Christian – he is sure to meet with the very same circumstances that this parable gives almost immediately. He may do his very best: he may spend his time, his money, his energy, his very soul, but he is certain to meet with the enemy who sows the tares. Sooner or later there is sure to be the enemy that follows after, as darkness follows light; someone is sure to come up who will question his motives, disparage his actions, assail his character. Wherever you sow wheat, the enemy follows you with the tares.

A.H. Stanton

Lord, keep my faith strong and my deeds obedient in all the dangers and difficulties of this life. Teach me to grow in grace and to trust in the assurance that all things work together for good in those who love you.

Proper 12

Human judgement is fallible and can lead into error when we feel most confident of our own strength. If we are open to discern the signs which come from God, our decisions will be governed by his will.

Matthew 13:31–33, 44–52

'Every scribe who has been trained for the kingdom of heaven is like the master of a household who brings out of his treasure what is new and what is old' (v.52).

Age, temperament, social life, peer pressure – all combine to thrust us into a corner when we make our response to the life of our time. Is what is new always an improvement and to be desired? Or what is old better and to be preserved? All through the history of Christianity, the same debate has gone on. There have been periods when nothing was allowed to change and the living spirit in the Church began to ebb. There have been times when everything was revised to conform to the spirit of the age. Jesus affirmed the truth of what had already been revealed and then challenged people to think of it in a new way. Seed, baking, treasure, jewels, fish, follow each other in a startling sequence of images of the Kingdom. All lead to the simple good sense of the person whose wisdom values both the new and the old, and makes use of both for an ordered, balanced life. Tradition – not just what was done yesterday but that which has been handed down through the ages – is the preserver and protector of the faith. Firmly grounded, the Christian is open to the guidance of the Holy Spirit into new insights of truth.

Reflections of this sort have gradually determined me not to grumble at the age in which I happen to have been born – a natural tendency certainly older than Hesiod. Many ancient beautiful things are lost, many ugly modern things have arisen; but invert the proposition and it is equally true. I at least am a modern with some interest in advocating tolerance, and notwithstanding an inborn beguilement which carries my affection and regret continually into an imagined past, I am aware that I must lose all sense of moral proportion unless I keep alive a stronger attachment to what is near, and a power of admiring what I best know and understand.

George Eliot

God of holy wisdom, give me the wisdom to live both in the stability of what is old and the opportunity of what is new. When I cling to the past and fear change, when I become impatient and rush towards novelty, keep me on the high road to the Kingdom where old and new are united in one eternal truth.

Proper 13

Faith is often incomplete, fearing that God will help us only in certain ways or to a limited extent. He meets all the needs of those who turn to him confidently and with the whole will.

Matthew 14:13–21
All ate and were filled (v.20).

It must have been a miserable crowd by the time evening began to fall and it grew cold in that desert place. The excitement of following this new healer and teacher had kept them buoyed up through the day, but now hunger and weariness set in and overcame their enthusiasm. Some of them muttered about these religious folk who care nothing about the needs of ordinary people. Their enthusiasm was turning to hostility. As for the disciples, they were sick of people crowding round their Master and wanted only to be alone with him. 'Send them away' was a cry that he heard from them all too often. The idea of sharing their meagre supplies among such a crowd was the last straw. But the voice of authority overcame their complaints, and they all sat down as he commanded them. He who had taught and healed many now fed them until they could eat no more. Tentative hope grew into total satisfaction. Replete and content, they did not then know that they had seen a sign of the Messiah. The miracle of the manna in the wilderness was even more bountifully repeated. The desert blossomed like a rose.

> Guide me, O thou great Redeemer,
> Pilgrim through this barren land.
> I am weak but thou art mighty,
> Hold me with thy powerful hand.
>   Bread of heaven,
> Feed me till I want no more.

> William Williams

Bountiful God, teach me to trust you for everything. When my hope is weak and my faith grows dim, make me remember how often you have overcome my fears and met my needs more abundantly than I could have imagined. All that is broken in me is made whole in you, and the desert of the heart is desert no more.

Proper 14

The great events of life, the happenings in the world, the extreme moods of nature, can dominate our minds. Even seeking to understand the deeper mysteries of faith can make us fail to see what is near to us. All that the believer needs is to be still and trust in the personal encounter with God.

Matthew 14:22–33
'You of little faith, why did you doubt?' (v.31).

Peter again, impetuous as ever, self-confident, failing when the going is suddenly hard. It is almost like a rehearsal for the eve of the Passion – the promise to follow even to death, the desertion, the denial. In each case the shame is followed by acceptance and restoration in the love of his Lord. There is a Sunday School chorus which exhorts, 'Fix your eyes upon Jesus'. As long as Peter did that he was safe, upheld above the peril of wind and water. When he looked down at the waves, his unsupported human weakness made him start to sink. The power that had fed the multitude in what had seemed a hopeless situation was forgotten as soon as the next crisis came. It is easy to feel superior about Peter, wiser to identify with him. Faith refers all to God, the source of life and its sustainer, and keeps him at the centre. Humanity left to itself keeps looking at the dangers, the conflicts and uncertainties. It is not easy to let the self go in absolute trust. For one day at a time, try not to look at the waves.

The Son of God will come to us, that He may prepare the sea for us, walking upon it. And when we see the Word appearing unto us we shall indeed be troubled before we clearly understand that it is the Saviour who has come to us, supposing that we are still beholding an apparition, and for fear shall cry out; but He Himself straightway will speak to us saying 'Be of good cheer, it is I; be not afraid.' And if, warmly moved by His 'Be of good cheer', any Peter be found among us, who is on his way to perfection but has not yet become perfect, having gone down from the boat, as if coming out of that temptation in which he was distressed, he will indeed walk at first, wishing to come to Jesus upon the waters; but being as yet of little faith, and as yet doubting, will see that the wind is strong and will be afraid and begin to sink; but he will not sink because he will call upon Jesus with loud voice, and will say to Him, 'Lord, save me'. Then immediately while such a Peter is yet speaking and saying, 'Lord save me,' the Word will stretch forth His hand, holding out assistance to such an one, and will take hold of him when he is beginning to sink, and will reproach him for his little faith and doubting. Only, observe that He did not say, 'O thou without faith' but, 'O thou of little faith', and that it was said, 'Wherefore didst thou doubt?' as he still had a measure of faith, but also a tendency towards that which was opposed to faith.

Origen

Blessed Jesus, let me at all times and in all places keep my eyes fixed upon you. In the storms and perils of life, strengthen my assurance that, as you have called me to walk with you and towards you, my feet will be guided and my whole being will be safe while I draw closer to you.

Proper 15

The promises of God were first made to the Jewish people. Their great prophets came to understand that he is God of the whole world, and the incarnation of Jesus Christ opened salvation to all who respond in faith.

Matthew 15:(10–20,) 21–28
'Even the dogs eat the crumbs that fall from their master's table' (v.27).

No sentimentality about 'little doggies' can soften the record of a discouraging and indeed insulting answer. It was not a society in which dogs were cherished pets, and the dogs of the Bible are usually images of pariahs and scavengers. What we do not know is how it was spoken – perhaps a tone of testing irony, a gentleness in the voice that challenged but did not dismiss the suppliant. The witty answer suggests that an understanding was already there. The encounter can be seen as one of the great turning-points in the ministry of our Lord. All people are now admitted to the fellowship of God's people and the benefits of his love. There is no more distinction between one race and another for all are his own. Jesus grants the gift of healing as completely as he had been giving it to those who were his own people after the flesh. From now on, the bounty of God would be given out not in crumbs but in the whole loaf, in the power that had already fed a multitude from a little bread, in the love that would make the broken bread a spiritual feeding for Christians in the generations yet unborn.

> Why should I call Thee Lord, Who art my God?
> Why should I call Thee Friend, Who art my Love?
> Or King, Who art my very Spouse above?
> Or call Thy sceptre on my heart Thy rod?
> Lo now Thy banner over me is love,
> All heaven flies open to me at Thy nod:
> For Thou hast lit Thy flame in me a clod,
> Made me a nest for dwelling of Thy Dove.
> What wilt Thou call me in our home above,
> Who now hast called me friend? how will it be
> When Thou for good wine settest forth the best?
> Now Thou dost bid me come and sup with Thee,
> Now Thou dost make me lean upon Thy breast:
> How will it be with me in time of love?

> Christina Rossetti

When I ask for little, my God, you often grant so much more than my expectation. Give me grace to ask always in the faith that makes your will my only desire for myself and for those dear to me. Let my trust never fail when I have to wait for the time of fulfilment that is in your purpose.

Proper 16

Careful attention to what is close and immediate is necessary in an ordered life, but our eyes should not always be looking down. We need also to look up to God for guidance every day and to learn as much as we need of his greater purposes.

Matthew 16:13–20
'Flesh and blood has not revealed this to you, but my Father in heaven' (v.17).

How far can human reason take us in knowledge of God? This is a question that has been debated by theologians for centuries. Most have agreed that it can take us a certain way, and indeed that we have a duty to use the gifts of intelligence that God has given us so that we can discern him at work in the world. But there is a point beyond which reason alone cannot go, and only the revelation given by God himself can make our knowledge of him complete – or as complete as is possible while we are still in this earthly life. What we need to know of the ultimate mystery is given to us by grace, not by seeking. The teaching and healing ministry of Jesus aroused many rumours and conjectures about exactly who he was. Even his closest followers were uncertain until Peter, always ready to offer an opinion, gave the right answer. Despite his many errors and failings, he was chosen to be the first to receive the revelation that their Master was the Christ, the Son of God. Or perhaps it was because of his frailty that he was chosen, a sign of the power of God working through the weak and fallible, and a hope for the generations of inadequate men and women who would yet try to love and follow Christ.

All this knowledge of God's creation and of God Himself, the Creator and Sustainer of the entire universe, which is infused into a soul by grace as I have mentioned, I call the fair words and communications of God to the soul chosen as His true spouse. He reveals mysteries and often offers rich gifts to it out of His treasury, and adorns the soul with them with great honour.

Walter Hilton

Heavenly Father, from you I have received the gift of reason and the power of questioning. Enable me to use them to the full, but not to rely on them alone. Make me ever more ready to look to you, more open to your calling and more worthy to receive the revelation of your will.

Proper 17

To follow our own way is comfortable and can too easily be mistaken for following the way set before us by God. The easy road may be leading us away from him. The committed life must continually beware of the call of self-will.

Matthew 16:21–28

'Those who want to save their life will lose it, and those who lose their life for my sake will find it' (v.25).

Peter is in trouble again. After the flash of divine revelation, his human instinct returns. What more natural than to want to turn his Master away from suffering and death? But the desire of human love would frustrate the purpose of divine love. Peter had not yet come to understand the great reversals of the gospel, the new laws of the Kingdom. To save is to lose and to lose is to find. To give all is to gain all, because the gifts are being offered back to the Giver. There on the road to Jerusalem Jesus gives a call to obedience which may come in any place and at any time: to let go of what seems good, in the faith that what comes after will be better. The ultimate sacrifice, the way to bodily death for the sake of Christ, is demanded of few. We reverence the martyrs who have given their lives at God's call. But if we fix our eyes on them for too long, we may be missing the

86

call to give up what is comfortingly familiar for the sake of something
equally unspectacular but part of God's plan for us.

'Tis so much joy! 'tis so much joy!
If I should fail, what poverty!
And yet, as poor as I
Have ventured all upon a throw,
Have gained – yes, hesitated so,
This side the victory.

Life is but life, and death but death.
Bliss is but bliss, and breath but breath
And if indeed I fail,
At least to know the worst is sweet.
Defeat means nothing but defeat,
No drearier can befall.

And if I gain – Oh gun at sea,
Oh bells that in the steeples be,
At first repeat it slow!
For Heaven is a different thing,
Conjectured and waked sudden in,
And might extinguish me.

Emily Dickinson

Lord, give me grace to follow always where you are leading me.
Grant me wisdom to know what is right in my way of life and what
is a hindrance to my faith. Strengthen me to let go of the old when
you are calling me to the new, knowing that in your will there is life
and not loss.

Proper 18

Christ is uniquely present in the soul of every believer, but he is not the property of any individual. His presence draws all Christians together in love of him and of one another, to share the comfort and the guidance that he gives.

Matthew 18:15–20
'Where two or three are gathered in my name, I am there among them' (v.20).

'Have we got a quorum?' may be the question at the start of a meeting – asked anxiously in case the meeting cannot be held, or perhaps hopefully, with the chance of getting home early. Are there enough people present for discussion and decisions? Jesus never counted to see how many people needed him. Teaching and feeding a great crowd or speaking to a single person in need, he gave his whole attention and his whole love. He promises to be present where Christians come together, not only for worship in public or private, but wherever people love him and are trying to serve and obey him. It does not need a formal act of prayer, a polite introduction, to bring him in. He is there among them, not on the outside looking in, not hovering at the edge of the group, but right at the centre. The Authorized Version reading 'in the midst of them' gives the stronger expression of his promise. He is not counting the number or taking notes, he is there teaching, guiding, drawing all to himself if we open our meeting for business or pleasure and let him in.

> I see his blood upon the rose
> And in the stars the glory of his eyes,
> His body gleams amid eternal snows,
> His tears fall from the skies.
>
> I see his face in every flower;
> The thunder and the singing of the birds
> Are but his voice – and carven by his power
> Rocks are his written words.

All pathways by his feet are worn,
His strong heart stirs the ever-beating sea,
His crown of thorns is twined with every thorn,
His cross is every tree.

Joseph Mary Plunkett

Lord Jesus Christ, I believe that you are present with me, now and always. As I praise you for your glory and thank you for all your mercies, let me honour other people for your presence in them, knowing that whatever time I share with them, you are there too.

Proper 19

The Bible often warns against judging and condemning other people. God is the only Judge, and it is he who shows mercy and pardons sin, and teaches us to show the same love to those who offend us.

Matthew 18:21–35

'"*Should you not have had mercy on your fellow-slave, as I had mercy on you?*"' (v.33).

'Forgive' is an easy word to say, for humorous dismissal of a trivial error or reconciliation after a serious quarrel. A word that can satisfy the ruffled nerves and keep social life smooth without going very deeply. So it must have been from the beginning of human relationships. As often in the teaching of Jesus, it takes a vivid story to bring home the difference between conventional life and the life of the Christian. His deliberate exaggeration is part of his method. A huge sum of money, in practice unthinkable for a slave in the ancient world, is contrasted with one so much smaller that the effect is almost absurd. The very absurdity makes the point. The debt of sin against the power and majesty of God can never be compared with the grievances between the people of his creation. The agony of the Cross is set against the daily response of men and women to each other. God's response to sin is to suffer and die in the person of the humanity that had so offended. Human response is too often the sulky rebuff, the refused hand, and worst of all the unspoken resentment that eats away the heart. It is not the debt that incurs the anger of the Lord: it is the unforgiving choice of satisfaction above compassion.

The Lord has clearly set forth the condition of such pardon; he has stated it as a law and expressed it as a covenant. We can only expect our sins to be forgiven according to the degree that we ourselves forgive those who sin against us. We are informed categorically that we will not be able to obtain what we ask for in respect of our sins unless we have acted ourselves in the same way to those who have sinned against us. Thus our Lord says in another place in Scripture: 'The measure you deal out will be dealt back to you.' Similarly, the servant who refused to cancel his fellow servant's debt, in spite of having had his own debts cancelled by his master, was thrown into prison. Because he refused to be generous to his fellow servant, he forfeited the indulgence that had been shown to him by his master. These ideas Christ sets forth even more directly and stamps it with his own authority when he says: 'Whenever you stand praying, forgive, if you have anything against anyone; so that your Father in heaven will also forgive you your debts. But if you do not forgive, neither will your Father in heaven forgive you your debts.'

Cyprian of Carthage

For your sake, Lord Jesus, for the free pardon that I have received by the power of your loving life and saving death, I desire my forgiving of others who have harmed or grieved me to be complete. Keep me so mindful of your mercy that I may forgive without seeking satisfaction, and love where love is not returned.

Proper 20

God's ways are not our ways: that is a theme right through the Bible. He shows mercy when people shout for judgement, makes suffering a privilege and does not weigh his love by merit. His Kingdom calls for a radical change in our human values.

Year A

Matthew 20:1–16

'"Take what belongs to you and go; I choose to give to this last the same as I give to you"' (v.14).

This is hardly to be recommended as an exercise in labour relations – the same pay for an easy hour in the cool evening as for a whole day in the heat; those who have been hanging around since the morning regarded the same as those who started work at the proper time. Strikes, riots and the fall of governments would follow such an exercise of equality in human terms. The Parables of the Kingdom set out to startle, to shake presuppositions, to turn expectations right around. Grace is a free gift of love, not a reward for good work or long perseverance. It is hard enough to kill the selfish instinct in ourselves, the desire for the best in material benefits and personal esteem. It is far harder to kill spiritual selfishness. Am I not more meritorious, more deserving of God's approval than those who go to church once a year, who think prayer is only an emergency call when all else fails, who repent at the end of a wasted and destructive life? Not at all. It is only by the grace of a Master whose ways are not our ways that I am allowed to walk into the Kingdom with them.

If the grace of God is at the beginning of all that we do for Him, so too it is the end and the reward. Almighty God gives us His reward, not according to what we have done, but according to what we wished to do; not according to what we are, but according to what we wished to be; not according to the works of our hand, but according to the inspiration of our soul; and the inspiration of our soul comes from Him. No earthly master, of course, can pay his servants in this way: whether it be by contract, or piece-work, they must be paid according to just exactly the work that they have done. But the Divine Master gives us our reward. He reads the very secrets of our hearts, and knows what we would do, and what we would be, and takes the will for the deed.

A.H. Stanton

Take from me, loving Master, the burden of self-righteousness. When I feel most sure of my faith and good works, then I am most in danger. Thank you for the love that is not measured, that brings sinners into the blessed company of saints.

Proper 21

G od works quietly, changing the lives of those who will hear his word. He is honoured by obedience and not by words of approval and acceptance that have no result.

Matthew 21:23–32
'Neither will I tell you by what authority I am doing these things' (v.27).

What are your qualifications? Have you got proof of your identity? What is your rank? Are you licensed to do this? Perhaps naturally suspicious of false claims, people have come to value the badge above the performance, the document before the deed. Leaders of the people, learned in their knowledge of religion, those who demanded the credentials of Jesus should have been convinced by the signs they had seen. The works prophesied of the Messiah, miraculous cures, proclamation of the Kingdom, had passed before them and they still wanted verbal justification. The Baptist had puzzled them, and now this man was agitating them by healing and preaching without a licence. As he always did when they were trying to trap him, he turned their question against them and made them their own accusers. If they could not cope with their uncertainty about the forerunner, how could they understand the status of the one whose coming he had prophesied? Sometimes the silences of our Lord were as powerful as his words. Those who do not respond to the signs of God at work in the world and in personal lives will never be satisfied by theological arguments.

> Dangerous it were for the feeble brain of man to wade far into the doings of the most High; whom although to know be life, and joy to make mention of his name; yet our soundest knowledge is, to know that we know him not as indeed he is, neither can know him, and our safest eloquence concerning him, is our silence, when we confess without confession, that his glory is inexplicable, his

greatness above our capacity and reach. He is above, and we upon earth; therefore it behoveth our words to he wary and few.

Richard Hooker

My Lord and my God, I know that all authority comes from you alone. Strengthen me to show my love by obedience to your will and my faith by trusting in the signs of your presence. Shield me from seeking refuge in words of adoration without responding to your call.

Proper 22

God made the world good and sustains it still in its fallen state. He has given a new hope in Christ, an ideal to follow and bring us back to grace. But he also gave us free will and many still reject his bounty.

Matthew 21:33–46
'The kingdom of God will be taken away from you and given to a people that produces the fruit of the kingdom' (v.43).

Christians have a long and shameful history of feeling superior to Jews and quoting their own scriptures against them. The Old Testament has many warnings of the anger of God against his people, and as many of his mercy when they repent and turn back to him. The New Testament, with its continued warnings, is not to be read complacently and with self-satisfaction. The charges brought against the Jews have been equally deserved by Christians, individually and in their churches. We have done it all: ingratitude, backsliding, disobedience, grumbling and rebellion, rejection of new prophets with unwelcome calls to repentance (think of the reception that John Wesley got, and the persecution of the Confessing Church in Germany). Assurance is a great thing and it is certain that God never rejects those who have kept faithful to him, even though they sin along the way. But rejection may come from the human side, and he wants people who love freely, not automata or puppets. It is well to look to the state of the vineyard and to cherish it as a sacred trust, not a

fortress. Those who now seem most clearly outside may be the next
to be invited in.

> He preached upon 'Breadth' till it argued him narrow –
> The Broad are too broad to define
> And of 'Truth' until it proclaimed him a Liar –
> The Truth never flaunted a Sign.
>
> Simplicity fled from his counterfeit presence
> As Gold the Pyrites would shun –
> What confusion would cover the innocent Jesus
> To meet so enabled a Man !

Emily Dickinson

*I know that I have been unfaithful to my calling and neglectful of
my duty. Lord, give me new strength to labour for you, feet swift to
follow, hands ready for service, so that I may produce good fruit for
your glory and the benefit of your people.*

Proper 23

For those who know and love God, life should be different. It is
to be lived in joy and hope, with love towards others, thankful
for what is past, obedient to the calls of the present and confident in
the future when God's whole purpose will be complete.

Matthew 22:1–14
' "Friend, how did you get in here without a wedding robe?" ' (v.12).

This is a popular text for sermons about people making excuses for
not coming to church or to some related activity. Unfortunately, it
is thus addressed to the wrong hearers, those who have already come.
As in all good stories, the strong point is at the end, the condemnation
of the man who accepted the invitation but came without respect to
his host. The question of how someone called in from the street could
get hold of a special robe is no more relevant than the equity of

paying the workers in a previous parable the same rate for unequal hours. This guest was being too casual, coming for what he could get at the feast and failing to be polite to the wedding couple in whose honour it had been prepared. He is the image of those who come to church casually, unprepared, not in love and charity with their neighbours, gossiping instead of making themselves ready for the time of worship. Do we make full preparation for our communion? And not only in church, but in the profession of Christian life that does not show the signs of obedience to the words of Christ? Those who accept the gracious invitation of God without truly responding to its obligations are not in a position to be patronizing about those who have refused it. There is not one of us whose wedding robe is immaculate.

> What is meant by the wedding garment? Surely it must refer to something that renders a man an acceptable guest at a wedding, and the absence of which would render his presence unsuitable at such a place, so that he were better away. The marriage garment is well explained of Christian joy of heart, 'the fruit of the Spirit is joy'; and we may add, delight at the presence of the Bridegroom; for this it is which occasions this gladness of heart.
>
> Isaac Williams

Gracious God, I am too often an unworthy guest at your table. I come to you carrying my doubt and anxiety, my resentment of other guests, my indifference to seeking your full purpose for me. Have mercy on my weakness and bring me to a right mind and a true heart in your service, so that I may not fall under judgement when I taste your feast.

Proper 24

Evidence for God is not found by looking for one who makes life go exactly the way we want it to be. We can come to know him only if we acknowledge him as one whose power is supreme and whose will is all-embracing.

Matthew 22:15–22
'Why are you putting me to the test, you hypocrites?' (v.18).

When discussion of religion gets too hot to be comfortable, it can be a relief to turn to specific issues. 'I asked God for something and he did not give it to me.' 'Why do people fight each other about religion?' 'What do Christians think about paying taxes that may be used for bad purposes?' A clear answer to every question would be so comforting: perhaps a Bible with an index in which one could look up a specific reference to the problem. But this kind of thing is putting God to the test of human values and limited desires, as the Israelites tested his protecting love in the wilderness by demanding food and water to be provided immediately. The enemies of Jesus thought that they could get him to give either a seditious answer or one not acceptable to Jewish religious nationalism. The divine wisdom that had borne with generations of rebellion and disobedience had no difficulty with that one. The demands of absolute trust can be troublesome, for most of us some of the time and for many all of the time. It is much easier to try out a few test cases before deciding whether to become a Christian – easier, but not the way to faith in Christ.

Sung Heavenly Anthems of his victory
Over temptation and the Tempter proud.
True Image of the Father, whether throned
In the bosom of bliss, and light of light
Conceiving, or remote from Heaven, enshrined
In fleshly Tabernacle and human form,
Wandering the Wilderness; whatever place,
Habit or state or motion, still expressing
The Son of God, with Godlike force endued
Against the Attempter of thy Father's Throne,
And Thief of Paradise.

John Milton

Forgive me, Lord, when I put you to the test by uncertain prayers and selfish thoughts. Teach me again and again to remember that you alone are the creator and sustainer of all that exists. Let not my vision of you become too small.

Proper 25

If we truly love God, we shall love the men and women of his creation. The way we treat other people is the measure of the faith which we profess.

Matthew 22:34–46

'You shall love the Lord your God with all your heart, and with all your soul, and with all your mind. This is the greatest and first commandment. And the second is like it: You shall love your neighbour as yourself' (vv.37–39).

'Love' is a misused word, a dangerous word, even sometimes a harmful word. It is spoken to convey everything from genuine unselfish affection to mere lust, and even to a liking for chocolate. We need more words than one, as there were in the Greek which the writers of the New Testament used. The kind of love which Jesus commands is *agape*, love which is not aroused by finding beauty or worthiness in its object, but truly desires the good of another and is willing to help that good to come about. As St Paul describes it, this love is free from the taints of selfishness, jealousy, possessiveness which can so easily take over what sometimes passes as love (1 Corinthians 13). The question that brought Jesus to give this answer was not a sneaky test like the one about the tribute money, but probably a genuine wish to find if this new Teacher could properly interpret the Law. The two commandments come from the Old Testament (Deuteronomy 6:5 and Leviticus 19:18). He who gave the Law was the one who could summarize it in these simple but infinitely demanding words. The heavy details of ritual obedience were being lifted, and all God's people were being called to love as he loved them. When he said this, Jesus was in Jerusalem, the week before his Passion, where *agape* would be shown in a supreme way.

So then in the beginning man loves God, not for God's sake, but for his own. It is something for him to know how little he can do by himself and how much by God's help, and in that knowledge to order himself rightly towards God, his sure support. But when tribulations, recurring again and again, constrain him to turn to God for unfailing help, would not even a heart as hard as iron, as cold as marble, be softened by the goodness of such a Saviour, so that he would love God not altogether selfishly, but because He is God? Let frequent troubles drive us to frequent supplications; and surely, tasting, we must see how gracious the Lord is (Psalm 34:8). Thereupon His goodness once realised draws us to love Him unselfishly, yet more than our own needs impel us to love Him selfishly.

Bernard of Clairvaux

When I say, 'Lord, I love you', let me remember the cost of salvation. If I do not see you in those around me, I have not seen you in the reality of your sacrificial love. Take away all that hardens the heart and make true love flow through me to other people.

Bible Sunday

God has revealed himself through the ages and given us the words by which we are to live. The revelation is complete and nothing can take it away.

Matthew 24:30–35
'Heaven and earth will pass away, but my words will not pass away' (v.35).

St Peter would remember these words of Jesus when he wrote in his pastoral letter, quoting from the prophet Isaiah, 'The grass withers, and the flower falls, but the word of the Lord endures for ever' (1 Peter 1:24–25; Isaiah 40:8). The constancy of God, his complete faithfulness and steadfast truth, is emphasized throughout the Bible. What he wishes his people to know of his own being and nature, of the perfect revelation in Christ, and of the way of life they should follow, has been given through the medium of those chosen to record his Word. The Bible is not a reference book with an index by which we can find a text for the immediate solution of every problem. Its deeper meanings need faith and understanding, prayerful reading and the help of wise commentaries. Knowledge of its background and of its application to new conditions are both important for the Christian today and in every age. But the centrality of its revelation, the truth of its teaching can never be superseded, whatever may happen to the world. Some sects have claimed to receive new messages from God which go beyond the Bible. Jesus tells us that we have all that we need to know.

> Welcome, dear book, soul's joy and food! The feast
> Of spirits: Heaven extracted lies in thee,
> Thou art life's charter, the Dove's spotless nest
> Where souls are hatched unto eternity.
>
> In thee the hidden stone, the manna lies;
> Thou art the great Elixir, rare and choice;
> The key that opens to all mysteries.
> The Word in characters, God in the Voice.
>
> O that I had had cut deep in my hard heart
> Each line in thee! Then would I plead in groans
> Of my Lord's penning, and by sweetest art
> Return upon himself the Law and Stones.
>
> Read here, my faults are thine. This Book and I
> Will tell thee so; Sweet Saviour, thou didst die.
>
> Henry Vaughan

Holy God, I give thanks for your Word revealed by the hands of your servants through the ages. As it stands steadfast and immutable, so let my faith be constant, my reading of Scripture diligent, and my understanding enlightened that I may be more fit for your service.

Fourth Sunday before Advent

The call of God is not just for a single task or a short time of obedience. Those who truly desire to serve him will work faithfully through all the changing conditions of life.

Matthew 24:1–14
'The one who endures to the end will be saved' (v.13).

Many of us probably have uncomfortable memories of childhood and schooldays when we were being told to 'Keep going', 'Stick to it' or 'Don't give up'. Excellent advice, no doubt, but words that are easier to utter from the sidelines of life than to follow when the going is hard. G.K. Chesterton said that the truth was not that Christianity had been tried and found wanting, but that it had been found difficult and not tried. It is often a sadness to believers, lay as well as ordained, to see how people fall away after making the solemn vows of baptism, confirmation or marriage. Even for those who remain constant in worship, there can be the unseen fading of enthusiasm and hope. Whether in the deep tribulations described in the Gospel or in the routine of ordinary days, perseverance is a necessary virtue. Our call is different from the urging of distant parents and teachers. He who exhorts us has endured the utmost that human malice can do. We have the promise, 'He will also strengthen you to the end' (1 Corinthians 1:8).

When Mr. Standfast had thus set things in order, and the time being come for him to haste him away, he also went down to the river. Now there was a great calm at that time in the river; wherefore Mr. Standfast, when he was about half-way in, stood awhile, and talked to his companions that had waited upon him thither. And he said, This river has been a terror to many; yea, the thoughts of it also have often frightened me. Now methinks I stand easy; my foot is fixed upon that on which the feet of the priests that bare the ark of the covenant stood while Israel went over this Jordan (Joshua 3:17). The waters, indeed, are to the palate bitter, and to the stomach cold; yet the thoughts of what I am going to, and of the convoy that waits for me on the other side, lie as a glowing coal at my heart. I see myself now at the end of my journey: my toilsome days are ended. I am going to see that head which was crowned with thorns, and that face which was spit upon for me. I have formely lived by hearsay and faith; but now I go where I shall live by sight, and shall be with Him in whose company I delight myself.

John Bunyan

Lord whose mercies never fail and whose love is unchanging, keep me firm in the faith that I have known, and in the way of true obedience. Support my weakness with your eternal strength, that your will for me may be done until the end of my days on earth.

All Saints' Sunday

Desire for God is at the heart of all true religion. Worship is real only if it is centred entirely on God and not on personal satisfaction or desire for merit.

Matthew 5:1–12
'*Blessed are those who hunger and thirst for righteousness, for they will be filled*' (v.6).

Many blessings are promised by Christ to those who truly follow him, but this one stands out in a particular way. All the others – except perhaps peacemaking, which can be very active indeed – are passive rather than active. They require patience, courage and endurance more than direct initiative. Here no special work or virtue is demanded, but only a fervent desire for what is good. The desire must be as sharp as hunger and thirst, like our desire for those things that are necessary to sustain life itself. It tells us that life without God is not real life but an unsatisfied state of being that has no ultimate purpose. Perhaps this is a glimpse of what sainthood means. The saints were not always easy people to have around and some of them were distinctly odd in certain ways. But they passionately desired to know God and to serve him. As St Augustine said, 'Our souls are restless until they rest in you.' That puts us all under obedience. It is not a heroic virtue but an act of the will that is demanded, a direction of the whole being towards the source of life and love. It may not be easy, but he who uttered the blessing gives the strength to obtain it.

You never enjoy the world aright, till you see how a sand exhibiteth the wisdom and power of God: and prize in every thing the service which they do you, by manifesting His glory and goodness to your Soul, far more than the visible beauty on their surface, or the material services they can do your body. Wine by its moisture quencheth my thirst, whether consider it or no: but to see it flowing from His love who gave it unto man, quencheth the thirst even of the Holy Angel. To consider it, is to drink spiritually. To rejoice in it as diffusion is to be of a public mind. And to take pleasure in all the benefits it doth to all is Heavenly, for so they do in Heaven. To do so is divine and good, and to imitate our Infinite and Eternal Father.

Thomas Traherne

My God, fill me with yourself, so that I may be truly your child. When I look at my decisions, my pleasures, my desires, give me your Spirit of truth to judge whether they are leading me to you. May your word be to me food and drink, sustaining me from day to day until I come to you wholly.

Third Sunday before Advent

Making a commitment to Christ means being continually open to his word and ready to obey. We can never say that we have done all that is required. Complacency is the enemy of faith.

Matthew 25:1–13
When the foolish took their lamps, they took no oil with them; but the wise took flasks of oil with their lamps (vv.3–4).

There may be a nice little lamp somewhere among our possessions. Perhaps it is inscribed with the name of our worshipping denomination or of the local church. Perhaps it has a place for the recording of some church office or regular duty, or a hard-earned qualification in knowledge of the Bible or Church history. Does it still give a good light when we have to go out into the darkness? When we need its light, do we find that the oil that once gave it power has all dried up, or shall we say that the batteries are spent and corroded? The dry shell of religion is a sad thing. Continual awareness of the call of the Spirit day by day is the only way to keep the light burning.

As so often in the Christian faith, it is not 'either or' but 'both and'. Oil needs to be contained in a lamp before it can give light, and the lamp needs oil to maintain it. The framework of shared faith is necessary for a full Christian life, but each individual must make the response that faith demands. When the Lord calls, it is no use depending on the faith of others who have kept their lights burning.

> 'Watch therefore, for ye know not the day nor the hour.' Seest thou how continually he adds this, showing how awful our ignorance concerning our departure hence? Where now are they, who throughout all their life are remiss, but when they are blamed by us, are saying, 'At the time of my death, I shall leave money to the poor'? Let them listen to these words, and be amended. For indeed at that time many have failed of this, having been snatched away at once, and not permitted so much as to give charge to their relations touching what they wished to be done.
>
> St John Chrysostom

Lord, keep me alert and vigilant, ready to hear your call to duty or to prayer. May my love never dwindle into outward signs that have no inner strength: sustain my faith, so that I may be a light to others.

Second Sunday before Advent

There is no limit to God's mercy except what people may choose to put upon it. Those who do not make their lives ready for his coming are liable to his judgement for failing to honour the good things that he has given.

Matthew 25:14–30

To all those who have, more will be given, and they will have an abundance; but from those who have nothing, even what they have will be taken away (v.29).

This is indeed a hard saying, apparently unjust and even in part self-contradictory – how can nothing be diminished? But much of Christ's teaching is a strong statement of reality. This is another of the stories intended to shock the hearers into knowing something more about the different values of the Kingdom, but it is also true for life in this world. It is not a lesson in investment policy, though stewardship of money may be part of our duty to God. The foolish servant knew that his master would have high demands but he did not know that playing safe would not be enough. So it is with many who think that keeping out of trouble is all that God requires of them. Life that is narrow, self-centred or suspicious, withers away like some frail thing buried away from air and light, and loses what it seeks to protect. Life that is open, outward-looking or hopeful grows richer and more enjoyable and has something in abundance to give to the world. A pessimistic French dramatist wrote that 'Hell is other people' but perhaps Hell is the self that has shut its doors and refused to come out until there is no one left outside to recognize and greet it.

We have much to be forgiven; nay, we have the more to be forgiven the more we attempt. The higher our aims, the greater our risks. They who venture much with their talents, gain much, and in the end they hear the words, 'Well done, good and faithful servant'; but they have so many losses in trading by the way, that to themselves they seem to do nothing but fail. They cannot believe that they are making any progress; and though they do, yet surely they have much to be forgiven in all their services. They are like David, men of blood; they fight the good fight of faith, but they are polluted with the contest.

J.H. Newman

Heavenly Father, break though the shell of my self-love before it grows too thick for me to hear and respond to your call. Whatever you have given me to do in this world, enable me to do it with firm resolve and joyful obedience, so that my life shall not end without your will being done through me.

Christct the King

We joyfully acknowledge Christ as King and Lord. Our worship is flawed if we do not also acknowledge his presence in humanity and treat all men and women with respect and consideration for their needs.

Matthew 25:31–46
'*"Just as you did it to one of the least of these who are members of my family, you did it to me. . . . Just as you did not do it to one of the least of these, you did not do it to me."*' (vv.40, 45).

There are many stories, told in many lands, of waiting for Christ to pass by and learning too late that he had come in the form of various people with needs that the watcher could have relieved. The coming of Christ to be born into this world was a humble emptying of divinity and at the same time an elevation of humankind. The dignity of original innocence, lost by sin, was restored. God finds in the human form a new meeting-place for the divine and the human to be together in love. When Christ gives some of his last teaching before his Passion, he presents himself as King and also as a caring member of a family. In our own lives we cannot deny or escape relationship. It remains a fact even when relatives do not please us. It cannot be evaded, and if we deliberately refuse its obligations, we are to that extent less than human. Because God so loved the little people he had created that he sent his Son to be their Saviour, so the little deeds of our compassion are precious to him. As Advent begins, we come to the time of waiting for the coming of Christ. As we wait, let us not miss him in others who pass by.

Let us then, beloved, love to practise charity. It is of this that Paul speaks to us: 'Love your fellow Christians always. Do not neglect to show hospitality, for by that means some have entertained angels without knowing it.' Peter also says: 'Be mutually hospitable without complaining.' And Truth himself speaks to us of it: 'I was a stranger and you welcomed me.' 'As often as you did it for one of my least brothers or sisters,' the Lord will declare on the day of judgement, 'you did it for me.' Despite this, we are so slothful in the face of the grace of hospitality! Let us appreciate the greatness of this virtue. Let us receive Christ at our table so as to be welcomed at his eternal supper. Let us show hospitality to Christ present in the stranger now so that at the judgement he will not ignore us as strangers, but will welcome us as brothers and sisters into his kingdom.

Gregory the Great

Christ my King, as I worship you for your great glory, give me grace to honour all people for your sake. Make me a channel of your love, open my eyes to see your image in the women and men around me, guide me to use my opportunities for compassion and to neglect none of your children who cry to you.

Year B

First Sunday of Advent

God has revealed himself in many ways, supremely in the coming of Christ as man, and will one day bring all things to the completion of his purpose. The great signs that he has given should make us alert to find him in the ordinary course of our lives.

Mark 13:24–37
'What I say to you I say to all: Keep awake' (v.37).

The words of Advent are dynamic: wake up; watch; wait; be prepared. Lent may be seen as a period of intensive spiritual training to make us vigorous and fit for the calls of faith. Advent is a time for becoming more aware of those calls. Perhaps the long Trinity season has made worship fall into a routine rather than an experience that is continually renewed. The prayer for the last Sunday before Advent is, 'Stir up, O Lord, the wills of your faithful people'. It is the call to return to the excitement and devotion of newly found faith, the *reveille* of the Christian year. The Disciples certainly needed the warning. They fell asleep during his agonized vigil in the garden of Gethsemane, and many times before then they were slow to understand who he was and what he was saying to them. But the call to keep awake was not given to them alone, but to all, to the generations of believers who would follow him in love but would nevertheless sometimes become slack in their following. We are not to try to discover when he will come again to judge the world, but we are to live as if the next hour was the last.

It has been said that there are on the battlefield, defeats as glorious as victories. That is true also of the daily defeats of the soul in the struggle which we begin afresh every day, making new plans to do better and experimenting with new ideas and methods in order to succeed. That is what the Gospel declares:'Happy is the servant whom when his Master cometh He shall find . . .' Find how? Victorious? Triumphant? His task fully accomplished? No! Rather he who shall be found watching, vigilant, wide awake; that is to say looking after the things which are not going well and putting them right, time after time. That is our really great merit in the sight of God.

Henri De Tourville

Stir up, O Lord, my will when it becomes weak, and set me back on the right path when I go astray. Keep me vigilant for the signs of your presence and the voice of your calling, so that I shall not be found inattentive and absorbed in my own concerns when you have work for me to do.

Second Sunday of Advent

God deals patiently with his people, waiting for them to return and repent of their sins, and leading them like a shepherd. But his mercy does not diminish the power that will come at last to judge the world.

Mark 1:1–8
'The one who is more powerful than I is coming after me; I am not worthy to stoop down and untie the thong of his sandals' (v.7).

John the Baptist could not be described as a shrinking violet – nor could the Old Testament Prophets whose style he followed. He spoke with confidence in his mission and sternly denounced the sins of those who came to him for baptism. But he knew his place in the divine scheme. Perhaps only one who has confidence in his commission can with full sincerity confess his lowliness in the great work of God. He who before birth had leaped in the womb when in the presence of Mary carrying the divine Child, now knew the true status of his cousin after the flesh. Like a herald going before a powerful king, he was to prepare people to hear the Good News of God's redeeming love. But the One whom he proclaimed had far greater humility, the humility of the Son of God taking human nature with all its limitations and troubles. We are waiting to celebrate the birth of a baby, and the work of many artists will help us to picture the Christ Child and his mother. But beyond the manger there is a vision of the Creator, the Ancient of Days, the Lord God Almighty.

Now had the great Proclaimer, with a voice
More awful than this sound of trumpet, cried
Repentance, and heaven's kingdom nigh at hand
To all baptized: to His great baptism flocked
With awe the regions round, and with them came
From Nazareth the son of Joseph deemed
To the flood Jordan, came, as then obscure,
Unmarked, unknown; but Him the Baptist soon
Descried, divinely warned, and witness bore
As to His worthier, and would have resigned
To Him his heavenly office, nor was long
His witness unconfirmed: on Him baptized
Heaven opened, and in likeness of a dove
The Spirit descended, while the Father's voice
From Heaven pronounced Him His beloved Son.

John Milton

Lord, I am not worthy to lift my eyes to you, but because you have walked on this earth knowing its stresses and temptations I have courage to draw close and look into your eyes of mercy. May I in my unworthiness yet be one of your messengers in this generation, a little herald of the great work of salvation.

Third Sunday of Advent

God has appointed his prophets and teachers to proclaim the good news of salvation, but all who have heard it receive in their turn the same responsibility to testify to their faith.

John 1:6–8, 19–28
He came as a witness to testify to the light, so that all might believe through him (v.7).

What witness can be needed for a light, which by its nature is visible and illuminating? This was the supreme light, the divine light, the light which is the work of God throughout the Bible, from the moment of creation to the eternal light of the heavenly city which is not the work of human hands. But God in his love created people as well as light. He uses them, works in the world through them, inspires human tongues to speak his word and opens human ears to receive it. Even as the light of Christ breaks through the darkness, a man is called to be its witness, to be the channel of the grace that cannot be contained except by the divine will. John the Baptist was the successor of the prophets, the herald of Christ, the forerunner of the Evangelists and of all Christian missionaries, preachers and teachers. But few jobs can be left entirely to the professionals, and generations of ordinary Christians, never thinking of themselves as specially chosen, have witnessed to the light by their lives of love and fidelity.

It was necessary to give John's testimonies to the light, and to show the order in which they took place, and also, in order to show how effective John's testimony proved, to set forth the help it afforded afterwards to those to whom he bore it. But before all these testimonies there was an earlier one when the Baptist leaped in the womb of Elisabeth at the greeting of Mary. That was a testimony to Christ and attested His divine conception and birth. And what more need I say? John is everywhere a witness and forerunner of Christ. He anticipates His birth and dies a little before the death of the Son of God, and thus witnesses not only for those at the time of the birth, but to those who were expecting the freedom which was to come for man through the death of Christ. Thus, in all his life, he is a little before Christ, and everywhere makes ready for the Lord a people prepared for Him.

Origen

Heavenly Father, I thank you for all the people who have guided me in faith, for the words and examples that have borne witness to you.

May your blessing be always with them, living in this world and to eternal life. And grant to me in my time some measure of that same grace to testify to Christ, the light of the world.

Fourth Sunday of Advent

Mary was the one chosen to make actual the promises of God that salvation would come to his people. Her human obedience and the divine love together brought God himself into the world, the Word made flesh.

Luke 1:26–38
'Here am I, the servant of the Lord; let it be with me according to your word' (v.38).

Again, the mystery of God's working, his choice of women and men to fulfil his purpose. Did the great plan of redemption depend on Mary's agreement? Would there have been no Incarnation if she had not been obedient? These are meaningless questions. He who chose her knew what her response would be, yet the response was still required. Mary accepts her calling with free will, using the gift that humanity has misused since the beginning of consciousness, and still misuses day by day. Though the divine gift is misused and perverted, it has been newly sanctified by the co-operation of human and divine in the coming of Christ. The new covenant of mercy was made on a day in Nazareth, a day that had seemed to begin like any other day. Mary answers God's messenger, sent after the long years of her people's waiting for the coming of the Messiah. Now that she has answered, the waiting will not be long. Advent moves to Christmas, and God's faithful people offer him their Yes to all that is to come.

> 'Come,' Thou dost say to Angels,
> To blessed Spirits, 'Come'.
> 'Come,' to the lambs of Thine own flock,
> Thy little ones, 'Come home.'

'Come,' from the many-mansioned house
The gracious word is sent;
'Come,' from the ivory palaces
Unto the Penitent.

O Lord, restore us deaf and blind,
Unclose our lips though dumb.
Then say to us, 'I come with speed',
And we will answer, 'Come.'

Christina Rossetti

Father of all the world, I am called to be your servant. Let my obedience be with desire, not resistance; with faith, not compulsion; with love, not fear. May your word work in me and through me, to make me ready to receive my Lord at this season and in all my life.

Christmas Day

See Year A p. 24.

First Sunday of Christmas

The glory of God fills all things, from the distant spaces of the universe to the depths of the human heart. Our response may be to make it known, or sometimes to be silent and wait for the fuller revealing of the divine will.

Luke 2:15–21
Mary kept all these words and pondered them in her heart (v.16).

The Gospel writers, especially St Mark, often tell how Jesus concealed his divinity and his ultimate purpose. The great showings of his glory, the Nativity, Presentation, Baptism and Transfiguration, and the miracles witnessed by many, are balanced by periods of withdrawal into the wilderness or some quiet place where he could be alone. Some of those he healed are told to make known what God has done for them, others to say nothing to anyone. Only at the end comes the greatest public showing of the Passion, followed by the Resurrection and Ascension witnessed by only a few. When he was born, and while he was growing up, his mother followed the divine example and kept to herself the mystery of her child. We are not to expect new orders, special revelations, every day. Sometimes we need to remember that 'you are a God who hides himself' (Isaiah 45:15). If we reflect on the things that we have learned, the great showings both of the Bible and in our own lives, God will work within us quietly, like the seed growing secretly to fruition (Mark 4:26–29).

> The Annunciation was secret; the Nativity was secret; the miraculous Fasting in the wilderness was secret; the Resurrection was secret; the Ascension not far from secret. One thing alone was public and in the eyes of the world – His death; the only event in which He seemed a sign, not of power, but of weakness. He was crucified in weakness, but He was not crucified in secret. His humiliation was manifested and proclaimed all over the earth. when he was lifted up indeed from the earth, He displayed His power; He drew all men to Him.
>
> J.H. Newman

Blessed Lord, revealed in glory, hidden in the secret workings of the heart, grant me the gift of quietness, the grace of meditation on the wisdom that I have received, to grow in faith day by day without restless seeking after signs and wonders.

Second Sunday of Christmas

See Year A p. 27.

Epiphany

See Year A p. 28.

Baptism of Christ

The Spirit of God works in many ways, often beyond human understanding. In their baptism Christians receive the grace of the Holy Spirit through faith in Jesus Christ, the Son of God.

Mark 1:4–11
'I have baptized you with water; but he will baptize you with the Holy Spirit' (v.8).

Anyone who wants a feast of biblical scholars disagreeing can read their various opinions about baptism in the New Testament and the Early Church. Was the Holy Spirit received with water baptism, or with a laying-on of hands that followed? Water was widely used as part of religious rites at the time of Jesus, a symbol of initiation or purification. As the passage from Acts (19:1–7) appointed for today shows, the baptism of John was still the only one known to some converts even after Pentecost. But the baptism that Jesus ordered his disciples to perform, when his work of redemption was completed, was more than a symbol. It was the beginning of a new life, a life filled with joy and also often with danger even to death. The Church in the first centuries took it very seriously, with long preparation. Behind it all, cutting through the controversy of different opinions, stands the Son of God accepting the act of obedience, the ceremony that his life and death will transform into a holy sacrament, both a sign and an effective means to bring the Holy Spirit into the life of all believers.

Dear be the Church that, watching o'er the needs
Of Infancy, provides a timely shower
Whose virtue changes to a Christian Flower,
A Growth from sinful Nature's bed of weeds!
Fitliest beneath the sacred roof proceeds
The ministration; while parental Love
Looks on, and Grace descendeth from above
As the high service pledges now, now pleads.
There, should vain thoughts outspread their wings and fly
To meet the coming hours of festal mirth,
The tombs – which hear and answer that brief cry,
The Infant's notice of his second birth –
Recall the wandering Soul to sympathy
With what man hopes from Heaven, yet fears from Earth.

William Wordsworth

Holy Spirit, giver of new life to the human spirit, fill me with your grace. As I was made clean by the water of baptism, keep me in purity of living and empower me for the work that is purposed for me to do in this world, following the example of the Lord Jesus, the sinless one who accepted the baptism offered to sinners.

Second Sunday of Epiphany

The Word of God is not contained by human prejudices and expectations. It is revealed when and where he wills, and no obstinacy can conceal it.

John 1:43–51
Nathaniel said to him, 'Can anything good come out of Nazareth?' Philip said to him, 'Come and see' (v.46).

Countries have their regions, regions their villages, villages their families that are a byword for stupidity, the butt of many jokes. Readers can supply their own contributions. Perhaps it was that way with Nazareth in Galilee, or perhaps Nathaniel had his own views about the town. Whatever the reason, the only wise answer was an invitation to come and examine the evidence rather than make a knee-jerk reaction to one name. As so often in the Fourth Gospel, seeing was believing, and Nathaniel found more than he had expected. If there was in fact a popular prejudice against Nazareth, the joke was eventually on the rest of Galilee, as the place came to be revered as the earthly home of the Son of God. Instead of displacing our scorn on to poor Nathaniel, we might reflect on the general folly of judging a product by the package. God has a disconcerting way of revealing himself where our assumptions would least expect him. It is always worth having a closer look when something new invades our experience. It might be a glimpse of the eternal glory.

Every soil is to a valiant man his own country, as the sea to the fishes. We are citizens of the whole world, yea, not of this world, but of that to come. All our life is a pilgrimage. God for his only begotten Son's sake (the true Mercury of travellers) bring us that are here strangers safely into our true country.

Fynes Moryson

Lord, drive out from me the prejudices that make me judge without experience, the complacency that will not recognize the good in what is alien to me. Give me the grace to find you in unlikely people and unexpected places, and to look always with the eyes of faith and not with the half-closed eyes of fixed opinion.

Third Sunday of Epiphany

God answers prayer with 'Yes', 'No' or 'Wait'. When we bring our devotion into his presence, we must be prepared to meet his response in reality, not in what we think will happen.

John 2:1–11

Jesus said to her, 'Woman, what concern is that to you and me? My hour has not yet come' (v.4).

An apparent snub, not so harsh as the familiar King James Version, 'Woman, what have I to do with thee?', but still distinctly discouraging. Yet there is a wonderful blend of the divinity and humanity of Jesus in the response and in what follows. The realization of his mission and destiny as Saviour is strong within him. The ultimate time, the time of Calvary, lies ahead and nothing must divert him from it. His Mother knows her son by now, knows that the strange thoughts that sometimes seem to possess him never keep out for long his deep kindness, his desire to relieve little troubles as well as great ones. 'Do whatever he tells you', she says to the servants – and the result is an abundance of wine such as none of the company had ever tasted. If our Lord becomes to any of us remote and out of our experience, we cease to come to him in prayer for the daily needs that may mean so much but seem too trivial to ask. If we see him as nothing but a good friend, a decent chap who is always ready to do a good turn, we have lost all the wonder of the Incarnation and the redeeming power that has rescued us from much more than a few odd annoyances. Prayer is not a means of instant gratification. If it is offered with confidence in God's love, the result may be unexpected, but it will be right.

Not in the Divine mission which He had roe from the Father, was He to be controlled or influenced by a parent to whom He had been subject according to the flesh. And for this manifestation of Himself by miracles the 'hour was not yet' fully arrived, though it was just about to be. But notwithstanding this, the mercies of God are so wont to overflow beyond their own appointed bounds, and the Virgin Mother had so well known our Lord's gracious condescension on every occasion of need, that she did consider these words as a refusal of her request. As she asked in faith, so she in faith received. For God often hears and answers even when He appears at first to decline.

Isaac Williams

Lord Jesus Christ, in your love you give more than we can desire or deserve. In seeking the little things, let me not forget that you are King of kings, Lord of lords. In adoring your majesty, let me not forget that you care for the least of your people, the most erring of your sheep, and give me confidence to wait upon you until your will is made known to me.

Fourth Sunday of Epiphany

The Bible tells in many places of the continual conflict between good and evil. God gives power to those who will work for his victory.

Mark 1:21–28
'He commands even the unclean spirits, and they obey him' (v.27).

Even the sceptic could not deny that Jesus had a great power for curing nervous disorders and calming those who were mentally disturbed. Does that clinical language tell the whole story of his healing ministry or is it a statement of symptoms rather than the underlying causes? No doubt our knowledge of psychological medicine can modify many of the accounts of demonic possession in the Bible and in later history. Do we then dismiss all thought of the reality of evil? It is the fashion, even in some Church circles, to do that and to talk of negation, the absence of actual good, or to blame everything on human weakness compounded by environment. This is simply to push the question farther away. Why do people sometimes prefer the bad to the good unless there is something seriously wrong with our human nature? The history of the last century does not encourage a complacent belief that evil is somehow not quite real. We can debate the matter for hours in our discussion groups and seminars, but the fact remains that Jesus believed in the reality of evil. He speaks many times of demonic attacks, the powers of darkness, the evil Prince of this world. Discount all that if you like – say that he was conditioned by the beliefs of his time as man. But if the unpopular bits of his teaching and practice are dismissed, why should we believe the rest?

Our Lord of His infinite goodness, who has pity and mercy on all His creatures, will in His own time lay to His hand and strike down the devil and all his power. He eases them of their trouble, and puts away the fear, sorrow, and darkness out of their hearts. He brings into their souls the light of grace, and opens their inward vision to see that all their trials were profitable. He also gives them new spiritual strength to withstand with ease all the efforts of the devil and all deadly sins, and leads them into the ways of good and holy living. If they are humble, He preserves them in these ways to the end, and then receives them wholly to Himself.

Walter Hilton

Eternal God, source of all goodness, use me in your service and give me the strength that I need and cannot find in myself. Give me grace to oppose evil, to love those who are enslaved by it and to work for the time when all shall be made whole in the triumph of your Kingdom.

The Presentation of Christ

See Year A p. 34.

Fifth Sunday of Epiphany

Human strength is soon exhausted, spiritually as much as physically. We must take the opportunities for quiet devotion, so that our strength shall be continually renewed.

Mark 1:29–39
In the morning, while it was still very dark, he got up and went out to a deserted place, and there he prayed (v.35).

Those demons are still around, taxing the strength even of the incarnate Son. He might have had enough of deserted places after those forty days of fasting in the wilderness. Yet we read of the mystery in which his humanity prays to the divinity which is also his own. How can these things be? It is too deep for our understanding, but the practical thought is surely that if he needed times of quiet withdrawal, we must need them a great deal more. Not that it is easy in the pressures of life today. Many of us would like to find a deserted place where we could give proper time to our prayers. There are also many for whom the desert of physical deprivation or emotional stress is only too real and overwhelms the whole being. The retreat, the quiet day with organized devotion, is a great source of strength, but even a day may be hard to find. But somehow we need to go apart if only for a short time, to open the inner space of ourselves, so that it may become God-filled. If that depth of being is neglected, it is the demons who are more likely to find their way there.

God's command, to *pray without ceasing*, is founded on the necessity we have of his grace, to preserve the life of God in the soul, which can no more subsist one moment without it than the body can without air. Whether we think of or speak to God, whether we act or suffer for him, all is prayer, when we have no other object than his love, and the desire of pleasing him. All that a Christian does, even in eating and sleeping, is prayer, when it is done in simplicity, according to the order of God, without either adding to or diminishing from it by his own choice. Prayer continues in the desire of the heart, though the understanding be employed on outward things. In souls filled with love, the desire to please God is a continual prayer.

John Wesley

Blessed Lord Jesus Christ, may your prayers be my example when I pray through you to the Father. Early and late, fill me with the spirit of peace, so that I may find calm in the storms of the world and quiet in the noise of every day, to be renewed for the service to which you have called me.

Sixth Sunday of Epiphany

Every request that we make to God in prayer is an act of worship because it recognizes his power and our need. Humility is the mark of asking in sincere faith.

Mark 1:40–45

A leper came to Jesus begging him, and kneeling to him he said, 'If you choose, you can make me clean.' Moved with pity, Jesus stretched out his hand and touched him, and said to him, 'I do choose. Be made clean!' (vv.40–41).

It is the classic pattern of a request made from the powerless to the powerful: deference, petition that recognizes that all depends on the goodwill of the giver, the petition granted. It is the pattern of many Gospel encounters when people come to Jesus for physical or spiritual healing. It is the pattern of prayer, beginning with an act of adoration before we open our needs to God. We all know about asking and hoping. Like the leper, we all know our need and the joy of the healing touch which does not shrink from the unclean. Few indeed are in the position of granting a really big favour, of conferring a major benefit. But there are many demands on our time, our money, our attitude. The things which depend on our goodwill may seem very small but may mean a lot to the one who is asking. From a generous donation to a few minutes of sympathy, there are things to be given which are precious in the sight of God, for our love is always a response to his love. 'If you choose, you can do something for me.' 'I do choose . . .' But which way does the choice go?

How full of instruction is all this incident to us, when by prayer and meditation we bring it home, as it is intended we should do, each one to himself. The same power is present to heal when we feel and know ourselves to be 'full of leprosy'. And the like humiliation of ourselves, and the like faith, will be heard as it then was. But, alas! leprosy of soul and uncleanness in the sight of God is not so known and felt as bodily disease would be. Otherwise there is the same remedy, the same nearness to that all-healing Presence, the same will to restore us. Nay, far more; there is the same life-giving Body in the Holy Eucharist, ready to communicate

Himself to us, as He touched the leper and made him clean. And then there is the same lesson of obedience that we may continue in that holy fellowship.

Isaac Williams

Lord, if you will, you can make me clean. I come back time after time with the same prayer, and it is never refused. Stretch out again your powerful hand to me, touch me with your healing power, and set me back again in the way of righteousness.

Seventh Sunday of Epiphany

The will of God is for pardon and reconciliation. A new way of life is always open to those who come in faith.

Mark 2:1–12
When Jesus saw their faith, he said to the paralytic, 'Son, your sins are forgiven' (v.5).

A vivid account, a short story with a happy ending, a story with a moral like one of the parables. St Mark, usually brief and economical in his narrative, here fills the outline of events with details. The bearers 'dig' through the roof, a word that corresponds with archaeological evidence of houses roofed with a layer of earth. What is easily missed in the excitement of the story is that Jesus meets to the faith of the whole party, first with pardon and then with healing. Did the initiative to seek him come from the sick man or from his friends? No matter, for they worked together and were rewarded. Faith is not a private matter to be cherished in isolation from others. The friends of the paralysed man followed literally the charge that St Paul would later write to his new converts, 'Bear one another's burdens, and in this way you will fulfil the law of Christ' (Galatians 6:2). There are other ways of obedience, that do not involve carrying stretchers or climbing up and breaking through roofs. There are other burdens than physical illness, though that can be a major call on our compassion. There are many ways of bringing people to Christ.

Forgive me O Lord; O Lord in the merits of thy Christ and my Jesus, thine anointed, and my Saviour; forgive me my sins, all my sins, and I will put Christ to no more cost, nor thee to more trouble, for any reprobation or malediction that lay upon me, otherwise than as a sinner. I ask but an application, not an extension of that benediction: 'Blessed are they whose sins are forgiven.' Let me be but so blessed, that I shall envy no man's blessedness. Say thou to my sad soul: 'Son, be of good comfort, thy sins are forgiven thee.' Let me be so blessed, that I shall envy no man's blessedness. O say thou to my soul, 'Son, be of good comfort, thy sins are forgiven thee.'

John Donne

Merciful Lord, strengthen in me the faith that does not fail in difficulty, the faith that overcomes all obstacles and brings me into your presence. May my faith reach out to find others in their trouble, to bear their burdens and meet their needs. Pardon and healing are in the power of your love: grant them to us when we lay our sin and our infirmity at your feet.

Second Sunday before Lent

The light of God, revealed to the world in Christ, has no limit of time or space. It shines through all things, seen or unseen by mortal eyes, and affirms the power of life.

John 1:1–14
The light shines in the darkness, and the darkness did not overcome it (v.5).

We cannot read far in the Bible without meeting the divine light. From the first word of Creation to the eternal light of the New Jerusalem, light is the supreme token of the presence and power of God. We would not value the physical light of this world if we had not experienced darkness – groping through an unfamiliar room, bumping into obstacles on the path, being unable to read words clearly. In the secret places of our lives day by day we return from mental and spiritual darkness to the clear light of God. In prayer, the way that had seemed unmarked is made clear. We do stupid things, build minor problems into great calamities and then find that they have shrunk. We cannot discern the meaning of what is happening and then suddenly it is all made plain. St John tells us that the darkness never did overcome the light, quench it, contain it. Jesus said, 'I am the light of the world' (John 8:12) and every step towards him is a step away from the darkness.

> Hail holy Light, offspring of Heav'n first-born,
> Or of th' Eternal Coeternal beam
> May I express thee unblamed? since God is Light,
> And never but in unapproached Light
> Dwelt from Eternity, dwelt then in thee,
> Bright effluence of bright essence increate.
> Or hear'st thou rather pure Ethereal stream,
> Whose Fountain who shall tell? before the Sun,
> Before the Heav'ns thou wert, and at the voice
> Of God, as with a Mantle didst invest
> The rising world of waters dark and deep,
> Won from the void and formless infinite.

John Milton

Jesus, light of the world, as I stumble and grope in darkness, break into my life, shine on my path and lead me in the right way. Give me the inner light of holy wisdom, to see the truth and to turn from all that is false until I come to the perfect light of your heavenly glory.

Sunday Next before Lent

God who is always with us, always working in the world, does not always reveal himself openly. Waiting for him to show the next step forward is a vital part of our faith.

Mark 9:2–9

As they were coming down the mountain, he ordered them to tell no one what they had seen, until after the Son of Man had risen from the dead (v.9).

Mark makes much of what has been called the 'Messianic secret', the way in which Jesus conceals his divinity during his ministry of teaching and healing. Those who are healed are often told not to speak about it – though they usually disobey the command. All the three Gospels that tell of the Transfiguration report that the Disciples said nothing about the amazing sight that they had just witnessed. There is inherent in Christianity a principle of reserve, of discretion in speaking about faith. It does not contradict the duty of mission, working to bring others to Christ, but it is a warning against speaking without consideration. A brash approach, demanding to know whether a person is saved, has often done more harm, and closed the ears to the good news of salvation. The gospel is for all, but it is received individually. Temperament and circumstance combine to make the best opportunity. Holy wisdom should teach us when to speak and when to be silent: tact is a Christian virtue. It is the message of a loving, caring response without pious words that often prepares the way for the word to be spoken.

Our Lord had secret messages when He spoke, and did not bring forth openly all His divine sense at once. He knew what he was about to do from the first, but He wished to lead forward His disciples, and to arrest and open their minds, before He instructed them. And thus, throughout the course of His gracious dispensations from the beginning, it may be said that the Author and Finisher of our faith has hid things from us in mercy and listened to our questionings, while He Himself knew what He was about to do. He has hid, in order afterwards to reveal, that we, on looking back on what He said and did before, we may see in it what at the time we did not see, and thereby see it to more profit.

J.H. Newman

Eternal God, revealed in glory, hidden in mystery, give me wisdom in your service. Teach me when to speak of my faith, when to be silent and wait for the time of your choosing. Keep me from idle talk of sacred things, so that my witness may be heard when it shall please you to use it.

Ash Wednesday

See Year A p. 42.

First Sunday of Lent

We are sometimes called to go apart from our usual way of life and accept some deprivation or discomfort, confident that obedience will bring new blessings.

Mark 1:9–15
The Spirit immediately drove him out into the wilderness. He was in the wilderness forty days, tempted by Satan; and he was with the wild beasts; and the angels waited on him (vv.12–13).

St Mark gives no details of the temptations as the other Evangelists do, but presents the stark contrast of the wilderness experience. What a picture it would make – and has made – for a painter of religious scenes. The beasts and the angels, our lower and higher natures, humanity torn between those created by God lower and higher than ourselves. Not the domestic animals of pleasure and companionship, but the ravening beasts that prowl in the desert places outside the security of the city. Without letting the unrestrained imagination take over, it can be a good picture to take into the forty days of Lent, the forty days in which we dare to join ourselves with the deep mystery of Christ in the wilderness. Lent always brings temptations, weariness in devotion, even resentment about what we have voluntarily undertaken in love. It also brings many blessings, spiritual growth, guidance of the kind traditionally associated with the angels, the messengers of God. As we begin, are we going in the confidence of our own strength, or are we truly driven by the Spirit?

The Temptation was real, not a mere semblance. Our Lord, under stress of genuine temptation, had to win the victory, in man and for man, by evincing self-denial, self-control, disregard for selfish advantage; absolute renunciation of power, honour, and self-gratification; and complete self-surrender to His Heavenly Father's will. If the struggle had not been an actual struggle, there would have been no significance in the victory. The Gospels represent Jesus as subject to temptations from without, not only at this crisis, but during all His life. He said to Peter, 'Get thee behind Me, Satan, thou art a stumbling block unto Me'; and He said to His Apostles, 'Ye are they which have continued with Me in My temptations.' The only difference between the temptations of Christ and our own is that His came from without, but ours come also from within. In Him the tempting opportunity could not appeal to the susceptible disposition. With us sin acquires its deadliest force, because we have yielded to it.

F.W. Farrar

Lord Jesus Christ, tempted as we are but without sin, draw me closer to you as this Lent begins. Give me strength to resist the wild beasts of temptation, and grace to hear the angels of guidance, so that day by day I shall grow more fully into the way of your example.

Second Sunday of Lent

The faithful followers of God in all ages have trusted in his promises and not been turned aside from the way set out before them, even when his will was difficult to understand.

Mark 8:31–38

Peter took him aside and began to rebuke him. But turning and looking at his disciples, he rebuked Peter and said, 'Get behind me, Satan! For you are setting your mind not on divine things but on human things' (vv.32–33).

Like a group of naughty schoolchildren, they all felt the rebuke directed at the ringleader. The Disciples probably all had the same thought – this suffering and death must not come to their beloved Master, he must turn back before it is too late, and stay with them as he is now. It was the impetuous Peter who voiced the thought, but Jesus looked at all of them as he uttered the terrible word – Satan! Blurting out a natural concern for one so much loved would not seem to merit being identified with the Prince of Darkness. But the humanity of Jesus spoke from knowledge of the challenge to divinity. This was the old temptation that kept coming back, from the wilderness to Calvary. Use your divine power to convince the world, jump from the top of the Temple, call legions of angels to rescue you, come down from the cross. He was tempted as we are but without sin (Hebrews 4:15) and if the temptations had not been very strong and real, there would be less hope when we turn to him for help. Peter could see only a little way, and the nearer view was terrifying. We all stand there, with eyes of Jesus turned upon us, as we panic at the thought of what seems to be happening. May this Lent strengthen us to trust in the greater plan.

As we make progress in our spiritual conflict, we shall see what occasions are most hurtful to us, in what way our sin most steals upon us or assails us; and so we can either by ourselves, or by help of some who has the care of human souls, form rules to ourselves, how we can keep off the occasion, or be strengthened under it. For to come into temptation with no fixed rule to guide us, nothing to appeal to against our biased judgement, is to give ourselves over to defeat.

E.B. Pusey

Gracious Lord, open my eyes to see the light beyond the darkness, to know the hope beyond the fear. When the road is rough and winding, keep my feet in the way of your will. Forgive my doubt and anxiety, the failure to learn from past mercies that the future is in your hands, and save me from rash judgement before the fullness is revealed.

Third Sunday of Lent

The Bible tells of the love of God. It tells also of his holiness and his anger. Mercy always follows repentance, but deliberate defiance falls under judgement.

John 2:13–22
Making a whip of cords, he drove all of them out of the temple, both the sheep and the cattle. He also poured out the coins of the money-changers and overturned their tables (v.15).

This is the most vivid and violent account of the cleansing of the Temple. St John alone mentions the whip that Jesus used, and he puts the event at the beginning of the ministry and not on Palm Sunday. It has been used in many ways: to justify violent action by Christians and to censure the presence of bookshops in churches and cathedrals. Can we venture to know the mind of Jesus at that time? In St John's account the cleansing comes immediately after the miracle at Cana, the generous production of good wine. As he comes to Jerusalem, does the capital city of Judaism seem corrupt and commercial after the villages of Galilee? Does he recall his childhood visit when he talked with the scholars and perhaps came to know whose Son he truly was? Was he angered by the profaning of the Temple, so lovingly rebuilt after the Exile, so jealously guarded against pagans and foreigners but abused by its own people? It is a stark and sombre episode. What comes from it is not worry about selling postcards in the church but the reminder that the wrath of God is as real as his mercy. We can do many wrong things and be forgiven, but we put up a fearful barrier if we go on being careless of his presence.

Then the disciples remembered that it was written, 'The zeal of Thine house hath eaten me up.' Because by this zeal of God's house, the Lord cast these men out of the temple. Brethren, let every Christian among the members of Christ be eaten up with zeal of God's house. Who is eaten up with zeal of God's house? He who exerts himself to have all that he may happen to see wrong there corrected, desires it to be mended, does not rest idle: who if he cannot mend it, endures it, laments it.

St Augustine

Lord God, infinite in power and glory, may I always worship you in the beauty of holiness. Grant to your people true reverence, to acknowledge your presence at all times and to make their places of worship worthy of the prayers and praise they offer.

Fourth Sunday of Lent

People have often rebelled against the guidance of God, and preferred their own ways to his ways. Faith in Christ is the only remedy for the human tendency to sin.

John 3:14–21
This is the judgement, that the light has come into the world, and people loved darkness rather than light, because their deeds were evil (v.19).

Like many who came to learn more of this strange new Teacher, Nicodemus got more than he had expected. Jesus revealed to him both the good news of the salvation for which the Father had sent the Son into the world, but also the bad news that many in the world would reject it. The challenge did not end when Jesus returned to the Father. Many seeking to know more of the Christian faith, searching the Bible for guidance, have learned that it is more than cosy benevolence and occasional churchgoing. It demands a clear and continuing choice between good and evil, realities not to be glossed over by sentiment. The image is plain: it is possible to prefer groping in the dark to moving freely in the light of God, with all the responsibilities of seeing what you are doing. To stay in the darkness because the light is too demanding is to create a personal hell which shuts out other people as well as God. Nicodemus had something to think about, and at the end he came to do the last service of love in burying the body of Jesus. But it is better not to wait until the last minute to come out of the darkness.

Dear Friends, prize your time and the love of the Lord to your souls above all things, and mind that Light in you that shews you sin and evil. Which checks you when ye speak an evil word, and tells you that you should not be proud, nor wanton, nor fashion yourselves like unto the world; for the fashion of this world passeth away. And if ye hearken to that, it will keep you in humbleness of mind, and lowliness of heart, and turn your minds within, to wait upon the Lord, to be guided by it; and bring you to lay aside all sin and evil, and keep you faithful to the Lord; and bring you to wait upon him for teaching, till an entrance thereof be made to your souls, and refreshment come to them from the presence of the Lord. There is your Teacher, the Light, obeying it; there is your condemnation, disobeying it.

George Fox

Lighten my darkness, Lord, I pray and raise my eyes to look upon you and know the only way of salvation. Defend me from the evil in myself that would turn me from following in faith, and be my guiding light until the end of the way.

Mothering Sunday

See Year A p. 48.

Fifth Sunday of Lent

All the promises of the Messiah were both fulfilled and changed in the coming of Christ. He revealed the glory of God and performed great works, but he also suffered even to death before the work of salvation was completed.

John 12:20–33
'I, when I am lifted up from the earth, will draw all people to myself.'
He said this to indicate the kind of death he was to die (v.32).

To be lifted up, to be elevated above the rest, brings a promise of honour and glory. Come up higher, climb to the top of the mountain, get up on the platform, and people will see you as someone important and listen to what you have to say. Jesus is lifted up, exalted above all creation, risen, ascended, glorified. But he knew that his coming for the salvation of the world demanded another lifting up, the agony of pierced hands holding a tortured body where all could see him. He knew not only the fact of his death but also its manner, the most shameful and dreaded way of execution that the Roman power could impose. That is the image by which his followers have known him, the image that fills our thoughts now as we enter Passiontide. The image of the rising in glory is never absent but the time to focus on it is yet to come. This is the time to begin again to follow Jesus to the terrible uplifting of the Cross. When we pray that our hearts may be lifted up, let it be with a full submission to the will of God who brings glory out of humiliation.

> Why, all the souls that were, were forfeit once,
> And he that might the vantage best have took
> Found out the remedy. How would you be
> If he, which is the top of judgement, should
> But judge you as you are? O think on that,
> And mercy then will breed within your lips,
> Like man new made.

William Shakespeare

Lord Jesus, lifted up on the Cross for the salvation of all, draw me closer to you at this time of penitence. Make me fall humbly before the vision of your suffering, so that I shall be ready to be raised to whatever purpose you have for me, and to praise you in the exaltation of your triumph over death.

Palm Sunday

As the Passion drew near, Christ was deserted by everyone. The humility of his human presence left him vulnerable to the scorn of his enemies and the cowardice of his friends.

Mark 14:1–15:47
At that moment the cock crowed for the second time. Peter remembered that Jesus had said to him, 'Before the cock crows twice, you will deny me three times.' And he broke down and wept (v.72).

The year of Mark in the cycle of readings may be called a bad year for Peter, for this is the Gospel in which he is most severely treated – a moving fact if the early tradition that Mark heard and recorded his memories is true. All the Gospels relate the moment of his denial, with the detail of the crowing cock. It was Peter who had led the chorus of Disciples promising to follow Jesus even to death, who had fallen asleep in the garden, attacked one of the party who seized Jesus, and then followed to the High Priest's house. It is typical of him, the blundering enthusiasm followed by the abject failure, as when he had asked to walk on the water to Jesus. Surely this was the end: no return from the shame of open denial. Was there a more unhappy man in the world that night than Peter? He is absent from the accounts of the Crucifixion, perhaps hiding his shame all through the terrible day. He next appears on the day of Resurrection, restored among the Disciples, given a new commission. Palm Sunday is the day of mixed feelings, when triumph and sorrow meet. It is the day of the confused, the inadequate, the failures, those who follow in love, fall over and try to go on again. It is the day for all of us.

These are the pillars that support the Church by their teaching, their prayers, their example of patience. Our Lord strengthened these pillars. In the beginning they were very weak and could not support either themselves or others. This had been wonderfully arranged by Our Lord, for if they had always been strong, one might have thought their strength was their own. Our Lord wished to show first what they were of themselves and only afterwards to strengthen them, so that all would know that their strength was entirely from God. Again, these men were to be fathers of the

Church and physicians who would heal the weak. But they would be unable to pity the weaknesses of others unless they had first experienced their own weakness.

St Aelred

Lord Jesus, betrayed, forsaken, denied, have mercy on me. When I am false to the faith that is in me, when I turn away from the truth, when I am ashamed to confess you before others, have mercy on me. Rouse me with the clear call of new hope, let me follow you faithfully in the coming week, through your sorrowful Passion to your glorious Resurrection that restores the precious things that have been lost.

Maundy Thursday

See Year A p. 52.

Good Friday

See Year A p. 53.

Easter Eve

See Year A p. 55.

Easter Day

The Easter story tells of a journey from sorrow to joy, from fear to confidence. Those who had failed their Master were made witnesses of his Resurrection.

Year B

Mark 16:1–8

'Go and tell his disciples and Peter that he is going ahead of you to Galilee; there you will see him, just as he told you.' So they went out and fled from the tomb, for terror and amazement had seized them; and they said nothing to anyone, for they were afraid (vv.7–8).

The earliest version of St Mark's Gospel ends here. The feeling of terror and bewilderment that he records is found in all the accounts of the Resurrection. The friends of Jesus did not go to his tomb in joyful hope of meeting him again, but in deep grief which turned to fear before he appeared to them in his risen body. The fact that they were not expecting anything of the sort is a strong support of the story. Yet even the solemn ending of St Mark gives words of hope. The Disciples, disgraced by their desertion in Gethsemane, were to be received back and given a new commission. Peter, the most vocal of them in promise and in denial, is specially mentioned, given the reassurance that he more than any needed. Jesus was bringing them back to the place where it had all begun, to give them a new start, another chance. He is going before you, leading you to where he is; there he will be ready to receive you, there you will see him. It was good news for the Disciples, and it is the promise made to all who believe in him.

Saviour of mankind, Man, Emmanuel!
Who sinless died for sin, who vanquished hell;
The first-fruits of the grave; whose life didst give
Light to our darkness; in whose death we live: –
Oh! strengthen thou my faith, convert my will,
That mine may thine obey; protect me still,
So that the latter death may not devour
My soul, sealed with thy seal. – So, in the hour
When thou (whose body sanctified this tomb,
Unjustly judged), a glorious judge shall come
To judge the world with justice; by that sign
I may be known, and entertained for thine.

George Sandys

Lord Jesus Christ, risen in glory from the tomb, forgive my many failures in your service, my anxiety, my fear, my doubt. Go before

135

*me in this life, make me a servant of your word, and bring me at last
to live with you for ever.*

Second Sunday of Easter

Joy and confidence are the marks of the Easter people of Christ.
Fear and anxiety are not far away. From the time of the Apostles,
there has been need for vigilance in faith.

John 20:19–31
*It was evening on the first day of the week, and the doors of the house
where the disciples had met were locked for fear of the Jews. Jesus came
and stood among them and said, 'Peace be with you' (v.19).*

Of course the Easter season is one of joy, for we know the whole story.
The Gospels of the day are full of fear, anxiety, bewilderment, incredulity. Joy dawns only slowly, as the truth of all that has happened comes
to be understood. We read of people who have come through deep sorrow and still do not know what to think. The appearances of the risen
Lord are full of mystery, the presence of one who can appear inside a
locked room but can eat and drink and be touched. Eleven men are still
afraid, still doubtful after all the teaching that these things would be.
He is patient with them still, he comes to them in the midst of their
fear and utters the word of peace, both greeting and benediction. We
too are his disciples, his Easter people, full of joy. People free from
all fear and doubt? People always open to his presence? People whose
inner doors are not locked for fear? He is still patient, still comes to
us and brings the peace that passes all understanding.

> I got me flowers to strew thy way;
> I got me boughs off many a tree.
> But thou wast up by break of day,
> And brought'st thy sweets along with thee
> The Sun arising in the East,
> Though he give light, and th'East perfume;
> If they should offer to contest
> With thy arising, they presume.

Can there be any day but this,
Though many suns to shine endeavour?
We count three hundred, but we miss.
There is but one, and that one ever.

George Herbert

*Risen Lord, break through the closed door of my heart, drive away
my fear, give me the blessing of your peace. In the joy of this Easter
season, keep me in the assurance of your presence and shield me from
the false confidence that fails when temptation comes.*

Third Sunday of Easter

The resurrection brought new power and confidence to those who
were its witnesses. The experience of personal encounter with
the risen Lord has been granted also to those who have not seen with
physical sight.

Luke 24:36b–48
*'Touch me and see; for a ghost does not have flesh and bones as you
see that I have'* (v.39).

The fear of ghosts occurs in all human societies. Ghost stories that
thrill and entertain are an ever-popular type of fiction. The ghost
calling for revenge appears in many famous tragedies, stories of a
murder which ends with more murders, violence breeding violence.
The Lord who appeared to them on the day of the Resurrection was
no ghost seeking vengeance for his killing, but a living friend with a
solid body whose call was that the message of pardon and salvation
should be preached throughout the world. The future is not one of
conspiracy and more violence, but of love openly declared to enemies
as well as friends. The fear of being haunted by the Master they had
deserted and denied soon turns to delight; the doubt becomes perfect
recognition. This was no ghost to be propitiated and laid to rest, but
an eternal living presence. Ghost stories have their day and fade, as
ghosts are said to fade at sunrise. This story is different, true at sunrise

and at sunset, in the dark night of the soul and in the bright light of celebration.

We must not think of Jesus Christ as behaving sometimes as God and sometimes as man like an actor appearing in two different roles. Whatever He did, He did as both God and man; in Him Godhead and manhood were indissolubly united in one perfect Person. This is illustrated, for example, by the appearance of Jesus to the disciples on the evening of Easter Day. He appears, suddenly, when the doors of the room were shut, and quiets their fears by showing them His hands and feet and side. He invites them to touch Him and eats before them. He also claims that the Scriptures have been fulfilled by His death and resurrection and He commissions them to preach forgiveness of sins in His Name. Here Docetism is rebuked – the theory that Jesus only seemed to be human. Here modern secularism is rebuked – the refusal to accept Jesus as God incarnate. But Jesus is showing himself as a complete Divine and human Person.

Edgar Dowse

Risen Lord, cast out my fear, my uncertainty, my unworthy thoughts. Let me feel your presence, strong and living empowering for the work of your Kingdom. Give me grace to tell the Good News, to convince those who doubt that you live and reign today, to bear witness that the gospel is the word of truth.

Fourth Sunday of Easter

In the Easter season, the reality of Christ's suffering does not fade. All preaching of the Resurrection is also a memorial of the Crucifixion.

John 10:11–18
I am the good shepherd. The good shepherd lays down his life for the sheep (v.11).

A picture of the Good Shepherd hangs in many churches and schools. Not always very good art, but moving and devotional. Usually in a long white robe with well-combed hair and beard, a crook in his hand, he leads some obedient sheep. There is abundant love and gentleness, little sense of the struggle against evil. The shepherd who embodies the work of Jesus is rather different: strong, brave, defiant in the face of danger. Shepherds whose flocks wander into wild places have to be different from those on the quiet hills of our country. Remember David who pursued any bear or lion to rescue a stolen lamb, killing the predator if it resisted (1 Samuel 17:37)? In that courage, he went on to kill Goliath. Our Good Shepherd is cast more in that mould than in the holy pictures. Here in the Gospel Jesus speaks words of love and comfort as well as warning against the hireling shepherds. He speaks also of the immeasurable price of redemption – life laid down willingly for the erring flock. The grace of God is not to be bought by any human endeavour, but it does not come cheaply.

> Lead me to mercy's ever-flowing fountains;
> For Thou my Shepherd, Guard, and Guide shalt be;
> I will obey Thy voice, and wait to see
> Thy feet all beautiful upon the mountains.
> Hear, Shepherd! – Thou for Thy flock art dying,
> O, wash away these scarlet sins, for Thou
> Rejoicest at the contrite sinner's vow.
> O, wait! – to Thee my weary soul is crying,
> Wait for me ! – Yet why ask it, when I see,
> With feet nailed to the cross, Thou'rt waiting still for me!

> H.W. Longfellow

Jesus, Good Shepherd, give me courage to defend the right, wisdom to see the approach of spiritual danger, grace to respond to the gift of sacrificial love. In the joy of this Easter time, let me never forget the price that was paid so that I and all your people might be led into the way of salvation.

Fifth Sunday of Easter

Fullness of life is found only through Christ. If we live in him and he in us, we are united with God whom we can never approach by our own efforts.

John 15:1–8
'Whoever does not abide in me is thrown away like a branch and withers; such branches are gathered, thrown into the fire, and burned' (v.6).

Few of us are vinegrowers. Most of us have some experience of gardening, so it is no use dismissing the image as outdated and irrelevant, a quaint piece of New Testament life that has lost its meaning. The odd branch of a rose tree or fruit bush, broken by a storm or cut off in pruning, does not keep its beauty for long. It is a piece of dead wood, ending up on the bonfire. When we think that we are doing rather well by ourselves, when good deeds become their own justification, when divine grace comes to be thought of as a helpful but not essential force in our lives – think of the broken branch and its fate. There is no life when the sap that rises from the roots to the smallest twig is cut off. All the power of the risen Lord is freely given to those who hold fast to him in love and trust. Life in God's garden is strong and beautiful. Nothing in it is destroyed wantonly or maliciously, though there is quite a lot of judicious pruning where it is needed. But there is a barren corner where no one comes who does not come knowingly and in proud self-confidence, defiantly separated from the true vine.

O my noble vine, give Thou Thy branch sap, that I may grow and flourish in Thine essence, by Thy power and nourishment. O sweet Love, art Thou not my Light? Lighten Thou my poor soul during her doleful imprisonment in flesh and blood. Lead her always by the right way. Break Thou the will of the Evil One, and lead Thou my body through the course of this world, through the chamber of death, into Thy death and peace, that it may, at the last day, arise in Thee out of Thy death, and live eternally in Thee. Teach Thou me what I should do, be Thou my willing, my knowing, and my doing, and let me go nowhere without Thee. I devote myself utterly unto Thee.

Jacob Behmen

Lord of the true vine, may I always remain firmly joined with you, rooted in the deep source of my being. Keep me safe from all that might sever us, all that might cause my love to wither. May my faith flourish in the garden of your love, to bring forth good fruit to your honour and glory, until I come to abide in you for ever.

Sixth Sunday of Easter

The divine calling is a mystery which brings obligations to service and the grace to fulfil them. To turn to God is to be born again.

John 15:9–17
'You did not choose me but I chose you. And I appointed you to go and bear fruit, fruit that will last' (v.16).

When he said these words to the Disciples did they remember their first calling? From the fishing boats, from the customs post and from other places, they had followed with a sudden abandonment of the daily routine which must many times later have made them wonder. Did they think of the time when he called them together on the hilltop and gave them their commission? In the months of hearing and obeying they had been prepared for the greater task, still only partly understood. Now he was sending them out into the unknown, the first heralds of the Kingdom. In the centuries to come, some Christians would know and remember the exact moment of their conversion; others would grow and follow quietly day by day. All who listened to the voice of God would come to understand that the Christian faith is not a human choice made after assessing the possibilities of various ways of life. It is not like joining a club or a political party. It is a response to a calling that has nothing to do with the merits or achievements of those who are called. Its consequences may not always be comfortable, there is no peace if they are rejected.

> We go to bring forth, and He Himself is the way wherein we go, and wherein He hath appointed us to go. Accordingly let love remain; for He Himself is our fruit. And this love lies at present in longing desire, not yet in fullness of enjoyment; and whatsoever

that longing desire we shall ask in the name of the only-begotten Son, the Father giveth us.

St Augustine

Heavenly Father, as you have called me to your service make me worthy of my calling. Give me your Spirit to guide and strengthen me in the way you have marked out for me, so that I may do your work and witness to your love all my life.

Ascension Day

See Year A p. 64.

Seventh Sunday of Easter

The will of God calls us towards his own eternity. Before we come to know him in his full glory, there is work to be done in the world, a duty to be fulfilled but not to turn us away from the greater future.

John 17:6–19
'I am not asking you to take them out of the world, but I ask you to protect them from the evil one. They do not belong to the world, just as I do not belong to the world' (vv.15–16).

What is the world? The creation of God, the place where humanity must learn to love and obey him. The place where he himself walked as man. The home place of sin and opposition to his will, the place of temptation, the realm of the evil one who is called by Jesus the 'Prince of this world'. How to reconcile the two senses has been a question from the time of the New Testament to this day. 'Worldly' has been a favoured word of disapproval for many strict Christians. Yet other Christians have accused some of their fellow-believers of being too 'unworldly' and neglecting human needs for the sake of their private spirituality. To be in the world, fully committed to its duties and opportunities, yet not conformed to its values, is not easy. The words of Jesus in his great prayer to the Father on the night before his Passion are our guide. His followers have to go on living in this world for their allotted time: they will experience no mystical lifting up into another sphere before death, although some of the mystics may have glimpses of it. But they are to live knowing that the world is not their final destiny, that they belong elsewhere when their time shall come. The world itself is not evil, but there is evil to be guarded against with prayer.

> People do that to others which they know would not be acceptable to themselves, either in exercising an absolute power over them, or otherwise laying on them unequitable burdens; here a fear lest that measure should be meted to them, which they have measured to others, incites a care to support that by craft and cunning devices which stands not on the firm foundation of righteousness: Thus the harmony of society is broken, and from hence commotions and wars do frequently arise in the world.
>
> John Woolman

Blessed Lord, grant that I may so walk through this world that I shall serve its needs and give love where love is most needed. Grant that I shall so walk through this world that I never lose sight of the world beyond, unseen, impenetrable, but the place where your people truly belong. Deliver me from evil, so that your will may be done though me until I come to you.

Pentecost

The Holy Spirit gives power and direction in our journey of faith. We cannot know the truth without divine guidance.

John 15:26–27; 16:4b–15
'When the Spirit of truth comes, he will guide you into all the truth' (16:13).

On the next day after he gave this promise, Jesus was asked by the Roman governor, 'What is truth?' Whether scornful, sceptical or genuinely enquiring, Pilate spoke for people long before his time and long after who have asked the same question. The ultimate answer, when philosophical speculation has come to an end, is that truth is in God, from whom we receive all our powers, including the power to ask questions about truth itself. Christians are as likely as others to make mistakes; even more likely, perhaps, to think that their particular church or group has the monopoly of divine truth. The Holy Spirit guides, does not compel, does not destroy our free will and make us into obedient puppets. A guide needs to be recognized, trusted and followed if we are to continue in the right way. On this day, let us renew our trust not only in the power of God to lead us into all the truth, but in his desire that we should respond to the love that reaches out to us.

> Consider that the Holy Ghost came down upon the apostles in the shape of tongues, to signify that he came to make them fit preachers of his word, and to endow them with the gift of tongues, accompanied with the heavenly wisdom and understanding of the mysteries of God and all the gospel truths, to the end that they might be enabled to teach and publish, throughout the whole world, the faith and law of Christ! And these tongues were of fire, to signify how his divine Spirit sets those souls on fire in which he abides, inflaming them with divine love, consuming the dross of their earthly affections, putting them in a continual motion of earnest desires and endeavours to go forward from virtue to virtue as fire is always in motion, and carrying them upwards towards the God of Gods in his heavenly Zion, as the flame is always ascending upwards towards its element.

Richard Challoner

Holy Spirit, bring me into the way of truth. Free my life from all that is confused and uncertain, all that hinders my life of faith.

Made free by the truth, may I follow where truth leads, to be made one with the Apostles and all the people of God in love and obedience.

Trinity Sunday

There is a deep mystery in the Holy Trinity which we cannot fully understand but must simply accept in reverence, knowing that God is at work among us at all times.

John 3:1–17
'The wind blows where it chooses, and you hear the sound of it but you do not know where it comes from or where it goes. So it is with everyone who is born of the Spirit' (v.8).

There is a word in Greek – and also one in Hebrew – that can mean 'wind', 'breath' or 'spirit'. In his conversation with Nicodemus, Jesus is making a play on words that give some idea of the mysterious working of God in the world. We know it by its effect, as we know the power of the invisible wind and the breath which sustains our life, as something invisible but unquestionably real. In that meeting at night, itself secret and concealed from others, Nicodemus came in fear of the opponents of Jesus yet determined to learn more of the teaching that had already attracted him. Instead of being given a privileged explanation denied to ordinary hearers, he is given a glimpse of mystery which can be perceived if not fully understood by a simple comparison. It is a good passage to meditate over on Trinity Sunday. God who is one and yet is Father, Son and Holy Spirit, has given us a faith by which to live and not a puzzle to solve. We shall never catch the wind by chasing after it and we shall know more of God by devotion within the mystery than by trying to reason out the details of the divine nature. What theologians have suggested about the Holy Trinity may indeed be helpful, but for most of us it is enough to know that God is as close to us as our own breath.

O holy, supreme, eternal, blessed and glorious Trinity, ever laudable, yet ever ineffable; Father of goodness, Son of love, Spirit of bounty, whose majesty is unspeakable and goodness inestimable, whose work is life, whose love is grace, whose contemplation is glory; Godhead, Divinity, Unity, Trinity, thee I adore.

Lancelot Andrewes

Holy and Blessed Trinity, breath of my life and source of my inner spirit, teach me so to reverence the mystery of faith that I shall live more fully as a child of God. Give me a thankful heart for what I know, humility not to seek that which is beyond my human understanding, and perseverance in this world so that I may come at the end into the presence of the eternal mystery.

Proper 4

One of the worst sources of error is corrupting what is basically good until it becomes harmful. We need continually to keep the balance between tradition and development.

Mark 2:23–3:6
The Pharisees went out and immediately conspired with the Herodians against Jesus, how to destroy him (3:6).

That was a dangerous alliance, ultimately a deadly one. It was also very strange – the Pharisees, strict and nationalistic in their upholding of the traditional Jewish Law, joined with Herodians who supported the puppet rulers of the land and were not ill-disposed towards Roman rule. It was not the last time that a common antagonism would create unexpected bedfellows, in politics and also in religion. Love draws people together, but sometimes hatred can draw them together for a time until their common purpose is fulfilled. Even in human terms, a man who could cause such a conspiracy of opponents was one to be reckoned with. But, though some of them at least may have believed that they were acting for the best, it was against God himself that they were conspiring. When a principle or an aspect of the faith is being challenged from different sides, it is well to look closely at motives. Sometimes the majority is right, but not always.

And while allies are always welcome, they may lead farther than we ought to go. What starts with negative emotions may lead to some very positive wrong.

> Why, what hath my Lord done?
> What makes this rage and spite?
> He made the lame to run,
> he gave the blind their sight
>   Sweet injuries!
>   Yet they at these
>   themselves displease,
>   and 'gainst him rise.

Samuel Crossman

Lord Jesus, hated and opposed by some of those you came to save, give me wisdom to discern the true from the false, in all relationships and especially those within the faith. Keep me from the easy way when flattery leads to pride, and pride to betrayal of the right. Teach me to examine my own motives and to be guided by nothing but desire for the will of the Father to be done and the glory of the Son to be honoured.

Proper 5

The power of evil is a reality, attested throughout the Bible and by Jesus himself. It threatens our human nature, and only divine power can overcome it.

Mark 3:20–25
He called them to him, and spoke to them in parables, 'How can Satan cast out Satan? If a kingdom is divided against itself, that kingdom cannot stand' (vv.23–25).

The tension is growing, the problem posed by Jesus of Nazareth is more pressing. How can this obscure man, with no official credentials, wandering from place to place, be the agent of God? Surely these healings are not divine miracles but the result of some diabolical possession. The reply is not deeply mystical but plain commonsense. Does evil want to get rid of evil? Is Satan using his power in the world to make the world a better place? It is a sharp skirmish, a brief victory in the campaign that will bring Jesus to the Cross and to the greater victory of the Resurrection. Beneath it there lies a warning that never goes away. It is too easy to find bad motives for what makes people uncomfortable, for what confronts them with questions they would rather not answer. It can lead to worse things, to seeing the bad side of everything, of refusing to believe in the reality of goodness in a fallen world. Rose-coloured spectacles can be misleading, but dark ones show a world without light. In the extreme, there may be the final alienation, of saying like Milton's Satan, 'Evil be thou my Good'.

For though that seat of earthly bliss be failed,
A fairer Paradise is founded now
For Adam and his chosen Sons, whom thou
A Saviour art come down to re-install,
Where they shall dwell secure, when time shall be
Of Tempter and Temptation without fear
But thou, Infernal Serpent, shalt not long
Rule in the Clouds; like an Autumnal Star
Or Lightning thou shalt fall from Heav'n trod down.

John Milton

Lord of healing, Lord of cleansing, cast out the badness that lurks within me, the darkness that menaces the light of faith. When I am afraid of the evil in the world, strengthen me with the assurance that good is the greater power and that in the end evil will not prevail against it.

Proper 6

Most of God's work in the world is done through the ordinary events of life, which attract little attention. Steady perseverance in faith is more important than seeking for spectacular signs.

Mark 4:26–34

'The kingdom of God is as if someone would scatter seed on the ground, and would sleep and rise night and day, and the seed would sprout and grow, he does not know how' (vv.26–28).

What we read of history deals mainly with the great events, the battles and the fall of dynasties, the new movements and discoveries that changed human perception. In fact for most of the time the majority of people were getting on with their own lives and hoping to avoid uncomfortable changes. General knowledge of the Bible focuses on the big stories: Noah and the Flood, Samson against the Philistines, David and Goliath. But the record of the Bible is largely about the gradual revelation of God, made known to people living the ordinary life of their time and not strikingly 'religious'. The work is secret, progressing at a pace that can be followed, coming from time to time to its fruition in a big step forward and ultimately in the full revelation of God as man, incarnate within the human situation. We are reminded that, 'Truly, you are a God who hides himself' (Isaiah 45:15). Desire for a great religious experience has been the temptation and the downfall of many good people. He gives in measure as we can bear it, and seeking a sign easily distracts us from the daily round of obedience and quiet spiritual growth which is required of most of us.

> I shall know why, when time is over,
> And I have ceased to wonder why;
> Christ will explain each separate anguish
> In the fair schoolroom of the sky.
> He will tell me what Peter promised,
> And I, for wonder at his woe,
> I shall forget the drop of anguish
> That scalds me now – that scalds me now.

> Emily Dickinson

Sleeping and waking, Lord, increase in me the fruits of the Spirit so that your will may be done in me and through me. Give me grace to seek you and light to find you in the little things and the hidden ways, to grow in love and to show your glory without seeking praise for myself.

Proper 7

Some think that we fully understand the universe and have mastered its laws. But human knowledge is limited, and God reveals himself through the mysteries of his creation.

Mark 4:35–41
They were filled with great awe and said to one another, 'Who then is this, that even the wind and the sea obey him?' (v.41).

The nature miracles of Jesus have aroused much discussion. We believe that we live in an ordered universe with laws of cause and effect. If we believe also in a Creator, the laws are not the result of random evolution but part of his design. The Lawgiver has power to suspend the laws which he has made. Jesus never worked miracles for his own benefit – remember how he refused the devil's suggestion of turning stones into bread when he was hungry in the wilderness. When he used his divine power it was to help or comfort others, by healing, by feeding or by freeing them from one of the natural dangers of this world. The Disciples needed something to strengthen their faith, which had fallen apart when they saw the peril of the storm. If the elements had got out of hand and needed to be kept in order, those who had been close to him in his ministry deserved a stronger rebuke. Humble in his Incarnation, accepting for himself the complete human condition, the Son still reigns over all things.

> The billows swell, the winds are high,
> Clouds overcast my wintry sky;
> Out of the depths to Thee I call.
> My fears are great, my strength is small.

O Lord, the pilot's part perform,
And guard and guide me through the storm.
Defend me from each threatening ill,
Control the waves, say, 'Peace, be still.'

Amidst the roaring of the sea
My soul still hangs her hope on Thee;
Thy constant love, thy faithful care,
Is all that saves me from despair.

William Cowper

Creator God, Lord of all things visible and invisible, let me find you in the wonders of your creation. Shield all your people from the pride that claims to understand the depths of your mysteries, and increase our faith through the things of this world, so that we may be guided to the world to come.

Proper 8

The will of God is for life and health. He longs for us to call upon him in faith and we need never fear the simplicity of our approach.

Mark 5:21–43
He said to her, 'Daughter, your faith has made you well; go in peace and be healed of your disease' (v.34).

This remarkable episode, which is told in three of the Gospels, includes details that support an eye-witness memory. The woman's long illness, her bold and desperate rush forward, the sudden halt, the impatience of the Disciples: all make it a vivid story. A wonderful cure, but less wonderful than raising the dead, is granted in response to faith. The humble, nameless woman and the influential man remembered by his name Jairus are equally accepted and answered. Perhaps we sometimes act and pray as if we think God is too busy to deal with our modest requests – after all, he has the whole universe to manage! Fortunately for us, God is not a celestial computer with a limited program but a loving Father who hears the cry of his children when they turn to him in faith. As Jesus could distinguish the touch of mingled hope and anguish in the press of the crowd, the sincere plea is not stifled by the uproar of the world and the indifference of many. Power goes out from God to pardon and to heal, but the supply is never exhausted: the divine battery does not need recharging.

It was a secret matter. There was the whole crowd pressing about Him, begging for a blessing. They did not want it. They were not looking for it. But she did want it, and she felt she wanted it. Nobody knew her. We do not know her name to this day. Only this: among the unknown notables, she is the woman that touched the hem of the Master's garment, and was made whole. And it is related in three of the Gospels, that you and I may know it as a sweet Gospel story to go right to our hearts. She crept up – nobody knowing her – flung herself down, and just touched the hem of His garment. She said, 'If I may . . . I shall be.' She had faith, and, therefore, our Lord crowned her testimony afterwards, and said, 'Thy faith hath made thee whole.' Oh, it is a beautiful story! If any of you touch the Saviour, will you feel He has touched you? That is the question.

A.H. Stanton

Lord, I know that you always respond to my most feeble cry, my most tentative reaching out towards you. Increase and strengthen this confidence in me, that I shall never fear to bring all my need to you and come in faith to receive healing of body and spirit. Make me whole, as it is your will that all your people shall be whole, to praise your wonderful love and witness to the world.

Proper 9

In all ages, God sends his messengers to proclaim his word. People do not always listen to them, but they are constrained to do his will and not expect a favourable reception.

Mark 6:1–13

Jesus said to them, 'Prophets are not without honour, except in their home town and among their kin, and in their own house' (v.4).

The local boy who makes good is not always popular when he comes back home. People remember things from his childhood and comment on his family's lack of status. Envy and resentment can mingle with pride in being associated with success, and that is a dangerous mixture. Jesus coming with this band of men around him, standing up to preach in the synagogue of his boyhood, seemed more an affront than a compliment to the town. Nobody really expects wisdom and new insights from the familiar: it is the distant, the unknown, that beckons with a promise of solving our problems. Those who have shared our locality, our experience – what can they know that we do not? We know that Jesus was a great deal more than a talented local boy. But do we know how much there is to be learned from the ordinary people who are close to us, from families, friends and neighbours we take for granted? It may sometimes be worth listening to them and not always waiting for the visiting preacher with a national reputation.

Full many a gem of purest ray serene
The dark unfathomed caves of ocean bear.
Full many a flower is born to blush unseen,
And waste its sweetness on the desert air.
Some village-Hampden that with dauntless breast
The little tyrant of his fields withstood;
Some mute inglorious Milton here may rest,
Some Cromwell guiltless of his country's blood.

Thomas Gray

Lord, open my ears to hear the voices that are familiar, to learn from the people I know well. When I look for novelty, when I listen for the distant call, give me grace to remember that your word is spoken in many ways and by many people who are not honoured in the judgement of this world.

Proper 10

Those who would serve God sometimes have to suffer for his sake. They are following the pattern of Jesus Christ, who was killed for the offence that he caused to the powers of his time.

Mark 6:14–29

The king sent a soldier of the guard with orders to bring John's head. He went and beheaded him in the prison, brought his head on a platter, and gave it to the girl. Then the girl gave it to her mother (vv.27–28).

Some plays have two plots running together, the minor one acting as a commentary and reinforcement of the major. *King Lear* is one of the finest examples. It could be said that the story of John the Baptist is like a sub-plot for the story of Jesus. The birth of each of them brings strange prophecies; they begin their mission with popularity and draw crowds to them; gradually the uncompromising nature of their preaching arouses hostility in the authorities and brings their death. The killing of the Baptist is told vividly and spares no detail of its horror, and it is not surprising that the story has attracted writers and painters. The malice of Herodias is more disquieting even than the brutality of the beheading – here is human spite and anger at its worst. There is much similarity to the story of Jesus, but of course the parallel is not complete because his death was not an end but a beginning. The story of the Baptist is a warning against the petty irritations that can swell into hatred, and the weakness that gives way to evil for the sake of peace and personal reputation. It is also a reminder to pray for those who still suffer for the name of Christ.

> I was angry with my friend:
> I told my wrath, my wrath did end.
> I was angry with my foe:
> I told it not, my wrath did grow.
>
> And I watered it in fears,
> Night and morning with my tears;
> And I sunned it with smiles,
> And with soft deceitful wiles.

And it grew both day and night,
Till it bore an apple bright;
And my foe beheld it shine,
And he knew that it was mine,

And into my garden stole
When the night had veiled the pole:
In the morning glad I see
My foe outstretched beneath the tree.

William Blake

Gracious Lord, shield me from the temptations of envy, anger and bitterness, and from the weakness that fears to speak the truth. Give me courage in the face of opposition, when I know that there is some work to be done in the name of Christ. Look with compassion on those who at this time are suffering for their faith and turn the hearts of their persecutors.

Proper 11

Even good works may bring the danger of distraction from worship and meditation. There is a time to go apart and be quiet.

Mark 6:30–34, 53–56
He said to them, 'Come away to a deserted place all by yourselves and rest a while.' For many were coming and going, and they had no leisure even to eat (v.31).

A scene of bustling activity, leaving no time for a proper meal – a scene of pressure so familiar in modern life. The Disciples are full of their accomplished mission, the crowd is making continual demands. Jesus knows that they need rest and calm before the work goes on again, and it is time for a quiet withdrawal, time to find space for thinking things over and sorting out priorities. No one can be a Christian in isolation, but faith that is to be effective needs its periods of solitude. There is need for the retreat, the structured quiet day or the simple withdrawal into a private room. People's needs are great and pressing, a continual duty, but we shall serve them better if we learn to set limits, to find the space for finding ourselves again. The Greek word behind the 'deserted place' is the one used elsewhere for the wilderness, where the Baptist prepared for his mission of preaching, where Jesus suffered temptation. It is not a negative place, meaning only desolation and deprivation. When other things are set aside for a time, there is space to be quiet with God.

> Where shall I find God? In myself. That is the true mystical doctrine. But then I myself must be in a state for him to come and dwell in me. This is the whole aim of the mystical life. That the soul herself should be in heaven, that our Father which is in heaven should dwell in her, that there's something within us infinitely more estimable than often comes out, that God enlarges this 'palace of our soul' by degrees so as to enable her to receive himself, that he gives her liberty but that the soul must give herself up absolutely to him for him to do this, the incalculable benefit of this occasional, but frequent intercourse with the perfect; this is the conclusion and sum of the whole matter, put into beautiful language by the mystics.
>
> Florence Nightingale

Teach me, dear Lord, when to be active and when to be still. Teach me to let go when cares and duties overwhelm me. Lead me into the quiet places, where to be apart is not to be alone, because you are there. When all around seems restless, teach me to rest in you.

Proper 12

Nothing is too small to be the means of God's bountiful love. No one is too insignificant to be a channel of his grace. All we need is faith, and he will do the rest.

John 6:1–21

One of his disciples, Andrew, Simon Peter's brother, said to him, 'There is a boy here who has five barley loaves and two fish. But what are they among so many people?' (v.8).

It is too easy sometimes to feel a little superior to the Disciples. The negative attitudes, pessimism and lack of understanding are displayed with brutal frankness by the writers of the Gospels. But we who know the whole story of Christ and his continuing presence with us, are still behaving in the same way. The sight of a hungry crowd advancing when there is nothing but one small packed meal on offer would not arouse much hope. But then, as always, divine grace uses what is to hand, accepts human endeavour and enriches it beyond all expectation. Gifts that are brought in love are not only accepted, but multiplied. Those who obey the command to sit and trust are not sent away empty. Bounty is not only adequate but overflowing, leaving more to be gathered up than was there at the beginning. All these things come into the story, the only miracle told in all four Gospels, which must have been very meaningful for the Early Church. We can see in the actions of Jesus with the food a figure of what is done at the Eucharist. We can also see that out of little things, slight talents offered in faith, great works may be done.

> Christ spoke of buying bread, when he intended to create or make bread; but did He not, in that bread which He made, intend further that Heavenly bread which is the salvation of our souls? – for He goes on to say, 'Labour not for the meat' or food 'which perisheth, but for that food which endureth unto everlasting life, which the Son of man shall give unto you.' Yes, surely the wilderness is the world, and the Apostles are His priests, and the multitudes are His people; and that feast, so suddenly, so unexpectedly provided, is the Holy Communion. He alone is the same, He the provider of the loaves then, of the heavenly manna now. All other things change, but He remaineth.
>
> J.H. Newman

Lord, may I learn to acknowledge my weakness and insufficiency, but not to think that there is nothing I can do for you. You have called me to your service, and your strength will prevail where I am weak, your love where I am indifferent. Guide me to use for you the gifts that you have given, confident that what I offer will receive power for good from you, the Giver of all good things.

Proper 13

The divine bounty that gives food to nourish the body is a sufficient cause for gratitude. Much more wonderful is the spiritual food which unites us with Christ.

John 6:24–35
Jesus said to them, 'I am the bread of life. Whoever comes to me will never be hungry and whoever believes in me will never be thirsty' (v.35)

Instead of feeling superior to those who first heard the words of Jesus, we might try to have some sympathy with them. There was a lot to take in – first a resounding miracle of feeding with real food that satisfied a very hungry crowd. Then thoughts turned naturally to another divine feeding known to them all, the manna that had sustained the Israelites in their long wilderness journey. Then they are taught that there is a still more wonderful kind of bread, which turns out to be the Teacher himself. He who has satisfied their physical hunger will satisfy their spiritual hunger, not once but for all time. The full meaning of that saying, the mystery of food given for eternal life, was not yet completed, but there was already too much for even the most pious members of the crowd to grasp. Christians have still not fully grasped it, but they have known the reality of Jesus Christ, the bread of life. Still we go on disputing about details, still we strive to understand and to agree together, but the Lord's Table to which the faithful are called is known by all to be the heart of our worship.

'Twas August, and the fierce sun overhead
Smote on the squalid streets of Bethnal Green,
And the pale weaver, through his windows seen,
In Spitalfields, look'd thrice dispirited.
I met a preacher there I knew, and said

'Ill and o'erwork'd, how fare you in this scene?'
'Bravely!' said he; 'for I of late have been
Much cheer'd with thoughts of Christ, the living bread.'
O human soul! as long as thou canst so
Set up a mark of everlasting light,
Above the howling senses' ebb and flow,
To cheer thee, and to right thee if thou roam –
Not with lost toil thou labourest through the night
Thou mak'st the heaven thou hop'st indeed thy home.

Matthew Arnold

Almighty God, giver of food for the body and food for the soul, may I never fail to honour you in the holy communion of your Son Jesus Christ. When I receive the bread and wine of his supper, grant that I shall receive him in the depth of my being, in obedience to his command and in thanksgiving for his life given for me and for many.

Proper 14

When we think that we can go on in our own strength, the demands of life soon begin to defeat us. The strength that only God can provide is our hope of continuing to the end of our earthly journey.

John 6:35, 41–51

'I am the bread of life. Your ancestors ate manna in the wilderness, and they died. This is the bread that came down from heaven, so that one may eat of it and not die' (vv.48–50).

Jesus does not let them go away easily. He repeats the claim, one of the great 'I am' sayings of this Gospel. He reminds them that even their distant ancestors, specially favoured by God and brought safely through the wilderness to the Promised Land, ended their mortal lives like all other flesh. What is now on offer is the promise not of a land flowing with milk and honey, not of unbroken prosperity and success, but of eternal life. The interweaving of death and life is powerful in the New Testament, most strongly so in the Fourth Gospel. The life of Jesus shows no release from the worst experiences of human life, including death itself, but it also brings new life in this world as well as the world of eternity. Communion with him does not save from the bodily death which he himself endured, but it starts a new life before death, which death as we know it does not end. This is deep mystery, realities that seem to conflict but that experience teaches to be true. The manna in the wilderness was given when it was needed and then disappeared. The bread of life is given for ever, because our spiritual need does not go away.

Christian worship was to develop around the sacred meal, the Lord's Supper, which Jesus had instituted on the night when He was betrayed. The Lord's Supper was never a mere memorial feast, looking back with sadness to a past event which had ended with death. It was a joyful meeting with a living, present Lord, and the act of worship was meaningless and unintelligible apart from the resurrection. This sense of the living presence is reflected in the ancient liturgies, and the central act of worship may be described as an extension of the resurrection appearances.

Edgar Dowse

Lord Jesus Christ, in whom whoever believes shall not die eternally, grant me in his world the faith to trust in you alone, and to receive the bread of life which you have promised to all who follow you. May I come to your Table in humility and go from it with confidence, knowing that with you at my side nothing on the journey will be too great for me.

Proper 15

The idea of eating and drinking as a religious act is traditional and expressed in many ways. It is perfectly fulfilled in the Eucharist which unites the communicant with Christ.

John 6:51–58
'Those who eat my flesh and drink my blood abide in me, and I in them' (v.56).

The mystery grows even deeper. Union with the divine as the motive and the result of sacrifice is not new. But sacrifice was usually elaborate, costly in material terms, often requiring the slaughter of victims. Now a simple act of eating and drinking, the performance of something that is not only familiar but necessary for survival, brings about what so many have desired. The blood that is shed to make the sacrifice complete is the blood of the divine Victim in whom the old sacrifices have their end and the new sacrifice its beginning. Generations of men and women will be lifted from their helpless human condition, to be made one with the divine. This section of the Gospel is closely packed, and unusually repetitive in recording the words of Jesus. They are a call to each individual Christian to honour the sacrament of his Body and Blood and to his whole Church to seek the outward unity which will be worthy of the inner unity that he has already given.

> You created everything, sovereign Lord, for the glory of your name. You gave food and drink to men for their enjoyment, and as a cause for thanksgiving. And to us you have given spiritual food and spiritual drink, bestowing on us the promise of eternal life. Above all we thank you for the power of your love. Glory to you throughout the ages.
>
> The Didache

Lord Jesus, abide in me and let me abide in you. By the power of your communion may I be made whole and lifted from the sin and weakness that would turn me from you. Keep me in the holy fellowship of all those who come to your Table.

Proper 16

The life of faith is a life of continual choice. God does not compel obedience, but he guides and strengthens those who keep their trust in him.

John 6:56–69

Many of his disciples turned back and no longer went about with him. So Jesus asked the twelve, 'Do you also want to go away?' Simon Peter answered him, 'Lord, to whom can we go? You have the words of eternal life' (vv.66–68).

It is easy to forget that Jesus had many more disciples than the twelve who are named in the Gospels. These famous ones do not get a very good report; they are often doubtful, frightened, seeking power and precedence, trying to keep other people away from their Master. They walked with him and listened to him, but at the end they too forsook him and fled. But in spite of all, they were the witnesses of his Resurrection, received back into fellowship and made the missionaries of the new Church. Many people from then until now have rejected Christianity when it became difficult. The excitement of Confirmation Sunday does not always lead to faithful weekly communion. The promises made at baptisms and weddings are often sadly neglected when going to church is no longer a special occasion, but a continuing duty that sometimes goes against inclination. The twelve disciples of whom we know give us the assurance that God can work with fallible people and make them his own. Immaturity, laziness and uncertainty are no bar to this grace if we know that there is no other to whom we can go.

Like as the fountain of all light created
Doth pour out streams of brightness undefined
Through all the conduits of transparent kind
That heaven and air are both illuminated,
And yet his light is not thereby abated;
So God's eternal bounty ever shin'd
The beams of being, moving, life, sense, mind,
And to all things himself communicated.
But see the violent diffusive pleasure
Of goodness, that left not, till God had spent
Himself by giving us himself, his treasure,
In making man a God omnipotent.
How might this goodness draw our souls above,
Which drew down God with such attractive Love.

William Alabaster

Dear Lord, you alone have the words of eternal life. When my feet begin to hesitate and my following grows slack, set me back in the right way. With the assurance of your love and the strength of your presence, may I never fail on the journey which I am making with you in this world and towards you in the world to come.

Proper 17

The commandments of God are unchanging. To keep them faithfully and remain open to fresh insights is our difficult but essential duty.

Mark 7:1–8, 14–15, 21–23
'You abandon the commandment of God and hold to human tradition' (v.8).

That really hurt. Those who most firmly believed that they were keeping and upholding the Law were accused of making their own laws and imposing them on others in a way contrary to what they professed. The conflict between Jesus and official religion was entering another phase. The same accusation has been made through the ages, most often between Christians of different confessions who accuse each other of corrupting the pure gospel by new doctrines and practices. The only answer must be to seek the guidance of the Holy Spirit. For the sake of unity, each denomination needs to look continually at itself and determine what is true tradition and what is later choice. But it is not a matter to be left to the Church leaders. Each Christian needs self-examination to know what is deeply held and what is only personal preference. How much of what we do plays into self-importance, love of the familiar, a sense of superiority? Are we being distracted by externals from the centrality of the atonement for sin? The question may still hurt, but it is not to be avoided. Not all that is new is wrong, but does it grow as a true development or is it a corruption?

People get influenced by the world and selfish, and proud, and idle, and there are also so many bad people that one is apt to become suspicious, and disbelieve in people, and so to treat them with a kind of hard reserve. But that is no good; a full disinterested love always ready to help, always longing to help most in spiritual things. This is what is wanted to raise people from the sour, unbelieving, materialistic thoughts, which the rough struggle of life too often produces.

Edward King

Almighty God, your word is everlasting and your will is unchanging. Help me to keep your word and to perform your will, neither running after novelty nor rejecting new guidance, but always seeking the Holy Spirit to make my worship pure and undefiled.

Proper 18

The will of God is for health and abundant life. Through Jesus Christ, the great works prophesied of the Messiah have been, and are still, accomplished.

Mark 7:24–37
Looking up to heaven he sighed, and said to him 'Ephphatha,' that is, 'Be opened.' And immediately his ears were opened, his tongue was released, and he spoke plainly (vv.34–35).

When St Mark gives us the exact words that Jesus spoke, as he does here and elsewhere in his Gospel, we feel very near to the event. The Aramaic word has a resonance even though we may not know anything else of the language. But what brings us even closer is the detail of the sigh as he looked up to heaven. What was the meaning of that typically human expression of disquiet? Was it the sorrow of God for human suffering, distress that people came more often for physical than for spiritual healing, or a moment of human weariness at the continual demands on him? Jesus Christ, true God and true man stands there before us. He was performing the works of healing which were to be signs of the Messiah, a witness to those around him and a sign to all ages. Still there is compassion for the suffering of the world, still prayers are too often for selfish ends, still people turn to God when there is trouble and forget him when things are going well. In all languages prayers are made and prayers are heard. If ears are truly open, the word of God comes to direct and to make whole.

164

The deaf may hear the Saviour's voice,
The fettered tongue its chain may break;
But the deaf heart, the dumb by choice,
The laggard soul, that will not wake
The guilt that scorns to be forgiven –
These baffle e'en the spells of Heaven;
In thought of these, His brows benign
Not e'en in healing cloudless shine.

John Keble

Lord, open my ears to hear your word and open my lips to make it known. I praise you for your patience that never fails, your love that meets the needs that I can only imperfectly express. As in the days of your human ministry you looked up to heaven, so let me now look to you where you are alive and reigning, still giving life and health to those who call upon you.

Proper 19

The saving love of Christ could have been given in many ways, but he chose the way of suffering and death for the redemption of the world.

Mark 8:27–38
Turning and looking at his disciples, he rebuked Peter and said, 'Get behind me, Satan! For you are setting your mind not on divine things but on human things' (v.33).

What terrible words for one chosen to be among the closest companions of Jesus, one who had just recognized and acknowledged his Messiahship. Did Peter for a moment appear as the power of evil? Or should the speech be divided – before the rebuke to Peter comes the confrontation with the Tempter? For the evil one was never far away, trying to divert the Lord from his purpose, working in the wilderness, in Gethsemane and on Calvary to make him declare his divine power and save himself from human suffering. It is easy to sympathize with Peter, appalled at the thought that his Master and friend should undergo such a fate, when it seems that he was about to be revealed as the glorious Messiah. But the victory was not to be won without a mighty struggle. Then and now, those who would follow him must find their way through this world, completely within it yet not conformed to its values. Here is a precious, sacred insight into the experience of Jesus, and a source of strength for all who are tempted to take the easier way.

> 'Does the road wind up-hill all the way?'
> 'Yes, to the very end.'
> 'Will the day's journey take the whole long day?'
> 'From morn to night, my friend.'
>
> 'But is there for the night a resting-place?'
> 'A roof for when the slow dark hours begin.'
> 'May not the darkness hide it from my face?'
> 'You cannot miss that inn.'
>
> 'Shall I meet other wayfarers at night?'
> 'Those who have gone before.'
> 'Then must I knock, or call when just in sight?'
> 'They will not keep you standing at that door.'
>
> 'Shall I find comfort, travel-sore and weak?'
> 'Of labour you shall find the sum.'
> 'Will there be beds for me and all who seek?'
> 'Yea. Beds for all who come.'
>
> Christina Rossetti

Lord, when I feel your rebuke for my sins and my lack of faith, guide me back into what is right. Shield me from betraying your purpose through fear and false judgement. Your ways are not my ways, but I pray that I may have grace to follow them.

Proper 20

Christ fulfilled the prophecies of the suffering Messiah and left a pattern of humble self-giving for his disciples in all ages to follow.

Year B

Mark 9:30–37

He sat down, called the twelve, and said to them, 'Whoever wants to be first must be last of all and servant of all' (v.35).

The Gospel record of the twelve disciples during the years when they walked with Jesus in the flesh seems to become more unfavourable as the time of his Passion draws nearer, and now they appear in a particularly bad light. Immediately after he has told them of the suffering and death that lie before him, they are quarrelling about precedence. He calls them to order, not with a simple command to behave themselves, but with a saying that reverses all human expectations, a paradox that can be resolved only with spiritual understanding. It is like some of the parables of the Kingdom, in which the same wages are given for one hour's work as for a whole day, or everything is sold to get possession of one precious pearl. Despite their knowledge of the scriptures, the disciples did not yet understand that the Messiah was to be a suffering servant, a victim not an earthly conqueror. Later, they would preach that message with conviction. How can any who desire to follow him do so except by sharing in some small measure his humiliation?

> Methought that in a solemn church I stood.
> Its marble acres, worn with knees and feet,
> Lay spread from door to door, from street to street.
> Midway the form hung high upon the rood
> Of Him who gave His life to be our good;
> Beyond, priests flitted, bowed, and murmured meet,
> Among the candles shining still and sweet.
> Men came and went, and worshipped as they could –
> And still their dust a woman with her broom,
> Bowed to her work, kept sweeping to the door.
> Then saw I, slow through all the pillared gloom,
> Across the church a silent figure come.
> 'Daughter,' it said, 'thou sweepest well My floor!'
> 'It is the Lord!' I cried, and saw no more.

George Macdonald

Jesus, meek and patient under human cruelty, forgive the many ways in which I have failed to honour your example. When I seek praise

167

for myself, set before me the image of your suffering, the recollection of your pain, and turn me away from the false values of this world.

Proper 21

The word of God is not limited to those who seem to have received special appointment. There are many who do his work without official recognition, and no one should try to stop them.

Mark 9:38–50
'No one who does a deed of power in my name will be able soon afterwards to speak evil of me' (v.39).

Chastened, but still not fully understanding, the Disciples have another objection. Someone has dared to use the name of their Master without being formally admitted to their little band. It is a complaint that echoes down the ages, in secular and sacred organizations. What are your credentials? Where were you trained and licensed? Are you registered with the proper authority? Because structures and organizations are necessary for good order, we make them into new gods from which all virtue must be derived. Jesus had reason to know about people speaking evil of him, as the conflict with authority was rising to its terrible conclusion. Any who had some glimpse of his greatness, who had seen his power for good at work, might share some of that power without being one of his inner circle. Such a one could hardly then turn against him and accuse him of doing bad things. Distrust of the unofficial is found both among Christians who observe a formal hierarchy and those who profess a more open ministry. We do not like the stranger who claims to be one of us without going through the proper process – but we may be wrong.

> There are a number of persons not members of the Church, who neither have themselves separated from it, nor oppose it, nor usurp its place, but who are more or less in the condition of the man in the text, 'not following us,' yet using the Name of Jesus. It may so happen they are exerting themselves for the cause of Christ in places where the Church is unknown, or where it does not extend itself. And, moreover, it may so be that they have upon them many

consolatory proofs of seriousness and earnestness, of a true love for Christ, and desire to obey Him and not to magnify themselves. Here, then, our Lord seems to say, 'Forbid them not in their preaching.'

J.H. Newman

Lord Jesus, open my heart and my mind to listen to your word from every source by which it comes to me. Keep me obedient to the church order in which I worship, but give me also the light which reveals you in other ways. In whatever form and through whatever people you have a message for me, guide me to attend and to act upon it.

Proper 22

God loves us as a father loves his children. We need the simple trust of a child if we are to respond to his love.

Mark 10:2–16
'Truly I tell you, whoever does not receive the kingdom of God as a little child will never enter it' (v.15).

The Disciples should have known better than to try keeping little children away from their Master who had so often shown his love for them. It was not a sentimental love, or even the spontaneous warm emotion that most people feel when a child comes close to them. It was deeper love for the innocence that brought them so close not only to his human person but to his Father and theirs. The child's simple trust is the basis of all faith, however much we may strive to understand. The child's single-minded attention to the present activity is the way to live each moment as it is given to us. There is a difference between being *child-like* and *childish*. St Paul reminds us that when we become adult we must put away childish things and find a mature faith (1 Corinthians 13:11). As life goes on there should be advance in the Christian life, spiritual growth and deeper prayer. But it will not be a true part of our inner being unless child-like simplicity is drawing us every day closer to the Kingdom.

A child's first sight of the ocean is an era in his life. It is a new world without him, and it awakens a new era within him. There is no other novelty to be compared with it, and after-life will bring nothing at all like it. A rapid multitude of questions rush upon the mind; yet the child is silent, as he needed not an answer to any of them. They are beyond answering; and he feels that the sight itself satisfies him better than any answer. Those great bright outspread waters! The idea of God is the only echo to them in his mind: and now henceforth he is a different child because he has seen the sea. So is it with us when we sit by the ocean of creative love. To gaze – to gaze is all we desire. The fact that so much is mystery to us is no trouble. It is love. That is enough. We trust it. But when we cease to be children and to be childlike there is no more this simple enjoyment. We ask questions not because we doubt, but because when love is not all in all to us, we must have knowledge, or we chafe and pine. We shall be children once again, and on the same shore and we shall then never leave it more, and we shall see down into the crystal depths of this creative love, and its wide waters will be the breadth and measure of our joy, and its glancing splendour will be the light of our eternal life, and its soft thunder will be the endless, solemn, thrilling music of our beatitude.

F.W. Faber

Heavenly Father, restore in me the trust which draws a child to a parent's side in perfect confidence. Help me to find again and to keep all through my life the simple love that comes from you and leads to you.

Proper 23

Although material comfort may not be evil in itself, it can too easily lead to indifference to the needs of others and to the real values of life. We must be continually on our guard against the temptations that it brings.

Mark 10:17–31

'It is easier for a camel to go through the eye of a needle than for someone who is rich to enter the kingdom of God' (v.25).

Much ingenuity has been used to explain this saying of Jesus. Was there a narrow gate in Jerusalem called 'The Needle's Eye' through which a loaded camel could not pass? Is a there a confusion in the original text between the word for *camel* and the word for *rope*?

Or is it not more likely that he intended to startle his hearers with one of his humorous exaggerations (he speaks elsewhere of those who try to strain out a gnat from the cup but could swallow a camel that was floating in it, and about worrying over a speck in another person's eye when a whole plank is sticking out of your own [Matthew 23:24; 7:3–5]? The thought follows on from the previous passage: if a child's simplicity brings us close to God, the state of being rich and successful may lead us away from him. It is possible to be a Christian in any condition of life, if it is taken as the will of God and offered in his service. We may rightly seek to improve our condition, more importantly try to improve the condition of others. The danger of being rich is its power to become an insulation against reality, a false assurance that being at ease in this world is all that there is.

> Truly a little is too much for him that knoweth not how to use much well. Therefore learn first the use of money and riches, and some other honester means to attain them, that this thine insatiable covetousness and unlawful desiring of other men's goods may be reduced to some reasonable measure, and that it do not exceed the limits or compass of honesty, and the bonds of brotherly love.
>
> Hugh Latimer

Lord, when I thank you for the comfort and security in my life, let me never hide behind it as a denial of what matters most. Grant me contentment with what I have, generosity to those who have less, and love without envy to those who have more. Bring me through the narrow way that leads to your Kingdom where the differences of this world pass into one equal glory.

Proper 24

The Suffering Servant described by the prophet Isaiah is often taken as a foretelling of the sufferings of Christ. It certainly reminds his followers of the great price he paid for our salvation.

Mark 10:35–45

'The Son of Man came not to be served but to serve, and to give his life a ransom for many' (v.45).

Going from bad to worse, two of the disciples want to claim the best places in heaven when Jesus enters into his glory. They all have to be reminded that there is a hard and bitter road to tread before the end. After the Resurrection, their preaching would have much to tell of the scriptural prophecies of sufferings that the Messiah would undergo, but the truth had not yet dawned on them, while visions of their own status in the Kingdom became ever more grand. Jesus is sure now of his destiny. The temptation to assert kingly power which began in the forty wilderness days, will never succeed. He comes not only as a servant but as one who suffers. His life is so humble that it does not shrink from the ultimate degradation, yet so precious that it will buy back the human race from its fallen state. By identifying with the most vulnerable and disadvantaged of his own creatures, the Son of God will lift them to the glory which his disciples have selfishly sought for themselves. And there, as the year of St Mark draws towards the end, we have the heart of the Gospel.

> Ah, my dear Lord! what couldst thou spy
> In this impure, rebellious clay,
> That made thee thus resolve to die
> For those that kill thee every day?
>
> O what strange wonders could thee move
> To slight thy precious blood and breath?
> Sure it was Love, my Lord; for Love
> Is only stronger far than death!
>
> Henry Vaughan

Blessed Lord Jesus, Son of God and Son of Man, I praise you for the love that suffered so that your people might be saved. Make me more worthy of so great a sacrifice, to live as one who knows the price of sins forgiven and the death that brought eternal life. By your grace, may weakness yet share in your glory.

Proper 25

The rejoicing that the Messiah was to bring would be for both physical and spiritual healing. In his earthly ministry, Jesus fulfilled the promise in every respect.

Mark 10:46–52
Jesus said to him, 'Go; your faith has made you well.' Immediately he regained his sight and followed him on the way (v.52).

Jesus is going to Jerusalem towards his Passion; he has just spoken of his coming suffering and death, rebuked James and John for seeking precedence. Yet he has compassion for a blind beggar, despised by others, whose persistence and faith is rewarded. We sometimes feel that we should not pray about little things, as if not to trouble God who has so much to do. He is not a remote tyrant, but the Lord of infinite love for the least of his creatures. If we draw courage for our own, slighter problems from the need and the faith of Bartimaeus we may remember that there is spiritual as well as physical blindness that needs to be cured. Rejoicing in the recovery of his sight, Bartimaeus wanted to stay with Jesus and followed him; the phrase 'on the way' may suggest discipleship as well as accompanying – the early Christians were known as those of the Way. How far did he follow? Was he one of those who fell away after the triumphal entry into Jerusalem and the menace of Holy Week, or did he stand firm and become one of the many unnamed believers recorded after Pentecost? We cannot know, so rather let us ask whether all the mercies that we have received make us truly wish to be always with Jesus and follow him in the way.

The faith of Heathens was *blind*; it was more or less a moving forward in the darkness, with hand and foot; – therefore the

Apostle says, 'if haply they might feel after Him.' But the Gospel is a *manifestation, and* therefore addressed to the eyes of our mind. Faith is the same principle as before, but with the opportunity of acting through a more certain and satisfactory sense. We recognise objects by the eye at once; but not by the touch. We know them when we see them, but scarcely till then. Hence it is, that the New Testament says so much on the subject of spiritual knowledge.

J.H. Newman

Lord Jesus who opened the eyes of the blind, open my eyes to see you in all your love and compassion. Bring your healing touch to clear my sight that is clouded by sin and failures, so that I may have the vision to follow you faithfully to the end of the way.

Bible Sunday

The Bible is the book of life for all who will receive it as the Word of God. It leads us to Christ, the only source of salvation.

John 5:36b–47
'You search the scriptures because you think in them you have eternal life; and it is they that testify on my behalf. Yet you refuse to come to me to have life' (vv.39–40).

It is hardly possible for a Christian to read the Bible excessively. But it is possible to become a 'Bibliolater', a worshipper of the Bible as a thing in itself rather than as the way into knowledge and love of God. It is also too easy to read selectively, attending to the passages that give immediate reassurance to the present way of things and ignoring those that give a more disturbing message. It is easy to rely on specific texts taken out of context. The Bible contains many types of writing from a long period of history, not all of equal value to the modern believer. Yet it is a whole, in that it tells of the gradual unfolding of God's purpose and human understanding of his nature. The Old Testament tells much of the preparation for the coming of Christ. He referred to it many times and it was the sacred scripture

174

of the very early Church, before the New Testament as we now have it was written. It is in the living Christ, killed and risen for our sake, that we put our trust. The Bible continually leads us to him, but faith depends not on passive reading but on an active response.

> I would have you every morning read a portion of the Holy Scriptures, till you have read the Bible from the beginning to the end: observe it well, read it reverently and attentively, set your heart upon it, and lay it up in your memory and make it the direction of your life: it will make you a wise and a good man. I have been acquainted somewhat with men and books, and have had long experience in learning, and in the world: there is no book like the Bible for excellent learning, wisdom, and use; and it is want of understanding in them that think or speak otherwise.

Matthew Hale

Lord of the Bible, revealed in words as the true Word of God, keep me faithful to the truth that I have learned and the wisdom that has been made known to me. Give me diligence to persevere in the study of the holy book, and grace to find it always the way to deeper knowledge and love of Jesus Christ as Saviour, Giver of eternal life.

Fourth Sunday before Advent

Religious obedience is not fulfilled in words or in outward observance. It must become part of life, a continual response to the will of God.

Mark 12:28–34
When Jesus saw that he answered wisely, he said to him, 'You are not far from the kingdom of God' (v.34).

A good deal of money, and a reputation for being clever, can be won nowadays by the rapid production of factual knowledge on the public media. It is considerably different from the wisdom which is described and praised in the Old Testament. Holy Wisdom is not a matter of knowledge or of intellect, but rather the ability to discern the will of

175

God and the resolution to act on it. It is a living relationship to the world as the place of his creation and his working, and not a pursuit of private fancies abut what it should be like. The scribe who made his contribution to the discussion was praised by Jesus not for his knowledge of the Jewish Law, which it was his business to teach and interpret, but for understanding its deeper implications. Anyone can go to church, join in the confession, say the creed and respond to the prayers. It is another matter to take them to ourselves, understand what we are saying about the nature and purposes of God, and shape our lives accordingly.

> There will be no ascent to God for you, no standing in his holy place, the gift of reason will have been bestowed upon you to no point, if like wild animals you follow the dictates of your senses while your reason just looks on. But the righteous tread the royal highway, turning neither to left nor right. These are the souls of whom the prophet writes: 'The way of the righteous is upright, and the path they tread is straight.' They pay heed to the timely warning and avoid the unprofitable maze. They make their choice to work efficiently, their effort focused through righteousness.

> Bernard of Clairvaux

Lord God, the source of all wisdom, give me grace to hear, to believe, and to obey all that you have commanded. Take my will and my mind, fill me with knowledge of your truth and make me a channel of holy wisdom for those whose lives touch mine.

All Saints' Sunday

In the blessed company of the saints in heaven we find the perpetual praise of God's glory and the pledge of our eternal life.

John 11:32–44
Jesus said to her, 'Did I not tell you that if you believed, you would see the glory of God?' (v.40).

We do not know much about Lazarus, whether he was a particularly good man, or influential in his community. He belonged to what was clearly a devoted and pious family, and Jesus felt for him an affection that brought tears to the eyes of his humanity. The point of the story as it is told in the Gospel is that Lazarus becomes a sign, an image of the glory of God shown in everyday life and in death. Jesus, the Lord of life, overcomes death as he would later overcome it in his own person. But Lazarus was restored to life for a few years and would die again, while Jesus would be raised to live for ever and bring his followers through death to eternal life. Our rejoicing in the saints is not for the lives of good people but for the fact that in their various ways their lives showed the glory of God. The power of the risen Christ was in them, and their memory on earth is more than a memorial of the past. They are the blessed company of heaven, greatly rewarded, but with a blessedness that the least worthy of faithful believers may hope to share.

> For, that thou mightest not think that He received the power of working from another, He taught thee this before, and gave proof by deeds, and said not, 'Arise', but, 'Come forth,' conversing with the dead man as though living. What can be equal to this authority? And if He doth it not by His own strength, what shall He have more than the Apostles, who say, 'Why look ye so earnestly on us as though by our own power or holiness we had made this man to walk?' (Acts 3:12) For if, not working by His own power, He did not add what the Apostles said concerning themselves, they will in a manner be more truly wise than He, because they refused the glory.
>
> John Chrysostom

Blessed Lord Jesus, joy of all the saints, friend of sinners, conqueror of death, grant me a deeper sense of your presence with me. Forgive me when I am cold and careless in devotion, and raise me from the death of sin to the life of holiness where I may praise you with your saints.

Third Sunday before Advent

The call of God may be unexpected and even unwelcome, but its consequences are inescapable. Whether we obey or resist, life will not be the same once it has been heard.

Mark 1:14–20
He saw James son of Zebedee and his brother John, who were in their boat mending their nets. Immediately he called them; and they left their father Zebedee in the boat with the hired men, and followed him (vv.19–20).

The word translated 'immediately' is a favourite with St Mark. His Gospel gives the impression of rapid and continuous action as the ministry of Jesus hastens on towards its climax. People hear his call and leave what they are doing so that they may follow him into the unknown. It is impossible not to feel sorry for some of those who were left behind. In this episode, Zebedee in the boat, alone with the paid fishermen while his two sons walk away with a stranger, is a sad figure. The call of God through the centuries has been costly for many, for those who have gone out into new ways and strange paths, and for those who have to remain. Yet the word 'immediately' will not be silenced. Few are in fact called to drop their work, leave their family and start a new vocation. But none who has put their faith in God will escape the call to do something for him – many calls perhaps that seem slight but may be important towards his purpose. The rapid response prevents the matter being put aside until tomorrow, when we shall be less busy and the chance of obedience may have gone. Sometimes the nets have to be dropped for a time.

The way of the cross is not the path from sorrow to joy but the path of suffering and joy, intermingling throughout, though contrasted dramatically as the meal gives way to the prayer in the garden and the long night of arrest and trial. Christianity, the faith in the Crucified One, is a religion for men and women in their strength, exhilarated, encouraged, walking tall – and a religion for men and women in their weakness – broken, disappointed, suffering, brought very low. And for most of us it is a religion for those who know strength and weakness, and seek God equally in both experiences.

Michael Perham

Lord Jesus, when you call, grant that I shall hear and obey. Forgive the excuses, the laziness, the selfishness which have too often made me neglect what I know should be done. Give me the grace to follow you where you will and when you will, so that both at work and in leisure I may be truly your servant.

Second Sunday before Advent

We know that Christ will come again, but our present task is to be faithful to the teaching and example of his Incarnation.

Mark 13:1–8
'Beware that no one leads you astray. Many will come in my name and say, "I am he", and they will lead many astray' (vv.5–6).

A Babel of seductive voices echoes down the ages. The deluded, the self-seeking, the evil, the sincerely misguided. It is not the claims to be Christ himself that are most to be feared – they are more easily dismissed as mental deviations. Those who have led many astray are the people who claim to have special revelation, to know for the first time what Christianity is about and to be divinely appointed founders of the true Church. They often come forward in times of trouble, prophesying the end of the world and promising that the only means of salvation lies in following them. Some have terribly misused their strange power, destroying by mass suicide or murder the community that they have gathered. Now we are looking towards Advent, when devotion focuses both on the first coming of Christ, incarnate in the infant Jesus at Bethlehem, and on his second coming to judge the world and bring all temporal things to an end. Let no one lead us astray: the end will come, but we have sufficient revelation for the present time, and that is all we need to know.

Keep us, O Lord, while we tarry on this earth, in a serious seeking after thee, and in an affectionate walking with thee, every day of our lives; that when thou comest, we may be found not hiding our talent, nor serving the flesh, nor yet asleep with our lamp unfurnished, but waiting and longing for our Lord, our glorious King, for ever and ever.

Richard Baxter

Lord Jesus, you will come again in glory to judge both the living and the dead. In the years of this present age, may the Holy Spirit preserve me from error and keep me in the way of truth. Guide me to prepare for your coming, not seeking to know the time but confident in your presence with me now.

Christit the King

The might and majesty of God are beyond our comprehension. As they are presented to us in the person of Christ, it is as an example of sacrificial love for us to follow.

John 18:33–37
Jesus answered, 'My kingdom is not from this world. If my kingdom were from this world, my followers would be fighting to keep me from being handed over to the Jews. But as it is, my kingdom is not from here' (v.36).

Kingship is an idea that troubles some people today. The days of absolute monarchy and hereditary rule seem to be over – is it right, then, to keep the name of 'King' in the language of the Church? The answer is plain enough in the words of Jesus himself. His Kingdom is not a place in which tyranny reigns and opposition is put down by force. It is a blessed state beyond this world, yet attainable within it, not by the exercise of power but by love and humility. In the last days before Advent, the mystery of the Passion is presented to us. It was for this that Jesus came into the world, not to conquer with the sword but to suffer without resistance so that there should be new

from beyond this world.

life for all the human race. He stood before the power of Rome, willingly vulnerable, refusing both human and divine intervention to save himself from death. On this day we praise his majesty at the same time as we give thanks for his humble obedience. The most ardent republican, the most committed campaigner for equality, need not fear to use his title of King.

> If Christ be a mere moral example, if the Church is a mere human society, then no wonder if the world is startled and perplexed when we speak of the Church as being to us more precious than our liberty, or even our lives; but if by the aid of the Holy Spirit we can see Jesus to be the Lord, if we can see Him, who is Head over all, to be the head of the Church, which is His body; if we can see that body to be the covenanted receptacle of the gifts and graces of Christ, then we know where true peace will be found – not where Christ is dethroned from His own Divinity, not where Christ is relegated to distant ages and looked upon merely as a moral, pattern man, but where Christ is present, full of grace and truth, looking to His own most true promise, 'Lo, I am with you always, even unto the end of the world.'
>
> Edward King

Lord Jesus, made vulnerable and condemned for the salvation of all people, give me grace to come into your Kingdom where the power of this world is set aside, and the only power is love. Reign in me as king, and draw me to yourself now in this life and in the life to come where your kingship is perfect and without end.

Year C

First Sunday of Advent

Death and judgement are unfashionable subjects today, even in the Churches, but they are emphasized all through the Bible and are traditional Advent themes. Our prayer is not to escape them but to be ready to meet them with hope in the saving power of Christ.

Luke 21:25–36
'Be alert at all times, praying that you will have the strength to escape all these things that will take place, and to stand before the Son of Man' (v.36).

'Alert' – a typical Advent word at a time when we are caught between the lethargy of deepening winter and the frenetic excitement of coming Christmas. Strength is needed when we are ready to let go, to decide that it will all somehow work out, or that we can manage quite nicely by ourselves. Christians are not promised exemption from trouble and danger, certainly not from the death of the body. The promise is of being protected and kept firm until the end, if we play our part with the response of obedience. Do not be afraid of the judgement, final or personal, but only of being unprepared when the call comes to stand before the Lord whom we have claimed to follow. It is not only the positive vices that can lead us against him. The warning is equally against the anxiety that eats into the mind, the excessive care for this world that closes the eyes to heavenly things. We are not to turn our backs on this world, nor on the delights of the coming season, but to be alert to what God is saying to us in the routine of the day.

'Now it is high time to awake out of sleep.' These are St Paul's words to the Romans, but is there any exhortation at this time more needed than that? Now, just a few reasons why it is high time to awake out of sleep. Because of the coming of the Lord. The Lord shall come with all His saints. We look forward to the coming of the Lord. Christians are ever like that, they stand waiting with their loins girt about, and their lamps burning. And do you say that the Lord delays His coming, and that a thousand years have past, and He has not come? Stand back and look out into eternity. Why do you talk like that, you who live under the Kingdom of God? What is a thousand years before the great range of eternity? It is but as a moment. It is as nothing.

A.H. Stanton

Father of all, you called me to duty and I often slept. Deliver me from the evil that grows from indifference and self-indulgence. May your Spirit guide me now to prepare to celebrate the coming of your Son to live among us, and at last to stand before him in the hour of my death.

Second Sunday of Advent

John the Baptist followed a line of Old Testament prophets and began a new line of witnesses to Christ. His mission reminds us to be ready to hear the word of God in unexpected places and from people who are little regarded by the values of the world.

Luke 3:1–6
The word of God came to John son of Zechariah in the wilderness (v.2).

Thirty years, a whole generation, and the strange events forgotten. His parents, old at his birth, were probably dead, and who would now recall the priest struck dumb in the sanctuary, the surprise naming of the child, and the prophecy of a new light for the world? Who remembered the rumours of angels in the fields outside Bethlehem? A new Caesar ruled half the world, new men clung to limited power in their territories, new priests maintained the old cults of sacrifice. The word came to none of them, only to a wild, half-naked man. Not to Rome or Jerusalem, but to the wilderness beyond Jordan, the barren land that seemed to be outside the favour of God. The word abides, in church and home and in the hearts of the faithful. If it grows too familiar and loses its challenge, listen for the new voice, crying perhaps in the wilderness of a world with the priests and rulers of its time. A popular evangelist with the power to make the old new again – or a passing word from one unknown except to a few, but known by God as one of his chosen messengers. It is a season to listen, to be prepared for the unknown, the improbable, a season for honouring the despised.

Through the roaring streets of London
Thou art passing, hidden Lord,
Uncreated, Consubstantial,
In the seventh heaven adored.

As of old the ever-Virgin
Through unconscious Bethlehem
Bore Thee, not in glad procession,
Jewelled robe and diadem;

Not in pomp and not in power,
Onward to Nativity,
Shrined but in the tabernacle
Of her sweet Virginity.

Still Thou goest by in silence,
Still the world cannot receive,
Still the poor and weak and weary
Only, worship and believe.

D.M. Dolben

Dear God, giver of the word of life, keep me open to hear that word. If it comes to me, to speak even a single thought, take my lips and use them. If it comes to me from another, take my ears and give me understanding. As I look again for the coming of the Son, grant that I shall not fail to recognize and honour the lowliest of his messengers and to know them highly favoured in the Kingdom.

Third Sunday of Advent

The gospel is truly good news because it brings assurance of forgiveness to all who repent and accept the salvation brought by Christ. Unless we recognize the reality of God's judgement, we cannot claim his mercy.

Luke 3:7–18
'You brood of vipers! Who warned you to flee from the wrath to come?' (v.7).

A very different greeting from the customary, 'I welcome you most warmly to our service this morning.' Sometimes our churches seem too bland in their proclamation of the gospel, too anxious to get people into a service and fearful of losing them if anything causes offence. John the Baptist did not shy away from giving offence. This first declaration of the coming of Jesus the Messiah certainly did not flatter the enquirers. Perhaps it may resonate still against coming to worship as an optional extra if there is time for it, of conferring a favour on the minister by being there to listen. Unless we come knowing our need, our weakness, we may do better not to come at all. Advent is a time to remember that the judgement of God is a reality and to give thanks for the mercy that is his gracious gift and not a natural right. No, the baptism family must certainly not be greeted at the church door as a brood of vipers! But a little more in the way of challenge, both from the pulpit and within our own hearts, may be in order.

> St John had the most sharply defined convictions, with which he went to work. He knew that a new spiritual society, to be called the Kingdom of God, was on the point of being set up upon the earth. He knew that his countrymen must either repent of their many sins against truth and grace, or perish. He knew that the One essential Figure in human history, a Being Who existed while he himself was yet unborn, was on the point of appearing among men. What mattered it to him if Jewish mobs, and Roman soldiers, if Scribes and Pharisees, Sadducees and Herodians, thought otherwise? He at least must go forward, come what might; his robust conviction was the secret of his courage.
>
> H.P. Liddon

When I come to you, my Lord, in the silence of my own prayers or in the worship of the congregation, may I never come casually, in pride and self-assurance. Keep before me knowledge of the judgement that I deserve, so that I may praise you for the mercy that releases me and the grace that enables me to love and serve.

Fourth Sunday of Advent

God's loving purpose was fulfilled when the Son came and took our human nature to himself. The promise of his coming had been spoken over many centuries but not all had believed, and few had understood.

Luke 1:39–45
'Blessed is she who believed that there would be a fulfilment of what was spoken to her by the Lord' (v.45).

Mary has been praised for many virtues: for humility, purity, obedience. Some Christians have made her cult excessive, and others in reaction have failed to honour her as they should. The quality that comes strongly through the accounts of the Annunciation, Visitation and Nativity is simple but too rare: she actually believed that God would do what he had promised. She accepted the startling, frightening message of the angel that she would be the human mother of the Son of God. People sometimes say that they are surprised when God does not answer their prayers – usually meaning that he has not given the answer they wanted. But often they seem equally surprised when he gives what they have asked, and when he is faithful to the promises made known in Scripture. Most of our faith is very far from removing mountains. We ask without real expectation, say the accustomed words but go on worrying and making plans for the worst. The time when Advent moves into Christmas is the time of all the year when we celebrate the fulfilment of the age-long promise of the Messiah. Most of those who were waiting for his coming did not recognize him. Millions who had never heard the promises were included in their completion.

Blessed she by all creation,
Who brought forth the world's salvation,
And blessed they – for ever blest,
Who love thee most and serve thee best.
Virgin-born, we bow before thee:
Blessed was the womb that bore thee;
Mary, Mother meek and mild,
Blessed was she in her Child.

Reginald Heber

Lord, help me to pray with faith, trusting in the promises of the Bible and the teaching that I have received, but above all in the experience of your love from day to day all through my life. At this time give me grace to know and feel that the Messiah, Jesus Christ, has come to the whole world and has come also to me as my personal Saviour.

Christmas Day

See Year A p. 24.

First Sunday of Christmas

God works among us not only in the great moments of life but equally in the days that seem unremarkable. His chosen ones who have been faithful at all times have left us an example of obedient service.

Luke 2:41–52
He went down with them and came to Nazareth, and was obedient to them (v.51).

While the baby is still in the Christmas crib, while we are still singing of the babe who has redeemed our loss and the little Lord Jesus asleep on the hay, we meet an active, enquiring boy. He is capable of finding his way around Jerusalem, of challenging his elders, of causing the anguish

known to every parent who has lost a child even for a short time. Then the
veil falls again for perhaps twenty years until we see him in full manhood,
beginning his ministry of teaching and healing. Two images dominate
our idea of Jesus, the baby in the stable and the man on the cross. But
between them were the years of growing up, the joys and sorrows of a
family, making friends, learning a trade, discovering about the world.
The beginning and the end are the pillars that bear up the whole edifice
of his life, God in our human condition. Most of his life on earth is
unrecorded, and that brings us closer to him, for most of our lives are
unrecorded too. He is Lord of the routine, the dull, the predictable, as
surely as he is the Lord of birth, and death, and eternal life.

Thy kingdom come! Yea, bid it come!
    But when Thy kingdom first began
On earth, Thy kingdom was a home,
    A child, a woman, and a man.

The child was in the midst thereof,
    O, blessed Jesus, holiest One!
The centre and the fount of love,
    Mary and Joseph's little Son.

Wherever on the earth shall be
    A child, a woman, and a man,
Imaging that sweet trinity
    Wherewith Thy kingdom first began,

Establish there Thy kingdom! Yea,
    And o'er that trinity of love
Send down, as in Thy appointed day,
    The brooding spirit of Thy Dove!

Katharine Tynan

*Heavenly Father, as this Christmas season draws on and life returns
to its familiar pattern of daily routine, may I keep the joyful mystery
always in my heart. Help me to grow day by day in obedience and
holy wisdom, and to walk in the way of the Lord Jesus who walked
this earth as child and man before me.*

Year C

Second Sunday of Christmas

See Year A p. 27.

Epiphany

See Year A p. 28.

Baptism of Christ

God's work in the world is usually silent and unseen, sometimes shown in a sudden and startling revelation. In daily work and in the moments of deep awe and devotion, the Holy Spirit guides the faithful.

Luke 3:15–17, 21–22
The Holy Spirit descended on him in bodily form like a dove (v.22).

What did they see in that moment of wonder? Was it truly the form of a dove in all its details, or a divine light that seemed like a beautiful white bird? Was the vision seen only by Jesus, or by John the Baptist, or by all who were standing there? Perhaps the thought of the dove that brought back to the Ark the evidence of life renewed helped to form the vision. Now the dove would signify for all time the Holy Spirit, silent, invisible, but felt as the powerful presence of God. On medals and banners, in stained glass, on pious postcards, the dove would be there. Artists would portray the Trinity, manifested at this moment as the Father looks down at the Son in the River Jordan and the Holy Dove descends. He came in peace and he would come again in wind and fire, to strengthen the Apostles, drive away their doubts and empower them for the work of the Kingdom. Deep peace and also continual calls to action come to those who are baptized into Christ, who honour the sinless One who accepted the baptism that is for the remission of sins.

Over our cleansed and blessed bodies willingly descends from the Father that Holiest Spirit. Over the waters of baptism, recognising

189

as it were His primeval seat, He reposes: He who glided down on the Lord in the shape of a dove, in order that the nature of the Holy Spirit might be declared by means of the emblem of simplicity and innocence. And accordingly He says, 'Be ye simple as doves.'

Tertullian

Come, Holy Spirit of God, to be my guide and my inspiration. Give me your peace, give me your empowering, so that the promises made at my baptism may be fulfilled now and in all my life to come.

Second Sunday of Epiphany

God does not disappoint his people. The promises of his care and the proclaiming of his glory are fulfilled in greater measure than we could ever imagine in our own minds.

John 2:1–11
'You have kept the good wine until now' (v.10).

The Gospels give us many insights into the daily life of New Testament times – and it is sometimes not so different from our own. The anxious host may relax by the end of the evening, when a general air of satisfaction has soothed the guests' critical sense. But in the Gospel narratives, especially in John, there is often a deeper meaning beneath the story, even when the story includes a miracle. This is the first miracle, a sign not only of human sympathy but also of divine glory, a revelation of power that had lain hidden for a long time; hidden for thirty years, but also hidden from the beginning of all things. There had been many prophecies that the Messiah would come, but the full wonder of his coming was not known. Not as unique man of God's favour but as God himself. Christ revealed himself, not in the Temple or the Royal Palace in Jerusalem but at a wedding in provincial Galilee, in a simple household where supplies ran short. It was good wine and plenty of it – something like 600 litres. God is not niggardly in his care for the body or for the soul.

That wine, which was produced by God in a vineyard, and which was first consumed, was good. None of those who drank of it found fault with it; and the Lord partook of it also. But that wine was better which the Word made from water, on the moment, and simply for the use of those who had been called to the marriage. For although the Lord had the power to supply wine to those feasting, independently of any created substance, and to fill with food those who were hungry, He did not adopt this course; but, taking the loaves which the earth had produced, and giving thanks, and on the other occasion making water wine, He satisfied those who were reclining at table, and gave drink to those who had been invited to the marriage, showing that the God who made the earth, and commanded it to bring forth fruit, who established the waters, and brought forth the fountains, was He who in these last times bestowed upon mankind, by His Son, the blessing of food and the favour of drink: the Incomprehensible acting thus by means of the comprehensible, and the Invisible by the visible; since there is none beyond Him, but He exists in the bosom of the Father.

Irenaeus

Father, your mercies are new every morning and your love exceeds all expectation. As I give thanks for all that is past, I thank you also that you do not leave me, you do not put an end to your generous gifts, but grace increases year by year until the best will be revealed in the life to come.

Third Sunday of Epiphany

The Bible is the word of God, open to all who will read or hear it. But we need the guidance of God himself in order to understand it fully and take it into our own lives. Bible study should be accompanied by prayer.

Luke 4:14–21
He began to teach in their synagogues and was praised by everyone (v.15).

191

A new preacher is always exciting, especially one already well known by reputation. This one turned out to be particularly good – and it was not just the pleasure of a new voice, or relief at not hearing a too-familiar old one. This one was special, giving a hitherto unrealized depth to the well-known texts. This was a regular worshipper, a local lad suddenly showing unexpected gifts of exposition. Although they did not know it, this was God who had inspired the scriptures from which he was reading, who had guided the prophets and was now here to expound them through a human tongue. Surely, even to the limited understanding of the congregation, this was the start of a brilliant career, a young rabbi whose name would be remembered with the great interpreters of the Law and the Prophets. This man would command an attentive congregation wherever he went. Nobody could have a word to say against him. But things turned out rather differently before his ministry had gone much farther.

> His words here ended, but his meek aspect
> Silent yet spake, and breathed immortal love
> To mortal men, above which only shone
> Filial obedience: as a sacrifice
> Glad to be offered, he attends the will
> Of his great Father.

John Milton

Lord Jesus Christ, gracious Teacher, it is your voice that speaks to me through the Bible, your words that are the word of God, because you are the Word made flesh. Teach me to listen not with the ears alone but with mind and heart and soul, so that I may truly learn of you and gratefully praise you.

Fourth Sunday of Epiphany

Those who are called to spread the word of God may suffer abuse, unpopularity and even persecution. The call may come not only to appointed preachers, but to any Christian.

Luke 4:22–40
When they heard this, all in the synagogue were filled with rage (v.28).

The mood soon changed when the words of the preacher came nearer home. Prophecy of the great works that would be done by the Messiah when he came was fine – they had heard it all before and it was an encouraging thought for some future time. But now the Messiah was standing in front of them, shaking their complacency, warning that the privileges of their religion might go out from them to people they thought were outside the care of God. Whatever the prophets may have done to help foreigners, nobody wanted anything to do with those across the border. It was time to get rid of this subversive young man before he did any more harm to those specially chosen for the divine favour. Preachers are not often lynched today, though many have suffered even to death for speaking the truth, but they can quickly become unpopular if they make the congregation feel less specially privileged. To have the Spirit of the Lord upon you is acceptable only if he does not upset comfortably established prejudices.

> One ever hangs where the shelled roads part,
> In this war He too lost a limb,
> But His disciples hide apart;
> And now the soldiers bear with Him.
>
> Near Golgotha strolls many a priest,
> And in their faces there is pride,
> That they were flesh-marked by the Beast
> By whom the gentle Christ's denied.
>
> The scribes on all the people shove
> And bawl allegiance to the state,
> But they who love the greater love
> Lay down their life; they do not hate.
>
> Wilfred Owen

Loving Jesus, keep me from being selfish in my faith. You are my Lord, my own personal Saviour, but you are not mine alone. Make me generous to share with others, with strangers and those outside my circle of believing friends, the love that you have for me and for them.

The Presentation of Christ

See Year A, p. 34.

Fifth Sunday of Epiphany

M any, perhaps most, of those who have been clearly called to serve God in a particular way have reacted at first with alarm and disbelief. All who claim to trust in him must be ready to respond if the call comes to them.

Luke 5:1–11
'Put out into the deep water and let down your nets for a catch' (v.4).

What an unpleasant suggestion, after a profitless night, to be told to go out and try again. Go right out, not near the shore where the return will be easy if nothing happens, but far into the deep water. There was the place of disappointment where nothing was found. There now is the place of success, so great that it is overwhelming, brings new peril, new fear, and a new command. There is the revelation that the voice which commands is the voice of God, that the companion in the boat is, reassuringly and terrifyingly, the Lord. It is obedience that matters, the trust which pushes out again when hope is feeble and the body is weary. The obedience that is pessimistic, even grudging gains more than the careless acceptance which makes no response and expects things to happen of their own accord. God does not give in half measures, and he does not want to receive them. If you have to leave the comfortable, familiar shore, be prepared to go well out until God's call is clear. The King James Version puts it even more strongly: 'Launch out into the deep.'

True faith is confident, and will venture all the world upon the strength of its Persuasion. Will you lay your life on it, your estate and your reputation, that the doctrine of Jesus Christ is true in every article? Then you have true faith. But he that fears men more than God, believes men more than he believes in God. Faith, if it be true, living, and justifying, cannot be separated from the good life; it works miracles, makes a drunkard become sober, a lascivious person become chaste, a covetous man become liberal; 'it over-comes the world – it works righteousness', and makes us diligently to do, and cheerfully to suffer, whatsoever God hath placed in our way to heaven.

Jeremy Taylor

Lord, here am I, not at all confident that I am ready to be sent. Give me the courage that only you can give, when I am called to some new task in your service. Strengthen me not to fear the deep water of life, for in its depth I shall find new challenges and new mercies.

Sixth Sunday of Epiphany

Life that turns away from God is empty. Even the slightest step towards him is drawn into his healing power and brings more blessings than we could imagine.

Luke 6:17–26
All in the crowd were trying to touch him, for power went out from him and healed all of them (v.19).

As we picture the crowd surrounding Jesus, pushing each other aside, pressing forward without regard for anyone else, it is tempting to shut out the unruly scene and dwell only on the teaching to his closest friends that followed. It is easy for the comfortable to dismiss the anguish of those for whom any hope of help is a last resort. It is easy from the security of church membership to feel superior to those, then and now, who do not know the reality of Jesus Christ, God and man. He gave his compassion freely, not only to his Disciples, not only to the religious people in his society – he often took a very poor view of them – but to all who came to him in hope, whatever their motives were. He is not the property of any devout individual, or of any congregation, or of the whole Church that he created. He is Lord of all, and his healing touch comes to those who do not know him as well as those who worship him. To acknowledge him as Master brings the obligation to share his love and to make it known.

> I was a stricken deer, that left the herd
> Long since. With many an arrow deep infixt
> My panting side was charged, when I withdrew
> To seek a tranquil death in distant shades.
> There was I found by One who had Himself
> Been hurt by th'archers. In His side He bore,
> And in His hands and feet, the cruel scars.
> With gentle force soliciting the darts,
> He drew them forth and healed, and bade me live.

William Cowper

Loving Lord Jesus Christ, source of all healing, let me feel your power to heal both body and spirit. When my hope and faith are broken, make them whole and draw me close to you. Give me the grace to see your love in those who do not know you as you are and to help them to understand that all love and life rest in you.

Seventh Sunday of Epiphany

To forgive enemies, not to use power for the hurt of others, may be the ideal of many who profess no religious faith. Christians know that they can hope to achieve the ideal only through strength given by God, who shows mercy when we deserve judgement.

Luke 6:27–38
'Be merciful, just as your Father is merciful' (v.36).

The precepts of our Lord are easier to read than to obey. Few people want to be mean, unkind, unforgiving – though it is sadly possible to choose the evil in preference to the good. Most of us would rather live in peace and love with others but, as we are inclined to say, the others often make it difficult! If we look away from ourselves and understand that this is the divine voice speaking, we may begin to understand that we are not being asked to perform some impossible operation on our natural human disposition. God who made us in his image gives us the strength to restore the image that sin defaces, to conform to what we are meant to be. Many philosophers have thought about God as impersonal or unknowable. Jesus reveals God in humanity, teaching that the ideal is not imposed by a distant tyrant but is in fact a share in the divine nature. We are being allowed to do the things that God does, to feel the compassion that he feels. A few minutes thinking about what we really deserve and the mercy which has so often spared us from the consequences of sin and folly should bring us to a better understanding of the commandments of love.

> The quality of mercy is not strain'd;
> It droppeth as the gentle rain from heaven
> Upon the place beneath. It is twice blest:
> It blesseth him that gives and him that takes.
> 'Tis mightiest in the mightiest; it becomes
> The throned monarch better than his crown;
> His sceptre shows the force of temporal power,
> The attribute to awe and majesty,
> Wherein doth sit the dread and fear of kings;
> But mercy is above this sceptred sway,
> It is enthroned in the hearts of kings
> It is an attribute to God himself;
> And earthly power doth then show likest God's
> When mercy seasons justice.

William Shakespeare

Lord Jesus, you have given me an example of the perfect love that pardons and shows mercy, and in pity of my failures you have continually brought me back into the right way. Give me the strength of your tenderness, the power of your compassion, so that when I am tempted to anger my response shall always be gentle and considerate.

Second Sunday before Lent

God made all things and sustains all things and cares for every individual life. If we are open to his calling, he gives all that we need and sets the limits that are right for us.

Luke 8:22–25

They went to him and woke him up, shouting, 'Master, Master we are perishing!' And he woke up and rebuked the winds and the raging waves; they ceased and there was a calm. He said to them, 'Where is your faith?' (vv.24–25).

Perhaps our habit of prayer is such that we need to carry a control marked 'Panic Button' or perhaps simply '999'. Too often we regard God as a kind of emergency service, to be alerted when things go wrong, when danger or distress afflicts us. The response of Christ to his panicking disciples was to calm both the sea and their fears. Once again, his power over the world and over the fearful hearts of men and women was revealed. But the calming was followed by a rebuke, not for having disturbed his sleep but for failure in faith. He had seen them through to this moment and he had a greater purpose for them, still to be revealed. His time had not yet come. A true relationship with God is continual, his care is constant in the quiet times as well as in the tumultuous, in the routine as well as in the excitement. Many people who say they are not 'religious' speak of having prayed when all other hope seemed lost. Better than not praying at all, but best to keep the line open all the time.

> For woe is me who walk so apt to fall,
> So apt to shrink afraid, so apt to flee,
> Apt to lie down and die (ah woe is me!)
> Faithless and hopeless turning to the wall.
> But yet not hopeless quite nor faithless quite,
> Because not loveless; love may toil all night,
> But take at morning; wrestle till the break
> Of day, but then wield power with God and man.

Christina Rossetti

Loving heavenly Father, you are so close, and I keep you so distant. You are in control of everything, and I am afraid that you are not noticing my need. Keep me open to hear and faithful to obey, in work and in rest, in calm and in turmoil, and to know that you are always near.

Sunday Next before Lent

We often do not understand what God is doing and we put our own interpretation on the signs that he gives. Faith requires patience, being ready to wait until the full meaning is revealed.

Luke 9:28–36
Peter did not know what he said (v.33).

The other disciples might have commented that this was nothing new. Peter, one of the closest companions of Jesus, had a habit of speaking without thinking, of being sure what was to be done next and letting everyone else know. He thought he could walk on water, be faithful to death, and now he wanted to hold this moment of glory for ever, to stay on the mountain with the heroes of the past and the Master he loved. He did not know what he was saying. If he had had his way, there would have been no Passion, no Resurrection, no Church, and no witness and martyrdom for Peter himself. This was the preparation – not the completion; the empowering – not the final test. Perfect confidence in faith is good, but it can have its shadow side if it leads to excessive confidence in self, in certainty that we know exactly what to do as soon as we have been given the first sign of his calling. 'They that wait upon the Lord will renew their strength,' says the prophet, and the constant renewal is needed more than the first ecstasy. Too often we do not know what we are really saying in prayer, but if we are sincerely open to be corrected, the next step will be shown.

In the story of the transfiguration we are told of the failure of the disciples to understand what was happening when they saw the figure of Jesus radiant with an unearthly splendour. It is not so much a story about lack of faith or the inability of the mind to comprehend the meaning of an event as a story about the failure of the imagination. Only the exercise of that power could have enabled the disciples to discern the reality of the experience and make some kind of coherent response to the vision that they had received. The gospels are full of examples of this kind of failure. Again and again there are instances of the people around Jesus failing to understand the parables or the purpose of the Lord. They have been given all the information they need but while 'they may indeed see' they 'do not perceive, and may indeed hear but do not understand' (Matthew 4:12). It is the same with our apprehension of a work of art. The failure to respond is a failure of the imagination. It is not the inability to understand, intellectually, the meaning of the words or the pattern of sounds or colours: one can grasp the 'content' of the thing (the 'information' supplied by the object) and remain 'outside' the work, not discerning the glory.

Brian Horne

Lord, I do not know how to pray as I should, but I know that you receive my words and use them according to your will. Save me from the self-assurance that makes me want to follow the way that seems immediately right, and teach me to wait upon you until the true way is made plain. In all my speaking with others, save me and them from the results of my speaking running before my thinking.

Ash Wednesday

See Year A p. 42.

First Sunday of Lent

There is no escape from temptation in this world, but there is an unfailing defence against giving in to it. If we sincerely call on God for help, he will give the strength we need.

Luke 4:1–13

When the devil had finished every test, he departed from him until an opportune time (v.13).

The use of the word 'test' here, instead of the more familiar 'temptation', is helpful. Temptation is a reality, not to be shrugged off by humorous reference to some harmless pleasure, but it is not itself sin. Thinking about the attractive possibility of something known to be wrong is leading towards sin and often to the yielding that is actual sin. Christ, the sinless one, knew its full force in the wilderness where body, mind and spirit had been taxed by days of solitude and fasting. Knowing our frailty, he tells us to pray that we shall not be led into temptation – that is, that we shall not be put to the test that may lead us away from God. Jesus saw off the devil, but temptation would return when the strain was even greater: in Gethsemane and on the Cross, where a miracle would release him from suffering but undo the great design of salvation. As he was firm to the end, so he will keep us firm in our less terrible testing. Lent is a time when temptation is often strong. As the old hymn says, 'one victory will help you some other to win', but only if you remember that the devil does not give up as easily as we are inclined to do, and that God never gives up at all.

> If the devil tempts you to do wrong, don't be out of heart all in a hurry. Don't think, because he tempts you, 'Ah, I am done for!' The devil went up to the Saviour, with great impudence, and told lies in His face; and notice how the Saviour beat him off – He quoted back to him a text out of the Bible. You remember that when the devil went to the Saviour, he wanted Him to turn the stones into bread. But the Saviour said, very quietly, 'No, I won't do it: it is written, Man shall not live by bread alone'. He brushed him off by quoting bits out of the Bible, which (I think we may say with reverence) most likely the Saviour had stored up in His mind when He was young. He used the Bible against the tempter. So when the devil comes to you, think of some text in the Bible.

Edward King

Father, as I pray, 'Lead us not into temptation', make me mean what I am saying, and let me understand the perils of this world. Defend my weakness when temptation comes, shield me from complacency when it is conquered. Be my guide though the wilderness when fear and anxiety press upon me and I am tempted to follow the easier way of self and to leave the way that lies before me to follow.

Second Sunday of Lent

God is our shield and defence against all that threatens and troubles us. He desires us, as his obedient children, to accept the love that is offered, but too often we refuse to hear him, and continue on our own way.

Luke 13:31–35
'How often have I desired to gather your children together as a hen gathers her brood under her wings, and you were not willing!' (v.34)

They were seeking to kill him, as they had killed many others who had brought the word of God to them in the past. As a baby he had escaped one Herod – now another Herod is afraid of the rival King. Jesus responds not with flight, not with anger, but with deep compassion for their folly and hatred. The memory of a loving mother's care in childhood, the memory of little chickens in the yard running for protection to the mother hen, brought a tender picture that made him cry out in sorrow for those who were his children and did not know it. There is debate and concern about the feminine element in our idea of God. This one homely image tells us that he is all that we can imagine of parenthood. The love, the sorrow for those who go astray, the endless will to forgive disobedience, the desire to comfort and protect, are all his own. How can we dare to think of God, unseen, almighty, creating and sustaining the whole universe, in this way? Because his Son has told us.

> Strong Sorrow-wrestler of Mount Calvary,
> Speak through the blackness of Thine Agony,
> Say, have I ever known Thee? answer me!
> Speak, Merciful and Mighty, lifted up
> To draw those to Thee who have power to will
> The roseate Baptism, and the bitter Cup,

The Royal Graces of the Cross-Crowned Hill,
Terrible Golgotha – among the bones
Which whiten thee, as thick as splintered stones
Where headlong rocks have crushed themselves away
I stumble on – Is it too dark to pray?

D.B. Dolben

Almighty God, stronger than any warrior, defend me from the evil in the world and in myself. Loving God, gentler than any parent, enfold me in your tender love. Merciful God, wiser than any prophet, show me the way and guide me into it.

Third Sunday of Lent

It is too easy to go on seeking pleasure and idly following what is most convenient, in the belief that there is plenty of time to change and become serious. God is patient, but it is not for us to take advantage of his patience.

Luke 13:1–9
'"If it bears fruit next year, well and good; but if not, you can cut it down"' (v.9).

'Give me another chance' is the cry of the naughty child and of the habitual criminal. When the cry is heard with mercy, it sometimes leads to a new beginning, but sometimes to repetition of the old ways. The Christian faith is a faith of other chances, continual pardon after repentance, and assurance that God never casts away those who cling to him in their falls and weakness. But with every promise of the Bible there is also a warning. Repentance, turning around and starting on a new road, may be forestalled by death or by the indifference that lingers too long without effort. If the sap is not rising in the tree because the roots have dried up, there will be no fruit. If the will to change becomes barren, the fruits of the spirit wither away. The Psalmist says that a righteous person is like a tree planted near water, which flourishes, while the ungodly are like dry chaff blown away by the wind (Psalm 1:3–4). Jesus promises the water of life to those who will receive it and, as always, the choice is ours.

It is a fearful thing to fall into the hands of the living God.
But it is a much more fearful thing to fall out of them.

Did Lucifer fall through knowledge?
oh then, pity him, pity him that plunge!

Save me, O God, from falling into the ungodly knowledge
of myself as I am without God.

Let me never know, O God
let me never know what I am or should be
when I have fallen out of your hands, the hands of the living
    God.

D.H. Lawrence

Lord, be patient with me, but save me from using your patience as an excuse for not trying to correct my faults. Give me the will to obey, to bring forth good fruit that will last and be a token of repentance. Let me not be cut down until my work here is done and you call me to eternal life.

Fourth Sunday of Lent

God reaches out to us, goes before us, hastens to welcome us when we turn to him. He receives with joy all who repent and seek a new life following his will, however long they have been away.

Luke 15:1–3, 11b–32
'While he was still far off, his father saw him and was filled with compassion; he ran and put his arms around him and kissed him' (v.20).

This long parable has been greatly discussed for centuries. Known as the story of the Prodigal Son, from a page-heading in the Bible, it is often said that it is really the parable of the Unforgiving Brother. Perhaps most of all it is the parable of the Loving Father. It begins with him as the father of two sons, and it ends with his words that tell of his love for both of them. He is a very human figure, continually looking out for his wayward son, hoping daily, recognizing him at a distance when a stranger would not be able to recognize him. His response is not anger, reluctant acceptance or even the mending of a severed love, but compassion. The Greek word behind it is a very strong one, the same that is used in the parable of the merciful Samaritan, and it tells of a deep inner feeling. The father cares most for what his son has suffered, the miserable state to which he is reduced. No longer young, he yet runs to meet his son. A very human figure – but a divine one as well. This is the God who never lets go, who sorrows with our sorrows and rejoices when we come home.

> For he was no stranger, but a son, and a brother of the child who had been well pleasing to the father, and he plunged into no ordinary vice, but went to the very extremity, so to say, of evil: he the rich and free and well-bred son being reduced to a more miserable condition than that of household slaves, strangers, and hirelings. Nevertheless he returned again to his original condition, and had his former honour restored to him. But if he had despaired of his life, and, dejected by what had befallen him, had remained in the foreign land, he would not have obtained what he did obtain, but would have been consumed with hunger, and so have undergone the most pitiable death: but since he repented, and did not despair, he was restored, even after such great corruption, to the same splendour as before, and was arrayed in the most beautiful robe, and enjoyed greater honours than his brother who had not fallen.

> John Chrysostom

Father of all, I have felt your loving embrace when I have failed and been away too long. I know that the least desire to return to the right way will lead me back into your arms. Bring me home again and again, until you call me to the eternal home from which I shall never stray.

Mothering Sunday

See Year A p. 48.

Fifth Sunday of Lent

Whatever is gained in this world, whatever good is done, it cannot be compared with the debt of honour and worship that we owe to God. Our lives have purpose only if they recognize his glory.

John 12:1–8

'You always have the poor with you, but you do not always have me' (v.8).

The end of the social gospel – a withdrawal of Christian action for the poor and deprived? As the fragrance of the precious ointment filled the house, Jesus foretold his coming Passion when the Disciples would be scattered and leaderless. The fellowship would be betrayed by the one who had professed sympathy for those outside it. There would be no soothing ointment in the hall of judgement or on the hill of Calvary. In the Church of the Risen Christ, the poor would find relief and a place of honour. Now was the time to recognize the reality of the Master by whom all would be accomplished. He was the Christ, the Messiah, the anointed one, and Mary's gift was a sign. He says to his disciples, then and now, 'Recognize the Lord when he is among you, honour him as Lord so that he may strengthen you in goodness. Know in whose name and for whose sake the works of charity are to be done. Do them with gratitude to the one who is the timeless, constant protector of the weak and vulnerable.'

To Mercy, Pity, Peace, and Love
All pray in their distress;
And to these virtues of delight,
Return their thankfulness.

For Mercy, Pity, Peace, and Love
Is God, our father dear,
And Mercy, Pity, Peace, and Love
Is man, his child and care.

For Mercy has a human heart,
Pity a human face,
And Love, the human form divine,
And Peace, the human dress.

William Blake

Lord God, help me to love you with my whole heart, and my neighbour for your sake. When I see in other people the needs of poverty, loneliness, depression, may I see also your presence in them. Let the fragrance of your perfect love purify me and fill me with compassion.

Palm Sunday

In the humility of his Incarnation, Jesus accepted the utmost of suffering. Few recognized that the Son of God was walking among them, and that in him the prophecies of the Suffering Servant were being fulfilled.

Luke 23:1–49
A great number of people followed him, and among them were women who were beating their breasts and wailing for him (v.27).

When he came into the city, they ran before him as if he was a king coming into his capital, a conqueror in triumph, an ambassador bringing news of joy and peace. He was all these things and more, but he disappointed the expectations of those who were hoping for a sudden revolution, and their adoration turned to hate. When he left the city, they walked behind him, following a group of criminals to execution. Some followed in mockery, some in morbid curiosity, a few in deep sorrow. For the faithful women who had been with him in the days of fame, when the crowd came not to insult him but to seek healing and pardon, it was the last chance to be near him. Death stood at the top of the hill, and the end of all their hopes. In a few days the King would come into his own, death would be conquered and the good news would start to go out into the world. But now, rising above the murmur of the mob, there was only the sound of women crying because the greatest beauty they had ever known was leaving them.

> Have, have ye no regard, all ye
> Who pass this way, to pity me
> Who am a man of misery?
>
> A man both bruis'd, and broke, and one
> Who suffers not here for mine own
> But for my friends' transgression?
>
> Ah! Sion's Daughters, do not fear
> The Cross, the Cords, the Nails, the Spear,
> The Myrrh, the Gall, the Vinegar,
>
> For Christ, your loving Saviour, hath
> Drunk up the wine of God's fierce wrath;
> Only, there's left a little froth,
>
> Less for to taste, than for to shew
> What bitter cups had been your due,
> Had He not drank them up for you.

Robert Herrick

Lord Jesus, by your grace I have followed you in times of joy and of trouble. Keep my feet faithfully in your footsteps, to follow you now in this Holy Week, sorrowing for your sufferings and for my sins and all the sins of the world that you carried on your shoulders. Bring me to the Day of Resurrection, to say again, Blessed is he who comes in the name of the Lord.

Maundy Thursday

See Year A p. 52.

Good Friday

See Year A p. 53.

Easter Eve

See Year A p. 55.

Easter Day

Christ is the Lord of all things. It is in his risen life that we find our true lives.

Luke 24:1–12
'Why do you look for the living among the dead? He is not here, but has risen' (v.5).

The search for the 'historical Jesus' has occupied many scholars. It is right and natural that we should want to know as much as we can about the life on earth of the man who was the Son of God. But there is a danger of becoming so fascinated with the quest that we turn attention from the fact that the centre of our faith is not the human ministry but the Resurrection. Our Lord is not in the archaeological evidence or the newly discovered documents, any more than he was in the tomb on the first Easter morning. Those who came in love to perform the last office for the dead were first dismayed and soon given a new mission to tell the good news that Christ had risen. The good news for a world where many are still without faith is not that great teaching was once given, but that it still has power because it was the word of incarnate God, who passed through death to be continually present with us and make us share in his glory. On this day above all, we know that we shall not find him among the dead.

> Up from the grave he arose,
> With a mighty triumph o'er his foes;
> He arose a victor from the dark domain,
> And he lives for ever with his saints to reign,
> He arose! He arose!
> Alleluia! Christ arose!

Robert Lowry

Lord Jesus Christ, risen from the dead to be the life of believers, keep me from an intellectual curiosity that forgets to find you ever present in all things. As I give praise on this day of Resurrection, fill my heart with yourself so that day by day and year by year I shall tell to others the good news that gives joy and salvation.

Second Sunday of Easter

Jesus Christ conquered death not for a few favoured friends or for the members of the Church, but for the whole human race. Those who know the peace of the Resurrection must make it known to all.

John 20:19–31
Jesus said to them again, 'Peace be with you. As the Father has sent me, so I send you (v.21).

The first divine greeting of 'Peace' was perfect joy. It was the word of salutation, the promise of the angels of the Nativity, the blessing to be given on entering a house, the word embedded in the name of Jerusalem. The second time of its utterance was more disturbing. This was not to be a return to the old ways, made sweeter now by the agony of loss that had been healed. Now they were still to follow, but in a different way. The broken fellowship was to begin again, now with a Master known and loved but also glorified. He was giving them the great commission, the power and the duty to follow in weariness and persecution, suffering and death, to the final glory. The disciples, the learners, were to become apostles, those who were sent to proclaim the King. The night before he went to the cross he had warned them that his peace was not the kind of peace that the world knew. Now they began to understand that the peace of God was not in the outer world but in the soul. There was work to be done. The Easter message was to be proclaimed, then and for generations to come.

> Then, gliding through th'unopening door,
> Smooth without step or sound,
> 'Peace to your souls', He said – no more –
> They own Him, kneeling round.
> Eye, ear, and hand, and loving heart,
> Body and soul in every part,
> Successive made His witnesses that hour,
> Cease not in all the world to show His saving power.

John Keble

Risen Lord, in the peace that passes understanding, in the peace that you alone can give, I know your peace and I rejoice in your love. Grant that my peace shall not be the peace of idleness, of complacency, of possessiveness, but the peace of confidence that reaches out to all who seek.

Third Sunday of Easter

The Lord makes his presence known in many ways. Those who recognize him respond at once in love and worship, to begin a new life according to his will.

John 21:1–19
When Simon Peter knew that it was the Lord, he put on some clothes, for he was naked, and jumped into the lake (v.7).

It must have seemed like a return to the past: another unprofitable night on the familiar lake and then a sudden catch beyond all expectations. It was a strange repetition of the time when Jesus had first met them, preached from their boat and then given them a miraculous gift. But this time the net did not begin to break or the boat to sink. This time Peter did not beg Jesus to depart from him, but leaped into the sea to meet him. He reacted with his usual impetuosity but now, in the power of the Resurrection, he had got it right. Jesus was calling them, the Master they had known and loved, still providing for their physical as well as their spiritual needs, wonderfully transformed in his Risen Body. The Easter joy transforms the routine days of life as much as the times of private prayer and public worship. Nothing had seemed to be going right through those weary hours of darkness and the new day was likely to be just a repetition of what went before. Then their eyes were opened and they knew him. Many who knew him only with eyes of faith have yet seen him waiting on the shore and cried out with the beloved disciple, 'It is the Lord'.

They sit down on the shore, face to face with Him, and eat their broiled fish as He bids. And then to Peter, all dripping still, shivering, and amazed, staring at Christ in the sun, on the other side of the coal fire – thinking a little perhaps of what happened by another coal fire, when it was colder, and having had no word changed with him by his Master since that look of His – to him so amazed, comes the question, 'Simon, lovest thou Me?' Try to feel that a little; and think of it till it is true to you.

John Ruskin

Risen Lord, you have so often called to me when the hour was dark and hopes have faded. May I never fail to hear your voice and to come to you, just as I am, trusting in nothing but your embracing love. Lighten me with the dawn of your presence at the beginning of every day and be my refuge at the coming of every night, until your last call to be with you for ever.

Fourth Sunday of Easter

The shepherd is a familiar Bible image of God. It expresses what we know of his love, his protection, his continual guidance and his patience when we go astray, and it is fully revealed in Jesus, the Good Shepherd.

John 10:22–30
'My sheep hear my voice. I know them, and they follow me' (v.27).

Sheep arouse double and somewhat contradictory ideas in us. They are a model of innocence and harmlessness, but they are also troublesome creatures who wander off and get lost and move about in a mindless crowd. There is a marked sheep syndrome in all of us, which is perhaps why we like to project these faults on to them. Following the crowd in the wrong way can lead to intolerance, persecution and war. Following in the right way brings a unity of purpose and the fellowship that our humanity needs. The Palestinian shepherd does not drive his flock but leads it, as in the promise that God will feed his flock like a shepherd and gently lead the ewes that are with young (Isaiah 40:11). The loving shepherd does not only lead those who agree to follow him. He seeks the lost one and carries it back on his shoulder (Luke 15:5). Christ is the Good Shepherd who leads his people because he has gone before them on the same road. He has known its perils and its anguish, even through the valley of the shadow of death. The Good Shepherd is also the Lamb who was slain.

The secret voice of Jesus is true, and it makes the soul true. There is no deception in it, nor pride, nor hypocrisy, but gentleness, peace, love and charity; it is full of life and grace. So when this voice speaks to a soul it may be so powerful that the soul puts aside what it is doing, whether it is praying, speaking, reading, thinking or working, and listens in rest and in love to the sweet sound of this spiritual voice. In this tranquillity Jesus reveals himself to the soul, sometimes as a master to be feared, sometimes as a father to be respected and revered, and sometimes as a spouse to be loved. The soul becomes absorbed in a wonderful reverence that cannot be transcended. It feels secure and at deep rest, and desires only to remain in this state. It is in touch with the goodness of Jesus and by the grace of that touch it is made whole and safe, knowing Jesus alone.

Walter Hilton

Loving Shepherd, lead me in the way of faith, the paths of righteousness; forgive the self-will that hinders me from following faithfully; shield me from the perils to which my own folly may bring me. Be my guardian and my guide through the uncertainties of this world, and bring me safely to the fold of God's people.

Fifth Sunday of Easter

Those who seek to do the will of God must be prepared for unexpected changes and new attitudes. It is his purpose to bring all things to perfection, and our part is to respond with unselfish love.

John 13:31–35

'I give you a new commandment, that you love one another. Just as I have loved you, you also should love one another' (v.34).

'Love' is one of the most misused words in the language. It can speak of empty sentimentality, of escape from serious understanding of another, of basic lust. It is used of pop stars, holiday resorts and chocolate. It can express the noblest human feelings, the mother's selfless care, the true union of man and wife. It is sometimes thrown around too freely in Christian circles, as when the phrase 'speaking the trust in love' (Ephesians 4:15) is a prologue to being disagreeable to another Christian. It is quite a surprise to think of it again as a new commandment, the consequence of the great love that Jesus was about to reveal in his sacrificial death. Things were not to be the same as they had been. The disciples, often competitive and quarrelsome, were to love one another without reserve, so that the love of God would shine through them to the world. It is of course a help to know that the Greek of the New Testament has more than one word for 'love' and that this is the total, unconditional love of which

St Paul writes (1 Corinthians 13). But it needs no language scholarship to try to follow the pattern of Jesus Christ.

> Of old time the people called of God dedicated themselves to him in a Covenant of law and promise, the shadow of better things to come. We are called to a life in Christ, in whom we are redeemed from sin and consecrated to God, having been admitted into the New Covenant of love which our Lord instituted and sealed with his own blood, that it might remain forever. On the one side this Covenant is the gracious promise of God in Christ, that he will fulfil in us, and for us, and through us, all that he has declared in Him who is the same yesterday, today, and forever. On our part the Covenant means that we willingly engage ourselves to live no more unto ourselves, but to him who loved us and gave himself for us.

> Methodist Covenant Service

Lord, it is so easy to say, 'I love you' and still to wound the loved one. Make my love like your love, free from selfishness, sincere in words, proved in deeds. Renew your spirit of love in me day by day, until I rest in the eternal love.

Sixth Sunday of Easter

In the stresses and turmoil of this world, and in the quieter daily routine of living, the vision of glory may break through. There are times when the heart is opened and we are filled with the power of the Spirit.

John 14:23–29
'Peace I leave with you; my peace I give to you. I do not give as the world gives. Do not let your hearts be troubled, and do not let them be afraid' (v.27).

How often they must have remembered it, that promise of peace and the command not to be afraid. Years of trouble lay before them, though they did not yet know it. Years of wandering, privation, mocking, persecution and for some of them eventually a martyr's death. There were many times when their hearts were troubled and they were afraid, until they remembered again that their Lord was still with them. How often his servants in later years would remember the promise – missionaries far from home, striving against discouragement; weary workers for the faith in unresponsive slum dwellings; simple Christian people stressed and facing an unknown future. Peace was the message of the angels of the Nativity, and in the world there was flight and massacre. Peace was the word of the Resurrection morning, to begin a new life and new responsibility. In the days of wars and rumours of wars there would be peace. A strengthening peace, an aggressive peace, breaking through resistance, demanding calm and assurance when the world had none to offer.

Be not thoughtful then about thine interests, but leave them to God. For if thou art thoughtful about them, thou art thoughtful as a man; but if God provide, He provides as God. Be not so thoughtful about them as to let go the greater things, since then He will not much provide for them. In order therefore that He may fully provide for them, leave them to Him alone. For if thou also thyself takest them in hand, having let go the things spiritual, He will not make much provision for them.

John Chrysostom

Lord Jesus Christ, Prince of Peace, I claim the promise of peace that is not of this world, the peace that passes all understanding. Come in the restless confusion of my days, come in the anxiety of my nights, come in the stillness of my prayers and let me rest in the assurance that all is well.

Ascension Day

See Year A p. 64.

Seventh Sunday of Easter

The word of God has come to people in many different ways, sometimes by a revelation of his power in daily life, sometimes by a vision of his glory, often by quiet reading or listening. By whatever means, it draws them into the Church of Christ.

John 17:20–26
'I ask not only on behalf of these, but also on behalf of those who will believe in me through their word, that they may all be one. As you, Father, are in me and I in you, may they also be in us, so that the world may believe that you have sent me' (vv.20–21).

The quest for Christian unity is a theme of our time, productive of much heart-searching, happy discovery, and also sometimes of fresh dissension. The scandal of division weakens Christian witness in an increasingly secular world. It was in the mission field that the need of unity was discovered and now all Christians have become missionaries. But as usual, we are liable to regard problems as unique to the modern age. There were disputes and divisions from the beginning: St Paul found rival claimants for leadership in the new church at Corinth; the great age of the Fathers was torn with bitter and sometimes violent disputes; the final break between the churches of the East and the West came in 1054; the Reformation divided the Western Church still further. Now as we draw closer together again, we need not fear bland uniformity and a loss of loved traditions. Our diversity in practice may be part of our glory, as diversity is the glory of God's creation. We can worship in different ways if we learn to say with one voice, 'Jesus Christ is Lord, to the glory of God the Father' (Philippians 2:11).

What shall I tell you to do in preaching to you on the unity of Christendom? Well, where strife ceases, love will begin. You deplore, we all deplore divisions in Christendom. Let us each one of us be a union, and make that the aim of life, union in Christ. Let us say to ourselves, 'Grace be to all those who love the Lord Jesus Christ in sincerity'. Speak a thought more kind than you have done before. Pray a little oftener, love a little more, cling a little closer to the God of Love. Life you know then will grow more like the life of Christ.

A.H. Stanton

Blessed Lord Jesus, one with the Father, let me never betray you by setting my own preferences before the good of all your people. I thank you for the faith that I have found through my own church membership. May it open me to greater fellowship with all who confess your name.

Pentecost

The Holy Spirit makes us aware of our sins and also gives us strength to overcome them. We have a powerful defender in all the adversities and temptations of this life.

John 14:8–17
'If you love me, you will keep my commandments. And I will ask the Father, and he will give you another Advocate, to be with you for ever' (vv.15–16).

The Greek word in the Gospel, here translated as 'Advocate', is *Paraclete*. The sense is of a defender for one in peril, particularly a person who will speak in defence of the accused in a legal trial. The Holy Spirit is our defence against evil, both the external perils of the world and the evil that comes from within. The King James Version renders it as 'Comforter', another important idea if we take it in the sense not primarily of making things easy but of exhorting and giving strength for greater effort. Here is the life of the Christian made plain. We need divine protection because our own strength will not prevail against the most severe pressures of life, and we need to be roused from complacency about being so protected and urged onwards in the service of God. Pentecost brings the celebration both of divine favour and divine demands. We shall not be asked to do more than we are capable of doing, because the ability to obey does not come from our unaided wills. Accused and vindicated by the same Spirit, we are free to go out and continue the good work that he has begin in us.

> The Holy Spirit, whose nature is always the same, simple and indivisible, apportions grace to each as the Spirit wills. Like a dry tree which puts forth shoots when watered, the soul bears the fruit of holiness when repentance has made it worthy of receiving the Holy Spirit. Although the Spirit never changes, the effects of the Spirit's action, by the will of God and in the name of Christ, are both many and marvellous. This action is different in different people, but the Spirit is always the same. 'In each person,' Scripture says, 'the Spirit reveals his presence in a particular way for the common good.'
>
> Cyril of Jerusalem

Holy Spirit of God, be my defence when I give way to temptation, and my guide when I seek to live according to the rule of faith. Increase in me the love of the divine will and the desire to perform it, knowing that I cannot trust in my own strength but that there is plentiful grace for all who will accept it.

Trinity Sunday

Faith moves between understanding and mystery. This is a day to accept the limits of our knowledge and simply to glorify the Holy Trinity.

John 16:12–15
Jesus said to his disciples, 'I have still many things to say to you, but you cannot bear them now' (v.12).

219

Even on the night before his Passion, the Disciples did not fully understand who Jesus was and what he was about to accomplish for the salvation of the world. He had taught them many things, and they believed that they were ready for anything that he might ask of them, but in a few hours they would all have deserted him and fled into hiding. It must have been in the forty days between his Resurrection and his Ascension that he unfolded to them the deep truths from which they could go out and begin to build his Church. In further time, the Church came to understand more of that which had already been partly revealed and which now became the developed doctrines of Christianity. But the human mind cannot bear the deepest mysteries except through faith and through images drawn from experience in this world. As we praise the Holy Trinity and sing the hymns of glory, we acknowledge that reason and intellect can take us a little way towards God, but that much remains beyond our understanding. The disciples were told all that they needed to know, at the time when they were ready to receive it. The grace of God does the same for us.

O holy, blessed, glorious three,
Eternal witnesses that be
In heaven, One God in Trinity!

As here on earth, when men withstood
The Spirit, Water and the Blood
Made my Lord's Incarnation good:

So let the antitypes in me
Elected, bought, and seal'd for free
Be own'd, sav'd, sainted by you three.

Henry Vaughan

Almighty God, you have given me knowledge of yourself through the Scriptures and through the teaching of the Church. Accept now the faith that is content to praise the assurance which passes understanding. Give me a peaceful spirit to rest in what I have been granted, and an open mind to receive what further teaching lies in your purpose for me.

Proper 4

The holiness of God may be felt even by those who do not consider themselves 'religious'. Wherever there is a desire for the good and a sense of the inadequacy of human effort, God's power breaks through.

Luke 7:1–10
'Lord, do not trouble yourself, for I am not worthy to have you come under my roof; therefore I did not presume to come to you. But only speak the word, and let my servant be healed' (vv.6–7).

No wonder that Jesus was moved by the faith of this man, an alien to Israel, a pagan, a man of rank in the army of the occupying power. The centurion came to the heart of our relationship with God. He is infinite in majesty, perfect in holiness, so far from the best of humanity that no one is worthy to approach him. He is compassionate, gentle, so close to us that the most intimate human relationship cannot compare with it. He hears the cry for help and responds to any who turn to him even with a faith that is inarticulate. The centurion knew what the exercise of power meant, and he could feel the difference in the power that is divine. Not soldiers obeying orders, but sickness, anxiety, guilt, fleeing before the Son of God. Words close to these of the centurion are often said before receiving Communion: Christ hears them, and comes to us. No one was worthy of the atonement that he brought, so why be hesitant about unworthiness in asking for lesser things?

I am not sufficient, O Master and Lord, that thou shouldest enter in under the roof of my soul, but since thou in thy love willest to dwell in me I take courage and approach. Thou commandest; I will open wide the doors, which thou alone didst create, that thou mayest enter with compassion as is thy nature; that thou mayest enter, and enlighten my darkened mind. I believe that thou wilt do this, for thou didst not flee away from the sinful woman, when with tears she came near to thee, neither rejectedst thou the publican who repented, neither didst thou cast away the thief who confessed thy Kingdom, neither didst thou leave the repentant persecutor to himself: but all those who had been brought to thee by repentance, thou didst set in the company of thy friends, O thou who alone art blessed, ever, world without end.

John Chrysostom

Lord, I am not worthy to receive you, but only say the word and my soul will be healed. I thank you for the love that responds to the weakest will, that meets with unmeasured care the slightest need. Lord, I will be bold to receive you, because you gave yourself for me.

Proper 5

The compassion of God is not remote and impersonal. The Christian story tells of the divine nature taking our human nature, experiencing our life with all its troubles and sorrows.

Luke 7:11–17
When the Lord saw her, he had compassion for her and said to her, 'Do not weep' (v.13).

It's easy to say, 'Don't cry, don't be upset.' Words are cheap and you can't know how I feel. A very human and reasonable response to words of comfort, however well meaning. And if Jesus was really God, how can he know what I feel? You have to experience grief before you can understand it. Exactly. And Jesus wept for Lazarus and the sorrow of his sisters. He wept for Jerusalem, soon to be destroyed and its people scattered. For the Jew and for the pagan philosopher, the idea of divine tears was a blasphemy or a nonsense. People pour out their tears before God, pleading for his comfort, but God made man sheds tears with them. He feels with them, not only with the fatherly love of God but with the brotherly love that itself has known sorrow. He has compassion on the bereaved mother – again that strong emotion in the Greek word so often used of him as he used it of the one we call the Good Samaritan. The compassion brings a miracle of restoration. We cannot work such wonder, but there is much that we can do. It is easy to speak, harder to respond with true compassion.

Who says the widow's heart must break,
The childless-mother sink?
A kinder truer voice I hear,
Which e'en beside that mournful bier
Whence parents' eyes would hopeless shrink,

Bids weep no more – O heart bereft,
How strange, to thee, that sound!
A widow o'er her only son,
Feeling more bitterly alone
For friends that press officious round.

Yet is the voice of comfort heard,
For Christ hath touch'd the bier –
The bearers wait with wondering eye,
The swelling bosom dares not sigh,
But all is still, 'twixt hope and fear.

E'en such an awful soothing calm
We sometimes see alight
On Christian mourners, while they wait
In silence, by some church-yard gate,
Their summons to the holy rite.

And such the tones of love, which break
The stillness of that hour,
Quelling th'embittered spirit's strife –
'The Resurrection and the Life
Am I: believe, and die no more'.

John Keble

Lord Jesus Christ, you have borne our griefs and carried our sorrows,
weeping with those who weep and mourning with those who mourn.
Raise up in me the compassion that feels another's pain and give me
your grace in words and deeds that show your love and bring your
comfort.

Proper 6

The forgiveness of sins is complete when they are recognized and acknowledged with repentance. Only those who trust in their own merits are in danger of rejecting the love of God in Christ.

Luke 7:36–8:3

'I tell you, her sins, which were many, have been forgiven; hence she has shown great love. But the one to whom little is forgiven, loves little' (v.47).

Forget about the old phrase about the greatest sinners making the greatest saints. It is too often an excuse for going on unrepentant and excusing the faults that mar our lives. A ranking of saints and sinners is not a job for human beings who all share to some extent the sinfulness of their race. Not many people really want to be bad, but there is that within us which leads us to follow the easy way, the way of personal advantage, the way of pleasure and privilege ranked above duty. Some people, even some church leaders, say that we think too much about sin, but no one can read far in the Bible without meeting its reality, a reality as strong today as it ever was. As one of the forms of confession puts it, we have sinned 'through negligence, through weakness, through our own deliberate fault'. The danger lies not in admission of sin but in the imposition and acceptance of lingering guilt after reconciliation with God. There is a narrow way between making excuses for ourselves and the kind of self-importance that magnifies our sins and acts of repentance. If we just recognize the unmerited and unbounded love shown on the Cross, we in our turn shall show great love, because so much is forgiven.

> What love is this of thine, that cannot be
> In thine infinity, O Lord, confined.
> Unless it in thy very person see
> Infinity and finity conjoined?
> What! hath thy Godhead, as not satisfied,
> Married our manhood, making it its bride?

O matchless love!

Filling heaven to the brim!
O'errunning it, all running o'er beside
This world! Nay, overflowing hell, wherein,
For thine elect, there rose a mighty tide!
That there our veins might through thy person bleed,
To quench the flames that else would on us feed.

Oh! that thy love might overflow my heart!
To fire the same with love: for love I would.
But oh! my straightened breast! my lifeless spark!
My fireless flame! What chilly love and cold
In measure small! In manner chilly! See!
Lord, blow the coal: thy love enflame in me.

Edward Taylor

God of all love, I have sinned much and not loved as I ought. Create in me a heart of love, sorrowful for offending, grateful for mercy, resolute for amendment. As the penitent woman washed the feet of the Lord with her tears, so may repentance bring me to his feet, so that he may raise me up again to a better life, following in his steps.

Proper 7

The wonderful freedom given by Christ is not to be jealously guarded and kept secret. The good news is not meant for a few favoured disciples but for all who will hear and receive it.

Luke 8:26–39
'Return to your home, and declare how much God has done for you' (v.39).

He wanted to follow Jesus, to be with his other disciples who were close to him every day. After the horror that he had suffered, he was not afraid of the privations and perils of their journeying together.

He was now free, and his place was surely with the one who had freed him. He knew that this was no ordinary healer, but the Son of the Most High God. His own people had rejected him, turned him out to live in chains and nakedness among the dead. If he went back, there would always be the shame, the memory of his former state. Go back, you newly born child of God, go back and stand before them as a witness to the good news of liberation. There are more ways of serving the Master than by following his daily path. There are people far off who need to hear the word of God: there are people near at hand who need it just as much. Go to them, be the living proof that God works to heal and to release. Then in Gadara, now in every town and village, those who are made whole in Christ have work to do.

I lost the love of heaven above,
    I spurned the lust of earth below,
I felt the sweets of fancied love,
    And hell itself my only foe.

I lost earth's joys, but felt the glow
    Of heaven's flame abound in me,
Till loveliness and I did grow
    The bard of immortality.

I loved, but woman fell away;
    I hid me from her faded flame,
I snatched the sun's eternal ray
    And wrote till earth was but a name.

In every language upon earth,
    On every shore, o'er every sea,
I gave my name immortal birth
    And kept my spirit with the free.

John Clare

Lord, I know you are as close to me in my home and in my work as you are to those who do great things for you in the world. Mine is not the mission that calls hundreds to your side or reveals new insights into your truth. Make me a sign of your glory, an instrument of your love, to those who know me well; for they will know best what difference you have made to me, and how little I can do in my own strength.

Proper 8

To begin the Christian way of life is not difficult, but to persevere in it needs the strength that only God can give. He will keep us firm to the end if we acknowledge the seriousness of our commitment.

Luke 9:51–62
Jesus said to him, 'No one who puts a hand to the plough and looks back is fit for the kingdom of God' (v.62).

It is very unwise to concentrate on the literal meaning of the words spoken by Jesus and to neglect the spiritual message that they convey. Few of us are likely to have problems of being short of oil for our lamps, or finding a treasure in the middle of a field. But sometimes the picture which he gives us is worth dwelling on. Imagine a ploughman walking forward with his head turned back, looking to the comfort of the farmhouse instead of the muddy field ahead. He will plough a very crooked furrow until eventually he trips over a stone or a root and lets go of the plough altogether. So it is with the Christian way, which requires a steady hand and a clear vision. A glance back at attractive but selfish possibilities left behind, a wistful thought that there are things that sometimes seem preferable to the duty of prayer and worship, can turn into a stumbling, half-hearted life that neither fully savours the easy way nor experiences the joy of following Christ. Like so many of his sayings, this is a piece of sensible advice which reveals a deep truth about the way things are. It is a hard saying when the soil is heavy and the plough keeps sticking and the end of the field is far away. But all the time, a stronger hand is guiding the plough.

O Lord God, when thou givest to thy servants to endeavour any great matter; grant us also to know that it is not the beginning but the continuing of the same until it is thoroughly finished which yieldeth the true glory. Through him who, for the finishing of thy work, laid down his life for us, our redeemer, Jesus Christ.

Anon, ascribed to Francis Drake

Lord Jesus Christ, strengthen me to keep my eyes fixed upon you and you only, the beginner and finisher of my faith. Keep me firm to the end, not wavering in allegiance, not regretting or desiring anything that does not come from you, but following all the way until the labour is over and the harvest is brought home in your everlasting Kingdom.

Proper 9

It is not easy to keep innocence and integrity in a busy and sometimes hard world. Only complete reliance on Christ as saviour and guide can keep us whole and bring us through all dangers.

Luke 10:1–11, 16–20
'I am sending you out like lambs into the midst of wolves' (v.3).

That was a hard one to take, a strange saying from one who was the Good Shepherd, the guardian of the flock. Not an encouraging message at the start of a journey which would inevitably be hard and weary at that time and in that country. He whom they had trusted to lead them into green pastures was sending them out among the predators who were waiting to feed. Not even as grown sheep, but as tender, helpless lambs, they had to start out alone. Were they clinging too closely to the Master, enjoying the privilege of being his best friends, taking the Good News too much for themselves and forgetting that there were others out in the wilderness? They were going to those who lived in the hard, dark places, even to the wolves whose names were anger and loneliness and fear. Go without comforts, without even basic needs, with no support but the assurance of faith, and no desire but to be offered in sacrifice; only then would they be worthy of their Master. We who go about our lives of work and recreation may not get eaten in the wilderness of the world, but we shall be attacked by temptation, perhaps mauled by mockery and sin. The Shepherd will not be seen, but he will not be far away.

It has been said that there are on the battlefield, defeats as glorious as victories. That is true also of the daily defeats of the soul in the struggle which we begin afresh every day, making new plans to do better and experimenting with new ideas and methods in order to succeed. That is what the Gospel declares: 'Happy is the servant whom when his Master cometh He shall find . . .' Find how? Victorious? Triumphant? His task fully accomplished? No! Rather he who shall be found watching, vigilant, wide awake; that is to say looking after the things which are not going well and putting them right, time after time. That is our really great merit in the sight of God.

Henri De Tourville

Lord, as I go out day by day I must depend on you alone. You would not send me into dark places unless there was work to be done and people to be helped: make me fit for the journey. If I must be as vulnerable as a lamb, make me as innocent too.

Proper 10

The commandments of God may sometimes seem intimidating and calling for heroic efforts. The opportunity for obedience often lies nearer than we think and if we aspire too far into the distance we may miss what lies immediately before us.

Luke 10:25–37
'When he saw him, he was moved with pity' (v.33).

Not by the command of the Law, not by social conscience, but by feeling for another human being in distress. 'Pity' is a weak word that can suggest superiority and condescension mingled with the concern. Even the Authorized Version's 'compassion' does not give the strength of the Greek word, which derives from the idea of being moved in one's inward parts, one's deepest being. To say 'It really turned him over inside' would come nearer to it. No matter either for the hostility between Jews and Samaritans, the religious disputes, the avoidance of personal relationships. Seeing was followed by action, emergency treatment, money given for further care. This was the neighbour, the one who was near and needed help. The Lord who told the story often reacted in the same way, and the same word is used of his response to suffering and calls for healing. It is not the conscious obedience to duty but the spontaneous act of love that most closely follows the example of Christ. But when the heart is cold and the first instinct is to pass by, the will can make us turn aside to do what we would rather ignore. And the acts of will often repeated will lead at last to true acts of love.

> Christ took our nature on Him, not that He
> 'Bove all things loved it, for the purity:
> No, but He dressed Him with our human trim,
> Because our flesh stood most in need of Him.

Robert Herrick

Lord of love, when the outward sight looks on another's need, give the inward sight which sees that all humanity is one in Christ and responds even against personal inclination and selfishness. When I say that everyone is my neighbour as a child of God, let it not be a pious word without feeling, but a truth that reaches into the depth of my being and out into the world where the journeys of so many are lonely and perilous.

Proper 11

Knowledge of Christ as the only source of hope saves us from getting lost in the distractions of the world. The active life of good works is sustained by having time to go apart and listen to God.

Luke 10:38–42

'You are worried and distracted by many things; there is need of only one thing' (v.41).

Is it so difficult to sit down, be quiet, and let God love and guide? Our whole way of life seems to answer with a resounding, Yes! There seems to be always something that must be done, a mounting pressure which can be as stressful when it calls to pleasure as when it calls to work. Perhaps it is some comfort to know that people were running around distractedly even in New Testament times, but the word of the Lord is still the same; 'there is need of only one thing'. Martha and Mary struggle inside us, divide our loyalty. It was Martha who welcomed the Lord, Mary who responded to his coming. Not to be always busy, yet not to neglect what really must be done; not to forget the times of prayer and reflection, yet not to be idle through laziness and selfishness – if those demands can be reconciled, the Christian life is being lived. There is need of only one thing – to be aware of the presence of Christ with us, in work, in recreation and in the times of rest.

> Our true light and power lie in the hidden source of interior grace in which God springs up ceaselessly within our souls. The soul is saturated with God's own life, His presence, His activity, His inspiration, His encouragement and the radiance of His presence. 'The Master is here and calls for you!' He speaks to you. It is very rare for the interior Master not to speak in the depths of the soul. The tone is varied as in the Gospel, but: always Divine. Nobler and loftier than ours, it is at the same time simpler, humbler, and more natural. No one speaks that language except our Lord Himself in His Gospel. Thus we each have at will the private, special, secret companionship of God, of the Divine Persons.

> Henri De Tourville

When I welcome you into my home and into my heart, dear Jesus, let me not then forget that you are there. I am so busy about many things that I feel as if the world cannot go on without me. Help me to be still, help me to listen, and then send me out again to do your

*work without stress and without self-importance. My need is in you
alone. Give me grace to know that, truly to believe it, and to live in
its security.*

Proper 12

God who is perfect love desires to forgive the sins of his people.
His mercy was fulfilled and confirmed in Christ, the sinless who
paid the price of sin. We have no price to pay but that of sincere
repentance. Professing sorrow for sin is only a form of words unless
it is proved by love for those who offend us.

Luke 11:1–13
*'Forgive us our sins, for we ourselves forgive everyone indebted to
us'* (v.4).

The Lord's Prayer is said many times every day, in shared worship,
in private devotion, and sometimes in gatherings where not all understand what they are saying. It is the gift and command of Jesus to
his disciples in all ages, and through them to the whole world. He
teaches us to praise and to ask without reserve, except for one thing
– forgiveness. In this alone is something demanded of us: it is a
two-way process, a contract, a covenant. As we pray to be forgiven,
we commit ourselves to a way of life. Debts, sins, trespasses – whatever we call them, they are the deeds of others that can diminish our
love for God if we leave them unresolved. Their offences and our
own are all one, all part of the deep human rebellion against the will
of God. If we treat them as we hope to be treated, prayer is sincere.
Free forgiveness is our credential, our token of membership in the
Kingdom of God. Jesus Christ, who needed no forgiveness, prayed
for his worst enemies and left us a legacy of love. We acknowledge
the gift, commit ourselves to follow his example, every time we say
the prayer that he taught us.

Endeavour to be patient in bearing with the defects and infirmities
of others, of what sort so ever they be; for that thyself also hast
many failings which must be borne with by others. If thou canst
not make thyself such a one as thou wouldest, how canst thou

expect to have another in all things to thy liking? We would willingly have others perfect, and yet we amend not our own faults.

Thomas à Kempis

Dear God, when I call on you as Father and ask for your gifts to be renewed, let me never speak falsely when I say that I too forgive as I hope to be forgiven. When the angry will rebels, come into my heart and make me a true disciple of Christ who taught his disciples to pray.

Proper 13

There are many pleasant things in this world which we may, and should, enjoy as part of God's love for us, but they are not permanent and if we value them too much and begin to trust in them, in the end we shall have nothing.

Luke 12:13–21
'One's life does not consist in the abundance of possessions' (v.15).

There is an old story of a fisherman who was granted fulfilment of wishes by a magic fish and who went from the desire for a more comfortable house to such outrageous demands for divine power that he found himself back in his old hovel. (Some versions blame the whole thing on his wife, but men have been making that excuse since the Garden of Eden.) Our society today is caught up in the same greedy spiral, following the lure of gambling and competitions which promise immense wealth. The harm is not only to those who get the riches that bring no happiness, but also in the emotions of greed, jealousy, malice that material success arouses in other people. It is easy to stand aside and feel superior to those who lose both money and dignity in the pursuit of money, but there are other ways of being too attached to material possessions. To enjoy the permitted pleasures of this world is as much a Christian duty as putting no ultimate hope in them. Whatever we are given is part of our human stewardship, in trust to use in God's service. It is evil when money and possessions become the meaning of life instead of the means to love.

Riches in the hands of individuals in society, is attended with some degree of power; and so far as power is put forth separate from perfect love, so far the government of the Prince of Peace is interrupted; and as we know not that our children after us will dwell in that state in which power is rightly applied, to lay up riches for them appears to be against the nature of his government.

John Woolman

Lord, let me not hear the false call of greed, the promises of lasting happiness that the riches of this world cannot fulfil. Make me truly thankful for all the blessings of this life: the things of beauty, the things that give ease and comfort, the things that make me able to help others, but let me never set them in the place of true joy that endures for ever.

Proper 14

The call of God may seem to draw us away from what is valued and desired. His purpose is better than we can understand, and his promises are faithful.

Luke 12:32–40
'*Where your treasure is, there your heart will be also*' (v.34).

A text often quoted, little observed. What do we really want from life, what are the goals that call out all our energy and make us single-minded? Human values are not constant. Today ambition is generally considered praiseworthy: in the sixteenth century it was a dangerous fault. Once the possession of land was the way to power and influence: now it is the possession of money. There was a time when the birth of many children was a desirable blessing; now we fear over-population. In all these changes, God alone is constant. The Bible speaks continually of his faithfulness, his steadfast love. Masters of the spiritual life write about the desire of the soul for God, and we respect the ideal but generally feel rather guilty about not getting very close to it. Fortunately, God knows us for what we are and is gracious in accepting the less than perfect which sincerely desires the good. As history has revalued human aspirations, a regular revaluation of our own immediate desires can lead to a new perspective on life.

> In my younger years my trouble for sin was most about my actual failings in thought, word or action; but now I am much more troubled for inward defects and omission or want of the vital duties or graces of the soul. My daily trouble is so much for my ignorance of God and weakness of belief, and want of greater love to God and strangeness to him and to the life to come, and for want of a greater willingness to die, and longing to be with God in heaven, as that I take not some immoralities, though very great, to be in themselves so great and odious sins if they could be found as separate from these. Had I all the riches of the world, how gladly should I give them for a fuller knowledge, belief and love of God and everlasting glory! These wants are the greatest burden of my life, which oft maketh my life itself a burden.
>
> Richard Baxter

Faithful God, Father of promises that never fail, lift my heart above the frail treasures which I may value too highly. Give me a deeper trust in your ways that are not my ways, and stronger hope in your purpose for me, even when it is beyond my understanding and seems to turn me aside from the path that my own desire would follow.

Proper 15

From the Old Testament prophets to the present day, those who seek to serve God faithfully have often found themselves at odds with the majority. Faith may lead to unpopularity and even persecution.

Luke 12:49–56
'Do you think that I have come to bring peace to the earth? No, I tell you, but rather division' (v.51).

There is a general opinion, shared by believers and unbelievers alike, that Christians should be 'nice' people, not rocking the boat, not upsetting anyone. But Christianity is not a matter of human fellowship at all costs. Jesus was not always 'nice'. He was tender, accepting, pardoning all who came to him knowing and confessing their need. But he could be challenging, disturbing, sometimes downright insulting to hypocrisy and self-satisfaction. 'Peace' is a lovely word, a Bible word, and one which he himself often used. He also reminded his disciples that the peace he gives is not as the world understands it (John 14:27). The Church of Christ is itself sadly divided, although the breaches are being repaired. But Christians may still need to cause division in other places, to say uncomfortable things, to stand out against wrong, both individual and social. They are likely sometimes to be part of an unpopular minority, in small matters as well as great ones. Loyalty to the truth does not always have nice consequences.

> He fumbles at your soul
> As players at the keys,
> Before they drop full music on.
> He stuns you by degrees,
> Prepares your brittle nature
> For the ethereal blow
> By fainter hammers further heard,
> Then nearer, then so slow
> Your breath has time to straighten,
> Your brain to bubble cool,
> Deals one imperial thunderbolt
> That scalps your naked soul.
>
> Emily Dickinson

Lord, keep me faithful to the truth that you have shown me. Give me strength to overcome my fear of being unpopular, laughed at, rejected, for your sake. But save me from covering my own anger and resentment with the cloak of faith. Guide me when to speak and when to be silent.

Proper 16

Formalism is always a danger in organized religion. The worship of God is never to be treated casually, but our love of him is best shown in being always open to the immediate needs of his children.

Luke 13:10–17

'Ought not this woman, a daughter of Abraham whom Satan bound for eighteen long years, be set free from this bondage on the Sabbath day?' (v.16).

The conflict with the religious authorities is becoming more frequent as the Gospel story unfolds. What an irony that the true Messiah, the long awaited, should challenge the rules so jealously guarded by those who claimed to know the mind of God. In one sentence, Jesus demolishes the rigid sabbatarian argument. This woman is of the same descent as the objectors and therefore deserves their total sympathy. Sickness is not the fault of the victim, but part of the evil in a world fallen from innocence. No day, however holy, gives exemption from performing works of mercy. It is a revolution in religious teaching, and one that has not yet gained its final triumph. We are still too liable to value the keeping of rules above the individual need, to reject the sufferers and the troubled ones who intrude into our ceremonies. We still turn away from the disabled, even when our words affirm their rights. Compassion should not become an excuse for slackness and irreverence in worship but the deepest order and reverence do not exclude compassion.

> If we do a thing because we think it is our duty, we generally fail; that is the old law which makes slaves of us. The real spring of our life, and of our work in life, must be love – true, deep love – not love of this or that person, or for this or that reason, but deep human love, devotion of soul to soul, love of God realized where alone it can be – in love of those whom he loves. Everything else is weak, passes away; that love alone supports us, makes life tolerable, binds the present together with the past and future, and is, we may trust, imperishable.
>
> Max Muller

Most holy God, create and keep in me always the spirit of reverence when I come to worship you. When reverence becomes an excuse for indifference, when I begin to value convention above compassion, forgive my fault and give me light to see that all worship must be grounded in love.

Proper 17

I f we are self-centred and make our own valuation of ourselves, forgetting the duty we owe to God and to his people, we are not following his will. He does not judge what is important by the standards of human judgement

Luke 14:1, 7–14
'All who exalt themselves will be humbled, and those who humble themselves will be exalted' (v.11).

It is the convention that religion and politics should never be discussed at a dinner party, and perhaps that is sound advice for the average social gathering. But when Jesus went out for a meal, his host and fellow-guests did not have an easy time. First he healed a sick man – a passage omitted from this selection of the Gospel – and aroused controversy about breaking the Sabbath. He went on to criticize those who were scrambling for the best seats, warned his host that he should be inviting the outcasts of society instead of his rich friends, and then told a story about people who insulted their host by not responding to his invitation. The point of it all is that those who came to the meal were thinking only of themselves instead of being aware of the needs of others for healing, food or shelter. They were too concerned with their own prestige and privilege, putting themselves at the centre of importance. We sometimes speak of Jesus as the unseen guest at every meal: it is a good thought, but not entirely a comfortable one. That unseen Presence may be telling us to look more closely at our attitudes and motives. He may be moving us down a little, not perhaps in seating, but in the height of our selfishness.

Give me the lowest place; not that I dare
Ask for that lowest place, but Thou hast died
That I might live and share
Thy glory by Thy side.

Give me the lowest place: or if for me
That lowest place too high, make one more low
Where I may sit and see
My God and love Thee so.

Christina Rossetti

Blessed Lord, whose example was always love and compassion and who did not regard the opinions of the proud and selfish, help me to look away from myself to the needs of others, and for your sake to regard them above myself. Let me look to you, and not to the values of this world, for my way of life.

Proper 18

There can be no rival to God in our loyalty. He grants us many pleasures and satisfactions in this world, but none of them should be allowed to come between ourselves and the absolute commitment of faith.

Luke 14:25–33

'None of you can become my disciple if you do not give up all your possessions' (v.33).

A hard saying indeed, and a challenge to those in the crowd following him who were moved more by curiosity or the hope of benefit than by faith. Many Christians have felt called to obey the command literally and, as hermits, religious or missionaries, given up all their worldly goods; and their response has been greatly blessed. The majority have seen themselves as called to play their part in a society where a certain amount of individual ownership is necessary for the sake of the whole. The deeper message is the same, and it rings through the whole of the Bible. Have no other gods but me, do not make idols of anything in the world, do not take what is not yours or envy other people's possessions. There is nothing good in this life, including the practice of religion itself, that cannot tend to usurp the absolute sovereignty of God. His true followers are those who accept with gratitude his gifts but do not come to love the gifts more than the giver. Yes, it is a hard saying and few of us are near to obeying it fully, but its challenge is for all. We are dependent creatures, and dependence on material things is a broad road that leads away from dependence on God alone.

On all accounts, whether we consider our fortune as a talent, and trust from God, or the great good that it enables us to do, or the great harm that it does to ourselves, if idly spent; on all these great accounts it appears, that it is absolutely necessary to make reason and religion the strict rule of using all our fortune. Every exhortation in Scripture to be wise and reasonable, satisfying only such wants as God would have satisfied; every exhortation to be spiritual and heavenly, pressing after a glorious change of our nature; every exhortation to love our neighbour as ourselves, to love all mankind as God has loved them, is a command to be strictly religious in the use of our money.

William Law

Heavenly Father, bountiful Giver, increase in me the thankfulness that I owe for all your goodness to me. Give me the grace to enjoy without selfishness the gifts that you have granted, and to use them wherever I may for the good of others. Let nothing come between your care and my need, no material thing draw me away from your spirit in me.

Proper 19

Sin is a reality of our fallen human nature which cannot be ignored. God's judgement is not diminished but his absolute pardon for repented sin is our hope and our joy.

Luke 15:1–10

'There is joy in the presence of the angels of God over one sinner who repents' (v.7).

The conflict is growing. This young teacher, who had seemed so promising, is keeping company with the outcasts of society – the collaborators, the notorious sinners, continual breakers of the Law – which alone makes us the chosen people of God. He actually welcomes them and seems to enjoy their company, and it's no good trying to get round it by stories about sheep and lost coins. Of course we try to find the lost things that belong to us, but this is really too much. He speaks of the angels, the heavenly host, God's nobler creation, close to his throne, rejoicing when a sinner repents. Not accepting back with reproof and warnings to do better in future, but actually rejoicing! Sin was very much in the minds of those who knew Jesus in his human ministry, and it was too often the basis for self-righteousness on the part of those who thought they were free from it. Sin and repentance are not fashionable themes today, sometimes not even in the churches. The Gospel teaching is not blurred: sin is serious, repentance is wonderful. Careful to avoid the smugness and hypocrisy of the scribes and Pharisees, let us not fall into the opposite error of thinking that sin is not all that important. The love of God is a cause for joy, not for presumption.

> Repentance itself is nothing else but a kind of circling; to return to Him by repentance, from whom by sin we have turned away. Which circle consists of two things; which two must needs be two different motions. One, is to be done with the whole heart; the other with it broken and rent: so as, one and the same it cannot be. First, a turn, wherein we look forward to God, and with our whole heart resolve to turn to Him. Then, a turn again, wherein we look backward to our sins, wherein we have turned from God: and with beholding them, our very heart breaketh. These two are two distinct, both in nature and names. One, conversion from sin; the other, contrition for sin. One, resolving to amend that which is to come; the other, reflecting and sorrowing for that which is past. One, declining from evil to be done hereafter; the other, sentencing itself for evil done heretofore. These two between them make up a complete repentance, or a perfect revolution.

> Lancelot Andrewes

Loving Shepherd of the sheep, you have so many times sought me and found me and brought me home. Let me not presume on your mercy or neglect your judgement, but let me hear your call and come to your arms of love. I am not worthy of the heavenly joy, but in the promise of the joy I resolve to do better.

Proper 20

What may seem to be minor faults are not excusable on the grounds that others are committing greater ones. There are duties and responsibilities for the simple as well as the powerful members of every human society.

Luke 16:1–13
'Whoever is faithful in a very little is faithful also in much; and whoever is dishonest in a very little is dishonest also in much' (v.10).

This is a difficult parable that has exercised the minds of many commentators. But that should not draw attention away from the very clear comment at the end. There have been sects that have maintained that the power of Redemption is so great that it does not matter what we do in this world, and others that have regarded the world itself as evil and therefore not to be served in any way. The Christian message leaves no doubt that we are to do our best with what is laid upon us to do, while never losing sight of the greater future that lies in God's purpose for the individual and for all humanity. If we grow careless over small matters of truth and honesty, the conscience starts to expand until it can accommodate far more serious offences. St Thérèse of Lisieux taught of the 'little way' to holiness by progressive, simple steps that daily bring the soul nearer to God. There is also a little way to evil, a gradual acceptance of things less than the ideal, which leads away from him. There is always a danger of 'scruples', of being so concerned with every detail that the liberty of God's love is forgotten, but there is an equal danger of becoming more and more unscrupulous in the popular sense. A good citizen of heaven will not be a bad citizen of earth.

It may be argued that dissatisfaction with our life's endeavour springs in some degree from dullness. We require higher tasks, because we do not recognise the height of those we have. Trying to be kind and honest seems an affair too simple and too inconsequential for gentlemen of our heroic mould; we had rather set ourselves to something bold, arduous, and conclusive; we had rather found a schism or suppress a heresy, cut off a hand or mortify an appetite. But the task before us, which is to co-endure with our existence, is rather one of microscopic fineness, and the heroism required is that of patience. There is no cutting of the Gordian knots of life; each must be smilingly unravelled.

R.L. Stevenson

Lord, help me to be faithful in the little things, so that I may be faithful also in the great. Keep me honest in word and deed, honouring the rules of this world but never holding them above your eternal law. May your spirit guard me against excuses and self-deceit and make me a good steward of all that you have entrusted to me.

Proper 21

Our attitude to material things helps to shape our attitude to things of the spirit. There is nothing wrong in enjoying the permissible pleasures of life so long as they do not turn us away from concern for the needs of others.

Luke 16:19–31
Remember that during your lifetime you received your good things, and Lazarus in like manner evil things; but now he is comforted here, and you are in agony (v.25).

This is one of the most vivid stories that Jesus told, with details ranging from expensively coloured garments and scavenging dogs to the mystery of life after death. Like many of his parables, it is a tale of the complete reversal of expected human values. At other times he tells of equal pay for unequal work, more delight in one straying sheep than in ninety-nine who behaved themselves, selling off all possessions to buy a single jewel. There will be some great surprises in the life to come, when everyone is seen through the all-knowing wisdom and judgement of God. It is not stated that the rich man has been punished simply for being rich. Jesus says elsewhere that great wealth makes it more difficult to live as one ready for the Kingdom of God. The story is told particularly as a warning to those Pharisees who thought a great deal of money and had come to trust it as a means of security and a sign that they were all right with God. Yes, it is only a story – but it has an uncomfortable edge for us all. When things are going well, we may feel that all is right with the world and ignore the suffering that is at our own gate. It may be a homeless beggar, but it may also be a rich person breaking under stress, or someone who seems important and successful but is lonely inside. There are many ways in which this world can be a rehearsal for the next.

(Jo, the little crossing-sweeper, is dying of deprivation and neglect. A kindly doctor is with him at the end.)

'Jo, my poor fellow!'
'I hear you, sir, in the dark, but I'm a gropin – a gropin – let me catch hold of your hand.'
'Jo, can you say what I say?'
'I'll say anythink as you say, sir, for I knows it's good.'
'Our Father.'
'Our Father! – yes, that's wery good, sir.'
'Which art in Heaven.'
'Art in Heaven – is the light a comin, sir?'
'It is close at hand. Hallowed be Thy name!'
'Hallowed be – thy –'
The light is come upon the dark benighted way. Dead? Dead, your Majesty. Dead, my lords and gentlemen. Dead, Right Reverends and Wrong Reverends of every order. Dead, men and women, born with Heavenly compassion in your hearts. And dying thus around us, every day.

Charles Dickens

Merciful Father, lover of the poor, refuge of the homeless, comforter of the afflicted, grant me vision to discern where I may give help and grace to offer it. I thank you for the good things of this life, and pray that I shall show my gratitude by compassionate love for those who have little joy in their lives.

Proper 22

Can we hope to see what is wrong with so many things in this world and try to show a better way, without feeling self-righteous? Whatever we do must be from love and duty, not to gain merit.

Luke 17:5–10
'When you have done all that you were ordered to do, say, "We are worthless slaves; we have done only what we ought to have done!"' (v.10).

Now that was another sharp answer for the Disciples. Perhaps feeling their inadequacy as they become more aware of the reality of who their Master was, and as he tests them with teaching beyond their expectation, they ask to make some progress in faith. Instead of a few simple hints on spirituality, they are told to remember that in themselves they are not important. They, who perhaps were beginning to feel proud of being so close to this Teacher whose fame was growing, are put on the level of slaves, the lowest in the world, with no rights and no rewards. There are no medals for service in the Christian conflict of good and evil, no prizes for not having broken the rules. We hear today much about the need for self-esteem to give people their proper dignity in society, and rightly so. But that is not the same as self-congratulation, a fault to which Christians are particularly liable. Getting up and going to church on Sunday, keeping the commandments, abstaining from quite a number of things that we would rather like to do but mustn't – surely we have a right to some approval from God. Now – the teaching is plain if uncomfortable. The old saying that virtue is its own reward is perhaps simplistic, but like many truisms, it happens to be true.

> Yield yourselves to the Lord, that is, as his servants, give up the dominion and government of yourselves to Christ. Pray that he put you to whatsoever work he pleaseth. Servants, as they must

do their master's work, so they must be for any work their master
has for them to do: they must not pick and choose, this I will do,
and that I will not do; they must not say this is too hard, or this
is too mean, or this may be well enough, let alone. Good servants,
when they have chosen their master, will let their master choose
their work, and will not dispute his will, but do it.

John Wesley

*Worthless, unprofitable – Lord, the words are not welcome and I
begin to fight against them, but in my heart I know that they are
true. They are my shield against the self-regard that shuts out your
love, the complacency that becomes deaf to the call of conscience. In
your service there is perfect freedom, and by your grace I will look
for nothing more.*

Proper 23

God does not care only for the people who openly praise and
worship him. His love is unbounded, and those who claim to
follow him have the greater duty to acknowledge it.

Luke 17:11–19
*Jesus asked, 'Were not ten made clean? But the other nine, where
are they? Was none of them found to return and give praise to God
except this foreigner?'* (vv.17–18).

'Foreigner' has a patronizing tone in these sensitive days, casting an
anxious shadow of discrimination and racism. In this saying of Jesus,
it was a word of mingled pleasure, surprise and sadness. The Samaritans were despised by orthodox Jews as people of mixed race, descend-
ants of those planted in the north of the country by a conqueror
generations ago, defective and heretical in their belief and worship.
Like the Roman centurion who felt unworthy to have Jesus in his
house, the Canaanite woman who pleaded for her daughter, here was
one who recognized the divine presence and by his response put to
shame many who professed to keep the Law. The Holy Spirit comes

as a particular gift of power to the Church, but it is a great mistake to think that power to be limited to the Church. The grace of God touches many who do not regard themselves as religious, who may express various shades of indifference and even actual unbelief. Perhaps they feel inside themselves the need of someone to thank for the gifts that have no human giver, and the way is opened for an act of faith that may not even be realized in this world. Praise to God for it, and also possibly an uncomfortable feeling about the depth of our gratitude to the God whom we claim to worship through his Son.

All that is required of the most perfect Christian may be contained in this 'giving him thanks'; giving thanks, always in word and deed, to Christ, for His great deliverance and salvation. Is he compassionate and merciful, active in giving of alms, fervent in prayer, careful in practices of mortification and self-denial; does he labour to offer up his whole body as a living sacrifice to God, acceptable through Jesus Christ ? All this is nothing else but a giving of thanks for his salvation. And therefore is it that love, joy, and peace are inseparable from every duty of a Christian, because his heart is the seat of thanksgiving. What more natural? what more easy? How much more so is this conduct of the thankful leper, than the miserable pride and forgetfulness of those who went their way and gave no thanks!

Isaac Williams

Loving Jesus, healer of souls and bodies, source of endless compassion, create in me a more grateful spirit for all your mercies. Help me to know your presence in those who do not seem to be in faith, and to make known my praise for all you have done for me.

Proper 24

Our encounters with God are often exacting and demand perseverance. He does not withhold his love, but he may test our sincerity and the depth of our faith.

Luke 18:1–8

Jesus told his disciples a parable about their need to pray always and not to lose heart (v.1).

Like many of his parables, it was a brief but vivid story, very human, somewhat amusing. It is easy to enter into the exasperation of the judge who eventually gives way to save himself from the continual demands of a petitioner. Most of us, with less authority, have agreed to something simply for the sake of peace and quiet. God does not become weary, but we can too easily become weary of asking. The prayer of petition, the prayer of asking for something desired, is a proper part of prayer but it can soon become a shopping list of what we should like to have, read out and passed on for action. The purpose of constant prayer is not to soften the heart of a tyrant but to test sincerity, to make the petitioner look again at what is desired and consider whether it is really the right thing to be asking. Selfishness, love of ease and comfort, a general wish to be free from the need to make an effort, can all corrupt Christian prayer. When people speak of wrestling in prayer, the violent word and the sense of conflict can cause disquiet, but there is good biblical warrant in the story of Jacob at the Jabbok (Genesis 22:22–31). The importance of prayer in challenging the conscience of the one who prays is not to be forgotten. But neither is the need to continue in faith when gifts do not come straight away.

God's command, to *pray without ceasing*, is founded on the necessity we have of his grace, to preserve the life of God in the soul, which can no more subsist one moment without it than the body can without air. Whether we think of or speak to God, whether we act or suffer for him, all is prayer, when we have no other object than his love, and the desire of pleasing him. All that a Christian does, even in eating and sleeping, is prayer, when it is done in simplicity, according to the order of God, without either adding to or diminishing from it by his own choice. Prayer continues in the desire of the heart, though the understanding be employed on outward things. In souls filled with love, the desire to please God is a continual prayer.

John Wesley

Father in heaven, keep me strong and firm in prayer. Give me the light to know whether what I ask accords with your will for me. Forgive the times when I have said or thought that my prayer was not answered, because I did get exactly what I wanted, and increase my faith that what is right for me will come in your time and your way.

Proper 25

There is no sin that will not be forgiven if it is followed by true repentance and resolve to do better. Those who believe that they have done nothing wrong are in greater danger.

Luke 18:9–14
'All who exalt themselves will be humbled, but all who humble themselves will be exalted' (v.14).

The Pharisees have got a very bad name in Christian tradition, and even in everyday language. The word is used as if it meant the same as 'hypocrite'. They were in fact a sect, or rather a religious guild, deeply concerned to keep every detail of the Law of Moses and interpreting it with new requirements which lay heavily on many of the people. Their belief that keeping the Law made them righteous too often led to complacency, and then to arrogance about the short-comings of others. It is not surprising that they clashed with Jesus, who taught that people must seek for righteousness deep within themselves. He did not condemn ritual observance, but made it uncomfortably clear that outward conformity was useless if it excluded humility and compassion. This parable is yet another example of the gospel reversals of social expectations: the despised tax-gatherer who acknowledges his sin is the one who wins approval. Self-righteousness is a continual temptation in the practice of faith and worship. Only confession of sin and desire for something better make 'religion' acceptable to God. The story is told of a Sunday School teacher who talked about this parable and then said, 'So now, children, let us thank God that we are not like that Pharisee.' Think about that one.

According to scholars, pride is nothing other than love of your own excellence; that is, of your own reputation. Therefore the more you love and delight in your own reputation, the greater is your pride, and the greater is this wicked image within you. If pride stirs in your heart, leading you to imagine yourself holier, wiser, better, and more virtuous than others, or that God has given you grace to serve Him better than others; or if you regard other men and women as inferior to yourself, and hold exaggerated opinions of your own excellence in comparison with others; or if as a result you feel complacent and self-satisfied, it is a sure sign that you bear this black image within you. And although it may be hidden from the eyes of other men, it appears clearly in the sight of God.

Walter Hilton

Lord, I am not worthy to lift my eyes to you, but it is your loving eyes that see into my deepest self, to reveal my faults and yet bring assurance of pardon. Guard me from being satisfied with myself, especially in matters of religious duty, and keep me humble so that I may rest in the peace of your mercy.

Bible Sunday

The Bible is the word of power, because it proclaims the power of Christ. It tells of his redeeming work, and it is through him that understanding is given.

Luke 4:16–24
Then he began to say to them, 'Today this scripture has been fulfilled in your hearing' (v.21).

It was a moment that seized the congregation in the synagogue with attentive wonder, soon turning to murderous anger. They did not know that their preacher that morning was the living fulfilment of all that the prophets had foretold of the coming Messiah – all that and a great deal more, for it was the incarnate Son of God who spoke to them, the living Word who expounded the word. We reverence the Bible not as a source-book for our religion but as the record of

God's purpose made perfect in Christ. It is he who gives light to the difficult passages, he whose Spirit enables us to discern the deeper meanings and leads us to shape our lives according to its teaching. To read only with the eyes, to hear only with the ears, is to miss the presence of Christ in the sacred text. Bible study is a worthwhile exercise for the mind, but it is time ill spent if it is not also, and principally, food for the soul. Church congregations today are not likely to rise up and try to kill the preacher. But do the preacher and the listeners always discern the living Christ in the words?

> Blessed Lord, by whose providence all holy scriptures were written and preserved for our instruction, give us grace to study them this and every day with patience and love. Strengthen our souls with the fullness of their divine teaching. Keep from us all pride and irreverence. Guide us in the deep things of thy heavenly wisdom, and of thy great mercy lead us by thy Word unto everlasting life; through Jesus Christ our Lord and Saviour.
>
> B.F. Westcott

Almighty God, giver of the holy word, make me more attentive to all that I read and hear of the Bible. May the voice of the Son speak to me through it, may the light of the Holy Spirit give me understanding. As I speak of the faith that is in me, may the words of Scripture be my guide and my inspiration, bringing Christ closer to those around me.

Fourth Sunday before Advent

The love of God is not static. He does not wait for his people to turn to him of their own accord, but reaches out to them and calls to them in the needs that they have not fully understood.

Luke 19:1–10
'The Son of Man came to seek out and to save the lost' (v.10).

Thirteen words of one syllable speak the whole gospel message. So many images of the parables that Jesus told are contained in this – the shepherd seeking one lost sheep, the woman happy to find a single lost coin, the father running out to meet his wayward son. Jesus himself says how he longs to gather the people of Jerusalem to himself as a hen gathers her chickens under her wings. Those who have power in this world may be prepared to receive requests by appointment, through a secretary, after a period of waiting before granting their favour. God in Christ comes out to look for the lost ones, that is to say, all of us. In his earthly ministry he finds his people in the prostitute, the tax-collector working for an alien power, the pagan, the orthodox member of the Jewish Council who comes secretly and in fear. It is all too much for the highly righteous. They are shocked by his behaviour, they censure him, in the end they kill him. When he has overcome death, he sends out his followers, filled with the Spirit, to seek out and save the lost.

> How hast thou merited –
> Of all man's clotted clay the dingiest clot?
> Alack, thou knowest not
> How little worthy of any love thou art!
> Whom wilt thou find to love ignoble thee,
> Save Me, save only Me?
> All which I took from thee I did but take,
> Not for thy harms,
> But just that thou might'st seek it in My arms.
> All which thy child's mistake
> Fancies as lost, I have stored for thee at home:
> Rise, clasp My hand, and come!

Francis Thompson

Lord Jesus, your voice has called me, your hand has touched me and made me know my need. When I stray from you, seek me in your patient, unfailing love and live in me again. In the strength of that love, make me a seeker in your name, to find those who do not know you and bring them back to their true home.

All Saints' Sunday

Mutual love is a principal mark of the Christian life. If we are to follow the example of Christ and his saints, we must act in love even when it is against our inclination.

Luke 6:20–31
'Do to others as you would have them do to you' (v.31).

This is sometimes called the 'golden rule', and honoured, in word more often than deed, as if it were the whole Christian gospel. If only it was so simple, if only we could always have pleasant thoughts about others, feel for their troubles and be considerate in every way. Few of us really want to be selfish and disagreeable, but our own concerns have a way of taking over and pushing other people's interests aside. If we had only the words of our Lord, or only the example of his love and compassion, there would be little hope of obeying this rule. But there is more: the spirit of Christ in us, which enables a response against which our nature revolts when left to itself. The saints were not all agreeable people, not always easy to live with, but the divine power that touched and called them shone through and made them lights in their generations. One of the most useless remarks to someone in trouble is, 'I know how you feel'. Nobody can fully share the pain of another, but self-regard can be purified to make us give as we would like to receive. Grace takes human nature and uses it in the service of the divine. That is what sainthood is about, and it is not just a few who are called to be saints.

The saintly man shares now to some extent the life of Heaven, with its sociability, with its capacity to fulfil our ultimate hopes and desires. This heaven is nearest at the moment of consecration in the Eucharist when Christ is in our midst, and we are not only here, but, being here are present to God in heaven. In the face of the multitude whom no man can number we stand here without some sense of obligation to become like them and their Lord. Which one of us would not be on the Lord's side? So we are by the demand for discipline, for a pruning so that we may bear better fruit. We have the assurance too that this is not to be merely our private enterprise. Called to be saints, we shall respond to our

Lord. And so, simply enough, we shall become luminous of His grace and, in spite of ourselves, vehicles for the self-manifestation of God.

John Bishop

Loving God, raise me above the selfishness which leaves too little room for the concerns of others. Following the example of the saints, and walking in the way where Jesus has led, may I hear the cry of need and respond as I would wish my cry to be heard, and as it is always heard in your mercy.

Third Sunday before Advent

God has revealed to us his gift of eternal life, but its nature is beyond our human understanding. We hold fast to that faith and do not try to impose our own theories upon it.

Luke 20:27–38
'He is God not of the dead, but of the living' (v.38).

Jesus says, 'Stop all this futile questioning and listen to me.' Pharisees with their trick questions about paying taxes, Sadducees with their legalistic denial of resurrection to eternal life. They are followed by generations of philosophers who despise the unknown and argue about the unknowable, by theologians who contend about a preposition. They are followed by church discussion groups who consider, 'What would you do if . . .' and 'What would happen if . . .' when the living Word is challenging their own lives. They are followed by all of us who profess the Christian faith but too often love the letter above the spirit, and prefer wondering about the possibility to facing the reality. It is the living God who has made us, who speaks to us and commands us here and now. We are not members of a debating society, but members of a living fellowship in the name of the risen Lord. He has given us minds to develop, reason to use, but he has also set the limits between reason and that which he has not yet chosen to reveal.

In the modern secularised world many people have abandoned a belief in a life after death in accordance with the saying 'you only live once'. Now if there is no life after death, all people who have lived and died are now completely extinct and this will apply to Jesus Christ as well as to everybody else. The fact that the resurrection has taken place and that Jesus is alive contradicts modern scepticism, but it does something more; it gives coherent expression to a doctrine of immortality which ensures that God has a purpose for us which extends far beyond the narrow limits of our life on earth. The resurrection appearances throw a flood of light on the question of a future life, for the 'Blessed hope of everlasting life' which Christians hold is bound up with the resurrection of Jesus.

Edgar Dowse

Almighty God, you have revealed yourself in the person of your Son, and it is enough. Through him you have promised the life of resurrection, and it is enough. In his words there is guidance of each day, and it is enough. Keep me firm in faith, living God, God of the living.

Second Sunday before Advent

The Bible never promises an easy life or a world free from trouble. It teaches that God has an ultimate purpose for his creation and that his people must be faithful until it is fulfilled.

Luke 21:5–19
'By your endurance you will save your souls' (v.19).

A cynic might say that prophecies of disaster are the ones most likely to be fulfilled. The onset of doom has been foretold throughout the ages, from the Old Testament prophets to both religious and secular pronouncements of the present day. The history of the world tells of natural disasters, persecutions, corporate and individual betrayals of trust, so is it likely that the future will be any different? The fear that everything is getting worse and that the world will soon come to an end has affected people in different ways. Some have retreated into solitude, some into inactive despair. Some have decided to have a good time while it is still possible and have turned away from all restraints. Some have taken their own lives, and there have been recent cases of mass killings in misguided sects. Jesus says to his followers, hold on, stand firm, get on with your lives in good times and in bad. It is not what is happening outside that matters in the end, it is how you are responding to it. If you want to fulfil the purpose for which God made you, live it out in the time and place that he has ordained for you.

After this, it was noised abroad, that Mr *Valiant-for-truth* was taken with a Summons by the same *Post* as the other; and had this for a Token that the Summons was true, *That his Pitcher was broken at the Fountain* (Ecclesiastes 12:6). When he understood it, he called for his Friends, and told them of it. Then said he, 'I am going to my Fathers, and tho' with great Difficulty I am got hither, yet now I do not repent me of all the Trouble I have been at to arrive where I am. My *Sword*, I give to him that shall Succeed me in my Pilgrimage; and my *Courage and Skill*, to him that can get it. My *Marks and Scars* I carry with me, to be a Witness for me, that I have fought his Battle, who now will be my Rewarder.' When the Day that he must go hence, was come, many accompanied him to the River-side, into which as he went, he said, '*Death, where is thy Sting?*' And as he went down deeper, he said, '*Grave, where is thy Victory?*' So he passed over, and all the Trumpets sounded for him on the other side.

John Bunyan

Give to me, dear Lord, the gift of constancy, so that I shall not fall away when times are hard. Keep me always firm in faith, certain in hope, and unswerving in love. Let me not fear the future, but guide me day by day until your will for my life is made perfect.

Christ the King

The promised Messiah came, but his kingship was not as his people had expected. He passed through suffering and death before his work of salvation was fulfilled.

Luke 23:33–43
There was also an inscription over him, 'This is the King of the Jews' (v.38).

Christ the King, crowned and robed in royal garments, pictured in paint and glass, spoken and sung with all the images of glory. Christ the King, dying on the cross naked, insulted with words of scorn and mockery. In the mystery of the Incarnation, the two Kings are one. His title was hung on his cross, the customary statement of the offence of a man condemned under Roman law to an agonizing and shameful death. This was a title of a different sort, a contradiction of what was being done there. Was Pilate adding his own mockery of a common man who had claimed kingly power? Was he stating his own concealed, suppressed feeling that the sentence had been unjust? Was he taunting those who had forced him to condemn Jesus by threatening Caesar with a rival power? Whatever his motive was, like many before and after him he uttered a truth greater than he could understand. As the Church's year draws to an end and the preparation for the Nativity returns, the last image of the cycle is stark and challenging. This is a dying man, this is our King and our God.

> Let all the world in every corner sing,
> My God and King!
> The heavens are not too high,
> His praise may thither fly;
> The earth is not too low,
> His praises there may grow.
> Let all the world in every corner sing,
> My God and King!
>
> Let all the world in every corner sing,
> My God and King!
> The Church with psalms must shout,

No door can keep them out;
But above all, the heart
Must bear the longest part.
Let all the world in every corner sing,
    My God and King!

George Herbert

Jesus, mocked and derided, scourged and pierced, rule in my heart as King. Give me your pardoning love, that I may love others; move me with sorrow for your agony, that I may share the pain of others; guide me with your royal power, that I may govern myself in faith and obedience to your will.

Festivals

Naming of Jesus

Names have their significance and their power. The name of Jesus is most sacred for Christians and a sign that he accepted every custom of human life.

Luke 2:15–21
He was called Jesus, the name given by the angel (v.21).

Not a very remarkable name in the view of any who may have been standing by and heard it spoken. They might have reflected that it meant 'Saviour' and recalled for a moment the conquests of their hero Joshua, but it was not an uncommon name at that time and in that society. Mary and Joseph knew that they were not making a private choice but obeying a divine command. Since the terrifying wonder of the Annunciation, since the trauma of Joseph's suspicions had been dispelled, they had been ready for a wonderful birth. Now their obedience brought them to fulfil the requirement of the Law, and also to take the next step that had been ordained. Even their great faith did not reveal to them the full mystery of the event. The Son of God was made obedient to the Law of God, and human obedience became a sharing with the divine. The invulnerable suffered pain, and suffering would draw God's people closer to him. The name that was given would become the Name that is above every other name, before which things in heaven and things on earth would bow (Philippians 2:9–10). The mystery of the Incarnation blends with the beginning of the calendar year: the gulf between God and the people of his fallen world has been for ever closed.

This name 'which is above every name' has all things in it, and brings all things with it. It speaks more in five letters than we can

259

do in five thousand words. It speaks more in it than we can speak today: and yet we intend today to speak of nothing else, nothing but Jesus, nothing but Jesus. Before his birth the angel announced that this child, born of Mary, would be great: 'he shall be called Son of the Highest, and the Lord God shall give him the throne of his father David.' The angel thus intimates that this was a name of the highest majesty and glory.

Mark Frank

Lord Jesus, increase in me reverence for your holy Name, so that I may rejoice in you as Saviour and serve you in imitation of your human obedience. Make me a constant witness to the New Covenant of your blood and a faithful member of the Church which you founded to be a perpetual servant of your Incarnation.

St Paul

The call of God may come early or late in life, but when it comes the change is greater than anything the human will could choose.

Matthew 19:27–30
Many who are first will be last, and the last will be first (v.30).

Boys were growing up, boys with names common in their society: Peter, John, Judas, Saul. They learned the Law by which their people had been taught to live. One of them, Saul, was a star pupil, marked out for distinction. They grew to manhood. One died disgraced, two found a new way to follow, one bitterly opposed the faith that they preached. Stopped in his tracks as he pursued the way of anger and destruction, he met his Master on the road. Later again, the opponents would meet, share the right hand of friendship. Saul the persecutor became Paul the Apostle, sharing the suffering of those whom he had wanted to destroy. A late convert became the first Christian theologian, a missionary to his own people and to the despised Gentiles outside the Law. God's power to change lives and to heal wounds has not left us. The feast of St Paul is the focus of the Week of Prayer for Christian Unity. May the Spirit who made enemies into friends draw into one those who love the Lord of love.

> The wise then, turn their eyes toward the One who is their head, but fools grope in darkness. No one who puts a lamp under a bed instead of on a lampstand will receive any light from it. People are often considered blind and useless when they make the supreme Good their aim and give themselves up to the contemplation of God, but Paul made a boast of this and proclaimed himself a fool for Christ's sake. The reason he said, 'We are fools for Christ's sake,' was that his mind was free from all earthly preoccupations. It was as though he said, 'We are blind to the life here below because our eyes are raised toward the One who is our head.'

Gregory of Nyssa

Blessed Lord, whose powerful light made Saul the persecutor into Paul the Apostle, grant that I may walk in that light and daily grow more fully in the life of the Spirit. Let me be a messenger of the gospel, confident in faith, loving in word and deed, a servant of the Kingdom.

St Joseph

Often perplexed, often disappointed and fearing the worst as we wonder what to do next, God shows the way and calms our fears by a new revelation of his purpose.

Matthew 1:18–25
An angel of the Lord appeared to him in a dream and said, 'Joseph, son of David, do not be afraid to take Mary as your wife, for the child conceived in her is from the Holy Spirit' (v.20).

Artists have liked to picture the dream of Joseph, often as an old man asleep with a little angel whispering into his ear. The reality will have been starker and less romantic. Joseph is torn with disappointment and grief at the idea that his betrothed has been unfaithful to him. Yet he cannot harm the woman he has loved, cannot make her a scorn to the neighbours, perhaps expose her to the penalty of the Jewish law. As he falls into an uneasy sleep, the truth is made known to him. God speaks to him in a dream as he had spoken to another Joseph long ago. Will things be as they were before this horror of supposed infidelity? No, for there is a greater call, a task that would be beyond unaided human strength – to be the guardian and protector of the Son of God. When we are too ready to think the worst of other people, to become distrustful even of those we should most deeply trust, we might reflect about Joseph's dream and consider whether the depth of despair may be the beginning of a new flight to God's service.

Here is the clearest of instances of the distinction between doctrine and devotion. Who, from his prerogatives and the testimony on which they come to us, had a greater claim to receive an early recognition among the faithful than he? A Saint of Scripture, the foster-father of our Lord, he was an object of the universal and absolute faith of the Christian world from the first, yet the devotion to him is comparatively of late date. When once it began, men seemed surprised that it had not been thought of before; and now, they hold him next to the Blessed Virgin in their religious affection and veneration.

J.H. Newman

Lord of love, give me a grateful heart for those whose human love I know. Forgive the mean temptations to put myself first, to find neglect and betrayal when the needs of others are greater than mine, and give me grace me to hear your call and to rise to the support that may be asked of me.

Annunciation

Our duty may be opened to us at a time and in a way that we least expect. If we are obedient to the call of God, he will do the rest.

Luke 1:26–38
Mary said, 'Here am I, the servant of the Lord; let it be with me according to your word' (v.38).

It started as an ordinary day when she did not expect anything special to happen. Angels had come to some favoured ones in the stories that she knew, but she did not expect any of them to pass through her home town. Perhaps she was thinking of her coming marriage to Joseph. When the angel came, she received the message at first with fear and incredulity – how can this thing happen to me? But the powerful words of reassurance calmed her. She accepted the divine will and began to form the human body of the divine Redeemer, the Son of God. She would nurture him, protect him, lose and find him, see him grow to manhood and a wandering life, see him at last in the agony of death when a sword pierced her own soul. But at that moment it needed her obedience, the willing co-operation of a human mind and body. She was highly favoured, but so are all those whom God calls to any task, those for whom there is no visible angel but only the still, small voice. Things happen when God wills them, not when we think it appropriate.

It is the most stupendous fact that ever has been announced on earth, God sent down the angel Gabriel – the angel's name, we are told, was Gabriel – to Mary, to make this announcement. And it was the greatest fact ever told to any mortal on this earth. And that is the fact which we this day commemorate: God sent His Son to be born of a woman, to be born into the world as all other creatures are. Now, my brethren, I will say this, that there is no miracle in the whole Gospel, of all the Gospel miracles, so great as this. Jesus Christ Himself is the very greatest miracle of the Gospel. Granting this, believing this, accepting this, then all the other miracles follow of course.

A.H. Stanton

Heavenly Father, I give you thanks for the example of the Blessed Virgin Mary, for her purity, her humility and for her obedience. As she heard the message of the angel, give me grace to hear your word and to follow your call, whether it be to great or to little work in your service.

St George

Persecution, whether slight or to the suffering of death, has been the lot of Christians through the ages. Following Jesus may be costly, but to suffer for faith is to suffer with him.

John 15:18–21
Jesus said to his disciples, 'If the world hates you, be aware that it hated me before it hated you' (v.18).

We do not know much about St George, although he has been the patron saint of England since the early Middle Ages. He was probably a Roman soldier, martyred at the beginning of the fourth century, to whom the legend of killing a dragon came to be attached. He takes his place in the calendar among the saints of the New Testament, a representative of the many Christians who have died for their faith since the time of the Apostles. When Christians meet the resistance of those outside the faith, they are following most closely in the steps of their Master. Jesus was hounded to death by those who could not bear his teaching and his accusation of their sins. Between violent death and a passing intellectual contempt there is a great distance, but even a little suffering can become holy if it is offered in love. A martyr is one who witnesses, and the witness of a quiet faith which firmly but gently is loyal to itself and does not give way, can work great changes in those who oppose it. Dragons come in many shapes and sizes, and sometimes with apparently pleasant faces.

> There can be no victory without a battle: only when victory has been secured through engaging in the battle is the victor's crown bestowed. The true helmsman is recognised in the midst of a storm. The true soldier is proven only on the battlefield. There can be no authentic testing where there is no danger. When the struggle is

real, then the testing is real. The tree which has sent down deep roots is not disturbed by gales, and the ship that has been made of decent timber may be buffeted by the waves but will not be broken. When corn is beaten on the threshing-floor, the solid and heavy grains rebuke the wind, whereas the empty chaff is carried away on the breeze.

Cyprian of Carthage

Lord Jesus, teach me not to exaggerate my little sacrifices in the cause of faith. Teach me also not to neglect the opportunities of showing love in the face of scorn and indifference. As I give thanks for the witness of St George and of all your martyrs, I offer myself to follow you in all ways, whether the path is smooth or rugged with difficulty.

St Mark

It is in the purpose of God that the good news of the Kingdom should be known to all. In his wisdom, he works through all kinds of men and women to be his chosen messengers.

Mark 13:5–13
The good news must first be proclaimed to all nations (v.10).

Mark was not one of the twelve disciples but almost certainly one who was close to Jesus during the last years of his incarnation. He was a young man who lost his nerve on a missionary journey and got into trouble with St Paul as a result. By early tradition, he eventually became the companion of St Peter at Rome, recording and interpreting his memories. The writer of the earliest Gospel, Mark was probably the first to use the word *evangelion*, 'good news', in its new Christian sense. Soon the good news was going out into the known world. In time, St Mark's words would be translated into languages and declared to nations of whom he had not heard. As we honour him, we honour all who from the beginning of the gospel to this time have worked as missionaries, evangelists, preachers, to proclaim the Good News. Their voice, as the Psalmist says, has gone out into all the world. The great work has not been left only to those whose lives have been devoted to it. In ordinary conversation, in argument and confrontation, in the quiet time of people who are close to one another, the Good News can be proclaimed.

O almighty and most merciful Father, who didst send thy beloved Son to die for the sins of the whole world, look down, we beseech thee, upon all nations who have not known his name, and in thine own good time lead them to his cross. Strengthen with the comfort of thy Spirit all who bear abroad the message of the gospel. Raise up among us a lively sympathy for their labours. Take away from those who hear all hardness of heart, and pride, and impenitence; and so move them, blessed Lord, with infinite love, that the day may speedily come when all the ends of the world shall be turned unto thee, and there shall be one flock and one shepherd; we ask all for the sake of Jesus Christ our Lord.

B.F. Westcott

Lord Jesus, make me a channel of the Good News that I myself have heard. Let not my joy in knowledge of your truth make me careless about those who do not know you, or who have heard the gospel and not regarded it. As St Mark was called to be your messenger, use me now according to your will for me in my own time and my own place.

St Philip and St James

The full glory of God, announced by the Prophets, was revealed in Jesus Christ. Even his Disciples did not understand; their ignorance should make us guard against failing fully to recognize his divinity.

John 14:1–14

Philip said to him, 'Lord, show us the Father and we will be satisfied.'
Jesus said to him, 'Have I been with you all this time, Philip, and
you still do not know me? Whoever has seen me has seen the
Father' (vv.8–9).

Philip might have been expected to be ahead of the other Disciples
in understanding. He was one of the first to be called, quickly recognized that Jesus was a very special person, and brought another man
to join the group (John 1:43–46). But he had not advanced very far,
and there is sadness in the words of Jesus: for it is always sad to find
that one whom you thought was intimate does not really know you
as you are. There are still many who respect Jesus Christ as a teacher
of morality, or as a pattern of loving human warmth, but fail to
know his reality. As the time of his Passion approaches, he reveals
his complete divinity to his chosen few. If they have not yet understood, they must be taught and prepared for the mission that will
soon be theirs. And what of James, sometimes unflatteringly described
as 'James the Lesser'? We know little of him except that he too was
numbered among the Disciples who became Apostles, messengers of
the new life in Christ. We are all slow to grasp the amazing central
truth of Christianity, that to know Jesus is to know all that we can
of the Father in this world.

You, who are beyond our understanding, have made yourself
understandable to us in Jesus Christ. You, who are the uncreated
God, have made yourself a creature for us. You, who are the
untouchable One, have made yourself touchable to us. You, who
are most high, make us capable of understanding your amazing
love and the wonderful things you have done for us. Make us able
to understand the mystery of your incarnation, the mystery of your
life, example and doctrine, the mystery of your cross and Passion,
the mystery of your resurrection and ascension.

Angela of Foligno

Jesus, Son of the Father, I acknowledge you as Lord and praise you
for the revelation of your divinity made human for the salvation of
the world. When I am slow to understand, increase my faith so that

I shall not walk with you through this world in ignorance, but may know that you lead me on to see your glory in heaven, in the company of Philip and James and all the saints.

St Matthias

We think that we have our priorities and our ways of deciding what is to be done. God sometimes works against all our expectations and brings to fruition something that we had not imagined.

John 15:9–17
'You did not choose me but I chose you' (v.16).

Drawing lots does not seem to us the best way to decide an important appointment. But it often appears in various forms in the Old Testament, as a way of determining the will of God if it is properly offered in his name. So the Holy Spirit, called upon by the eleven remaining Apostles, spoke through human action. The gap was filled, the wound in the faithful band of followers was healed and the symbolic twelve, the number of the tribes of Israel, was made up. Matthias appears for a moment and then is lost to view – not another word of him in the Acts of the Apostles – nothing else but legends and the use of his name for a lost Gospel. But if he was called and chosen, there will have been work for him to do. Numbered among the Apostles, in history and in commemoration, he is the hope of all who find a late vocation, or who come to the Christian faith after many years of doubt and unbelief. He leaves no place for regrets about the wasted years, no resentment about a promising start that brings no fame. His brief story is one that many can understand.

> Grow old along with me!
> The best is yet to be,
> The last of life, for which the first was made:
> Our times are in His hand
> Who saith, 'A whole I planned,
> Youth shows but half; trust God: see all nor be afraid!'

> Robert Browning

Lord, take the lost time, the neglected opportunities, and make them not a source of regret but a strength for better work in years to come. As Matthias was called to serve in a hidden ministry, so may my life be hidden with Christ, that his glory may shine through the quiet words and the secret deeds of love.

The Visit of Mary to Elizabeth

God's power is infinite and beyond our understanding, but he accepts simple faith from the people of his creation. If we trust in his promises, we shall indeed be his children.

Luke 1:39–49
'Blessed is she who believed that there would be a fulfilment of what was spoken to her by the Lord' (v.45).

A simple human response to a great mystery, a journey that brings yet another revelation of that mystery. Mary, astonished but faithful after the message of the angel, goes to confide in her kinswoman Elizabeth. The older woman, already expecting a child, will surely give her advice and reassurance. But before Mary has told her story, Elizabeth knows that strange events are unfolding. This is not just the young woman she has known so well – this is the mother of the Lord, the bearer of God's Messiah. She recognizes a faith greater than she has ever seen before and honours the blessing it has brought. Where do we find such faith again? Never perhaps in its fullness, but often in a simpler way if we will see it – in family and friends, the fellowship of believers, sometimes from those who hardly know that they have faith. There is more holiness around us than we know, more cause for rejoicing that God works through the weak and humble, and the divine is present in the human encounter.

St Mary is our pattern of faith, both in the reception and in the study of divine truth. She does not think it enough to accept, she dwells upon it; not enough to possess, she uses it; not enough to assent, she develops it; not enough to submit the reason, she reasons upon it; not indeed reasoning first, and believing afterwards, with

269

Zechariah, yet first believing without reasoning, next from love and reverence, reasoning after believing.

J.H. Newman

Gracious Lord, I thank you for the love of so many who are dear to me, for their sympathy in my times of trouble and their delight in my times of rejoicing. Give me grace more and more to see the divine in them, and in others who are less known to me, to feel the holiness of faithful human lives and to honour life itself, the continual miracle of your bounty.

St Barnabas

To work for peace and reconciliation is one of the most blessed Christian ministries. Suspicion and hostility can be removed by love better than by confrontation.

John 15:12–17
'I am giving you these commands so that you may love one another' (v.17).

Barnabas, like Matthias and Paul, was an Apostle who had not been one of the Twelve who accompanied Jesus in his earthly ministry. He soon became one of the most active messengers of the new faith. He sold his possessions for the common use, brought Paul to Jerusalem for a reconciling council with the suspicious members of the church there, and worked in Antioch to bring Jewish and Gentile Christians together. He is a model of the convert or the freshly appointed missionary whose zeal is directed not to scorning what has been left behind but to drawing out what is good in the old and the new. The Early Church, already torn by personal and doctrinal differences, needed a man like him to bring harmony. The Church today, still seeking unity and still composed of very fallible individuals, also needs people like him – a Barnabas in every parish or church community would not be excessive. Sometimes the leaders seem too busy to remember the Lord's great command to love one another; it is good that he still raises up women and men for the less spectacular work of reconciliation.

> Love is the source of friendship – not love of any sort whatever but that which proceeds from reason and affection simultaneously which, indeed, is pure because of reason and sweet because of affection. A foundation of friendship should be laid in the love of God, to which all things which are proposed would be referred, and these ought to be examined as to whether they conform to the foundation or are at variance with it.

Aelred of Rievaulx

Lord, give me the spirit of love, the gift of gentleness, so I may be an instrument of your peace. Teach me to put aside my own prejudices, so that I may be a guide and witness to those who are divided, and may take my part in seeking the unity of all Christians which is your will.

Birth of St John the Baptist

John the Baptist can be seen as the last of the Prophets and as the first to proclaim Christ in the flesh. God's purpose is still being worked out through the agency of those he calls to his service.

Luke 1:57–66, 80
They began motioning to his father to find out what name he wanted to give him. He asked for a writing-tablet and wrote, 'His name is John.' And all of them were amazed. Immediately his mouth was opened and his tongue freed, and he began to speak, praising God (vv.62–64).

The first son would be likely to take his father's name, or a name well established within the family. The Baptist's parents were obedient to the command which had come secretly to Zechariah in the Temple, and gave him the name which in its Hebrew form meant 'God has been gracious'. It was a deeply significant name, for God had indeed been gracious to the old couple by giving them a son, but a much more wonderful gift was on its way. Some thirty years later John would be the forerunner of the Messiah, announcing the Good News which was greater than any earlier prophet had dreamed of. The centuries of preparation were over and the divine light was coming into the world. The promises of God are not always met with the faith and obedience of Zechariah. There is a preference for the easier way, the familiar solution, doing what has always been done before. But from that day to this lives are being prepared for service that is to be revealed when the time comes. There may not always be much significance in a name, but there is no telling what is being offered as a token of obedience.

Hail, harbinger of morn:
Thou that art this day born,
And heraldest the Word with clarion voice!
Ye faithful ones, in him
Behold the dawning dim
Of the bright day, and let your hearts rejoice.

John – by that chosen name
To call him, Gabriel came
By God's appointment from his home on high:
What deeds that babe should do
To manhood when he grew,
God sent his angel forth to testify.

Bede

Heavenly Father, I thank you for the examples that you have given to guide us on our way: for the trust and obedience of Zechariah and Elizabeth, for the zeal of the Baptist, and above all for the pattern of living through your Son made human for our salvation. May the same Spirit who inspired John boldly to speak your word lead me to bear witness to you and share your love for all who are born into this world.

St Peter

God does not always choose those who have already proved their ability and leadership. He does not see with our limited vision, but knows the hidden gifts that can be drawn into his service.

Matthew 16:13–19

Simon Peter answered, 'You are the Messiah, the Son of the living God.' And Jesus answered him, 'Blessed are you. Simon son of Jonah! For flesh and blood has not revealed this to you, but my Father in heaven' (vv.16–17).

Simon Peter, next to his Master, is the person most often named in the Gospels: one of the three who were closest to Jesus; always the first to speak without thinking, often rebuked for it, the loudest voice of those who promised to follow Jesus even to death; the man who three times denied knowing him. It is a record that would make a selector for the ordained ministry feel very dubious. But the end of the story sees him as a witness to the Resurrection and one of the leaders in the new Church. Sometimes he got it right, and it was he who first openly acknowledged the divinity of Christ. Where a human employer or trainer would have given up, Jesus patiently worked on the man until he was made new. Even later he was still sometimes hesitant, changing his opinions according to his company, but basically he was the solid rock which is the meaning of his name. Glory this day to God who knew where to find, under the weakness and the folly, one of his greatest Apostles. And if we are open to him, he can make something of each one of us.

> While faith is with me, I am blest;
> It turns my darkest night to day;
> But, while I clasp it to my breast,
> I often feel it slide away.

> What shall I do if all my love,
> My hopes, my toil, are cast away?
> And if there be no God above
> To hear and bless me when I pray?

Oh, help me, God! For thou alone
Canst my distracted soul relieve.
Forsake it not, it is thine own,
Though weak, yet longing to believe.

Anne Brontë

Lord Jesus, I have often spoken foolishly and without thought, I have trusted too much in my own strength, I have denied you by my failures to live up to my faith. I praise you for the witness of St Peter, and for the reassurance that your call is greater than any human frailty. As I have known your risen presence with me, may I too serve the gospel and remain firm to the end in your service.

St Thomas

The call of God does not always come when it is most expected but his timing is perfect and he makes himself known when his servants are ready to receive him.

John 20:24–29
Thomas answered him, 'My Lord and my God!' (v.28).

It is a little hard to be labelled 'doubting Thomas' for being unable to believe that everything is really as wonderful as your friends tell you. They had been through a lot together, and had shared a loving fellowship, but the memory of the time when they had all run away and left their Master was still intolerably painful. To be told that they had not lost him, that he was there to receive them back into a greater and more wonderful union, was too much to take in. It was Thomas, the temporary outsider, the one who had not shared the first encounter with the Risen Christ, who was given the privilege of acknowledging his full divinity. Lord and God, the refutation of those who say that Jesus was only an inspired man, a human teacher, a pattern of good living. The later understanding may be better than the earlier. God sometimes withholds one gift, so that he may give another even greater. And there is something to be said for the life of the pessimist. There may be some pleasant surprises when they are least expected.

> O God, by whom the meek are guided in judgement, and light rises up in darkness for the godly; give us, in all our doubts and uncertainties, the grace to ask what thou wouldst have us to do; that the spirit of wisdom may save us from all false choices, and that in thy light we may see light and in thy straight path may not stumble; through Jesus Christ our Lord.
>
> William Bright

Jesus Christ my Lord and my God, forgive my hesitation, my doubt, my uncertainty. May I learn from the experience of blessed Thomas that the Good News is true in the times of desolation as in the times of devotion. As I have known you to be my Saviour, keep me firm in that knowledge and let me make your glory known to others who are seeking the way.

St Mary Magdalene

Great love may bring sorrow as well as happiness. In the power of the Resurrection, we know that Christ lives for ever and that in him all is made joyful.

John 20:1–2, 11–18
Mary Magdalene went and announced to the disciples, 'I have seen the Lord' (v.18).

Mary Magdalene is one of the most misunderstood and misrepresented people of the Bible. Without proper evidence she has been equated with other women in the Gospels and eventually has been seen as a reformed prostitute, the model for all 'fallen women'. All we know is that Jesus had cast out seven devils from her, which suggests some mental disturbance, addiction or besetting sin that need not have been sexual. Grateful for her deliverance, she loved much, mourned deeply and was rewarded by being the first witness to the

Risen Christ. On that morning when despair turned to delight, she knew that her Master and Friend would not be with her for much longer and yet that he would never leave her. She who had followed faithfully even to the cross and the tomb was given a new relationship, a deeper reverence. It was woman's love that received the privilege of being the first to tell the Good News, to comfort the men whose desertion had left them in despair. As we honour her, we praise God for our knowledge of Christ, our assurance that he is always with us.

Mary Magdalene standing by the grave's side, and there weeping, is brought to represent unto us the state of all mankind before this day, the day of Christ's rising again, weeping over the dead. But Christ quickened her, and her spirits that were good as dead. You thought you should have come to Christ's resurrection today, and so you do. But not to his alone, but even to Mary Magdalene's resurrection too. For in very deed a kind of resurrection it was that was wrought in her; revived as it were, and raised from a dead and drooping, to a lively and cheerful estate.

Lancelot Andrewes

Blessed Jesus, known to Mary Magdalene as human friend and as Risen Lord, give me a portion of the love which brought her to your feet on the Resurrection morning. Cast out the evil things that lurk in my life, give me the constancy that follows to the end, and grant me at last the full glory of your presence which I now know by faith.

St James

The way of Christ leads to joy and also to sorrow, for to share his love is also to share his suffering. It is not for reward in this world or the next that we must follow him.

Matthew 20:20–28

He said to them, 'You will indeed drink my cup, but to sit at my right hand and at my left, this is not mine to grant, but it is for those for whom it has been prepared by my Father' (v.23).

James figures prominently in the Gospels as one of the three disciples who accompanied Jesus at particular times, and he is usually named before his brother John who, with Peter, has a leading place after Pentecost. Encouraged by such favour, and prompted by their mother, the two brothers felt confident that they could do anything that their Master did. What he offered them was the way of suffering as well as joy, the bitter cup of the agony as well as the blessed cup of the Last Supper. Beyond the ways of this world lies mystery, the unknown that is not for mortal eyes to see. James, so sure of his privileged status, was killed by Herod in the persecutions that began with the preaching of the Apostles (Acts 12:2). Self-confidence may be a useful gift in getting on socially and professionally but it can be a disaster in the life of faith. Those who presume upon the strength they have been given and believe that their own strength is enough, soon discover their mistake. James got it right at last, and we may be thankful for the warning of his first error.

> Lord, who shall sit beside thee,
> Enthroned on either hand
> When clouds no longer hide thee,
> 'Mid all thy faithful band?
>
> Who drinks the cup of sorrow
> Thy Father gave to thee
> 'Neath shadows of the morrow
> In dark Gethsemane;
>
> Who on thy Passion thinking
> Can find in loss a gain,
> And dare to meet unshrinking
> Thy baptism of pain.

William Romanis

Blessed Lord, let my confidence be in you alone, and my faith be constant in sorrow and in joy. As James learned the way of obedience, so keep me from pride and desire for honour. Bring me to that eternal life in glory which is the pure gift of love and which none can deserve, but where even the unworthy can worship with the saints.

Transfiguration

The appearances of God in the Old Testament are surrounded by mystery and the distinctive glory of the divine presence. In Christ the glory is seen in human form, as he opens the way between humanity and God.

Luke 9:28b–36
Suddenly they saw two men, Moses and Elijah, talking to him. They appeared in glory and were talking of his departure, which he was about to accomplish at Jerusalem (vv.30–31).

There are many mountains in the Bible, often bringing that sense of wonder, of being somehow nearer to the mystery of God, on the threshold between earth and heaven. Moses on Sinai and Elijah on Carmel had known the immediacy of God in all his awe and majesty. Now they stood with the One long awaited, shared his glory, that great word which tells of the near presence of the divine, the glory that shone when the Son of God was born as man. Now, as the divinity of Christ was revealed, they spoke not of glory but of suffering, of the last journey to Jerusalem and its culmination in human death. The glory and the pain are never separated when Christians meditate on their Lord. It was the Son of God who would suffer at the hands of men – not a hero or an ordinary good man, or an innocent victim, but God Incarnate. The glory fades for a time; the disciples must return with Jesus from the mountain to the plain. Peter, typically, wants to stay, but the time has not yet come. But that which has been revealed for a moment is the undying truth, the glory of God manifested in one man, so that all his people might be glorified in him.

How truly was this a glimpse of Heaven! The holy Apostles were introduced into a new range of ideas, into a new sphere of contemplation, till St Peter, overcome by the vision, cried out, 'Lord, it is good to be here; and let us make three tabernacles'. He would fain have kept those heavenly glories always with him; everything on earth, the brightest, the fairest, the noblest, paled and dwindled away, and turned to corruption before them; its most substantial good was vanity, its richest gain was dross, its keenest joy a weariness, and its sin a loathsomeness and abomination. And such as this in its measure is the contrast, to which the awakened soul is witness, between the objects of its admiration and pursuit in its natural state, and those which burst upon it when it has entered communion with the Church Invisible.

J.H. Newman

Lord Jesus, revealed in glory as the Son of God, suffering as man for the sake of the whole world, grant me the inner vision of that which the disciples saw with mortal eyes. Give me grace to be with you in the times of devotion, to follow you in the times of daily work and to feel your presence in the times of trouble and anxiety, so that at the last I may come to you in the glory that is for all eternity.

Blessed Virgin Mary

God redeemed the world by making the divine incarnate in the human as a perfect sacrifice. He chose the Virgin Mary to be the mother through whom the purpose would be fulfilled.

Luke 1:46–55
Mary said, 'My soul magnifies the Lord, and my spirit rejoices in God my Saviour, for he has looked with favour on the lowliness of his servant. Surely, from now on all generations will call me blessed' (vv.46–48).

Mary: sometimes highly honoured and sometimes scorned, extravagantly adored and totally neglected. She is the pattern for the praise of virginity, the example of the nobility of motherhood; the most favoured of human beings, sharing the desolation of the most

279

sorrowful. It is not surprising that Christians have gone to extremes as they try to find her place in their worship. She is the supreme proof that God, who is all-powerful and needs nothing outside himself to effect his will, chooses people to co-operate with him in the great work of salvation. In her service, higher than any other in the history of the human race, there is the assurance that the simplest may be called to do great things for God, and that those who seem to be leaders may be required to do the humblest tasks. Her song of praise tells how the divine purpose reverses our expectations, changes our values. It is a day for rejoicing in the wonderful ways of God, not for trying to understand the depth of the mystery. It is through the humanity of her son who is the Son of God that we call her blessed.

> What dignity can be too great tribute to her who is as closely bound up, as intimately one, with the Eternal Word, as a mother is with a son? What outfit of sanctity, fullness and redundance of grace, what exuberance of merits have been hers, when once we admit the supposition, which the Fathers justify, that her Maker really did regard those merits, and took them into account, when He condescended 'not to abhor the Virgin's womb'?
>
> J.H. Newman

Holy God, since it is your will to draw humanity into the sublime working that makes all things new, I offer myself for whatever service you call me. May the example of the blessed Virgin Mary inspire me with humility and obedience, and fill me with rejoicing in the wonder of your love that sent the Son to be our Saviour.

St Bartholomew

The service of God does not bring status or human honour. Many of his chosen followers are unknown in this world and offer only their obedience.

Luke 22:24–30

'The kings of the Gentiles lord it over them; and those in authority over them are called benefactors. But not so with you; rather the greatest among you must become like the youngest, and the leader like one who serves' (vv.25–26).

We know little of Bartholomew. Associated with Philip, he may be the same man as Nathaniel in St John's Gospel. He has no outstanding part during the years of ministry or in the record of the missions which followed. But he is one of the Apostles, a witness of the Resurrection, honoured by the Church. The little band who walked with Jesus represents the whole company of Christian people. If some of them were chosen to be with Jesus at special times like the Transfiguration, or if they feature more often in the Gospel stories, they are not to feel more important but rather to seek the lowest place. Rank, achievement – even good works – fall away before the sacrificial love that gives new life. Christians are those who know their need, and rely on nothing but the mercy and grace of God. We need to know nothing about Bartholomew except that he was called and that he obeyed. His gift to us on his feast day is the reminder that the call of God is not to honour but to humility.

> If you would know whether a person is truly wise, learned and generous, observe whether his gifts make him humble, modest and open. If so, the gifts are genuine. If they swim on the surface, however, always seeking attention, then they are less than true. If we stand upon our dignity about places, or precedence, or how we should be addressed, besides exposing ourselves and our gifts to scrutiny and possible contradiction, we render those same gifts unattractive and contemptible. Honour is beautiful when it is freely bestowed: it becomes ugly when it is exacted or sought after.
>
> St Francis de Sales

Blessed Lord, teach me to serve without desiring any reward except to do your will. As Bartholomew was obedient and was made a witness of the Resurrection, so let me follow in humility until I come to share in that eternal life.

Holy Cross

The Christian faith rests on the suffering and death of the Son of God, accepted for the salvation of the world. The cross which was the instrument of that death is the sign of all our hope.

John 3:13–17
God did not send his Son into the world to condemn the world, but in order that the world might be saved through him (v.17).

The cross which we venerate on this day would have seemed the least likely symbol for a new religion. It was the instrument of the most shameful and prolonged death imposed in the Roman world. It is as if a group of believers today were to take a model of a gallows or an electric chair and wear it around the neck, embroider it on sacred vestments, carve it in wood and marble. But there was One who died on a cross who was like no other, and the cross became the symbol of sacrifical love, the sign of joy after suffering, life after death. The cross stands above all our Christian worship, whether the occasion be sorrowful or joyful. This day originally commemorated the supposed discovery of the True Cross in Jerusalem by St Helena in the fourth century. There is no day on which the cross of Christ does not throw its shadow of suffering and its strength of hope. Its arms reach out to embrace the world, it points up from earth to heaven. It is good to make a special memorial today, to thank God that the sins of the world were visited not with condemnation and destruction but with the most costly pardon.

> Lord, by this sweet and saving sign,
> Defend us from our foes and thine.
> Jesus, by thy wounded feet,
> Direct our path aright:
> Jesus, by thy nailed hands,
> Move ours to deeds of love:
> Jesus, by thy pierced side,
> Cleanse our desires:
> Jesus, by thy crown of thorns,
> Annihilate our pride:
> Jesus, by thy silence,

Shame our complaints:
Jesus, by thy parched lips,
Curb our cruel speech:
Jesus, by thy closing eyes,
Look on our sin no more:
Jesus, by thy broken heart,
Knit ours to thee.
And by this sweet and saying sign,
Lord, draw us to our peace and thine.

Richard Crashaw

Blessed Lord Jesus, grant that I shall glory in nothing but the Cross which brought salvation. When I worship in its presence, fill me with sorrow for your suffering and with joy in your love. May the Cross be my guide through this world and the sign that at last leads me to eternal life.

St Matthew

The things of this world are not evil in themselves, but they can become objects of worship and stunt spiritual growth. Following Christ day by day puts them in the right perspective.

Matthew 9:9–13
As Jesus was walking along, he saw a man called Matthew sitting at the tax booth; and he said to him, 'Follow me.' And he got up and followed him (v.9).

Busy about his daily work, not much troubled by what his fellow-citizens were thinking of him, it seemed like an ordinary day for Matthew – or Levi as he is also called. He was not like a modern official of the Inland Revenue, honest if not always deeply loved. He was collecting taxes or custom dues on behalf of an alien, occupying power. Such men, who bought a franchise for taxes and made the best profit they could, were numbered among sinners by the righteous Jews of the time. Had he seen Jesus before, was he already partly convicted in his conscience, or was this the first encounter? We do not know, but a simple command as the Master passed by was enough to change his life. The subsequent dinner party brought a mixed assembly of guests, some awkward questions from the Pharisees, and a saying that has since comforted many. Christianity is a religion for sinners, not for people who think they are good, but for those who know they are not good and cry out in their need. Matthew's shrewdness and skill may have sometimes been useful for the Disciples, but there was only childlike trust and the knowledge of irresistible grace when he first got up and followed Jesus.

> The feast which Levi gave to our Lord on his conversion is such a cheerful type to me of the Christian life. It is a festival of joy and gratitude for a conversion. We are sinners forgiven; *there* is a reason for perpetual praise. A feast represents a forgiven sinner's whole course; he is welcomed home, and he has brought more joy to heaven than there was before. His sorrow for sin is not a mortified, humiliated, angry disgust with himself. It is a humble, hopeful sorrow, always turning into joy. So if his very sorrows are the material of joy, his life may be represented by the feast which Levi the publican gave to Our Lord, who had forgiven and called him.
>
> Fr Congreve

Lord Jesus, I have promised to follow you, and I ask you now to keep me firm in the way that you have commanded. Whatever gifts I may bring to you, use them in your service. Whatever things may hinder my following, help me to forsake them and no longer desire them. Thank you for your call to sinners: empower me to make known to others that your door is always open, and your table always ready.

St Michael

The heavenly beings we call angels sometimes come to our world as messengers and protectors. St Michael stands as the representative of wonderful works of God beyond our understanding.

John 1:47–51

'Very truly, I tell you, you will see heaven opened and the angels of
God ascending and descending on the Son of Man' (v.51).

The archangel Michael is a heavenly being numbered with the human
saints. He is one of the few angels actually named in the Bible and
the account of his victory over the dragon (Revelation 12:7–9) has
made him appear as the protector of Christians against the forces of
evil. The existence of the angels reminds us that there are more things
in God's creation than we can know with our mortal senses. Jesus is
not a specially high angel as some heresies have suggested, but the
Son of God made human for our salvation. When he speaks to Nathaniel, he refers to the story of Jacob's dream of a ladder between
earth and heaven, with angels going up and down on it (Genesis
28:10–12). By his Incarnation, and all the life and death that culmi-
nated in his Ascension, he is the everlasting link between this world
and the world of eternity, the way by which our mortality can gain
immortality. In honouring Michael and all angels, we are praising
God who has not left us in our fallen state but has drawn us into the
totality of his creation.

> Consider a little the state of heavenly and divine creatures: touching
> Angels, which are Spirits immaterial and intellectual, the glorious
> inhabitants of those sacred palaces, where nothing but light and
> blessed immortality, no shadow of matter for tears, discontent-
> ments, griefs, and uncomfortable passions to work upon, but all
> joy, tranquillity, and peace, even for ever and ever do dwell; as in
> number and order they are huge, mighty, and royal armies, so
> likewise in perfections of obedience unto that Law, which the
> Highest, whom they adore, love, and imitate, hath imposed upon
> them, such observants they are thereof, that our Saviour himself,
> being to set down the perfect idea of that which we are to pray
> and wish for on earth, did not teach to pray or wish for more,
> than only that here it might be with us, as with them it is in heaven.

Richard Hooker

Almighty God, you have granted to mortal beings the protection of
the angels, working through the power of Jesus Christ who has

opened our way to heaven. As I commemorate this feast of St Michael and all angels, I express my trust in your loving care, in the redemption brought by the Son of God, and in the mystery of your creation which passes the ultimate limits of my understanding.

St Luke

S ome have given all in this world for the service of God. Everyone who believes in him has something to be used if it is freely offered.

Luke 10:1–9
'The harvest is plentiful but the labourers are few; therefore ask the Lord of the harvest to send out labourers into his harvest' (v.2).

Was he one of the unnamed seventy who went out on that first missionary journey? Who exactly was this man to whom we owe so much? He alone tells one of the precious Nativity stories, records some of the best-loved parables, and carries the history on into the work of the Apostles. A companion of St Paul, staying close to him until the end, Luke was a physician and by tradition also an artist. With so many talents, he was called to hard service, the perils of long journeys, the violence of the crowds, the final exile with his leader in a hostile foreign land. Women and men whose secular careers seemed full of promise have given up everything for the service of their Lord. The labourers have always been few, but they have been faithful and zealous, offering back to God the gifts that he had given them. Praise be to St Luke for his Gospel and for his example! Not many are called to the special work of God's harvesting, but many are called to give up a little for the sake of the greater. There is no human ability that cannot be used in the divine service.

I look upon all the world as my parish; thus far I mean, that, in whatever part of it I am, I judge it meet, right, and my bounden duty, to declare unto all that are willing to hear, the glad tidings of salvation. This is the work which I know God has called me to; and sure I am that His blessing attends it.

John Wesley

Bountiful Lord, giver of all talents and of all grace, take what you will of your gifts to me and use them in your service. Let my labour for the harvest of the gospel be in great or little measure according to your will. Keep me faithful through all my life, after the example of blessed Luke who never forsook his calling and stood firm to the end.

St Simon and St Jude

All are made one in Christ and no human honour can compare with being called to his service. We have no power that does not come from him.

John 15:17–27
'Remember the word that I said to you, "Servants are not greater than their master." If they persecute me, they will persecute you; if they keep my word, they will keep yours also' (v.20).

If the saints were like us, Simon and Jude might be grumbling that they have only one day between them, while most of the other Disciples have one to themselves and a few such as Peter are always being mentioned in the Gospel readings. In fact, we read of several occasions when they were all falling out over precedence and claiming power rather than humbly accepting privilege. But we may trust that things are not like that in heaven, and that they are united in the worship that they sometimes failed fully to grasp in this world. The privilege of being in the service of God is far greater than any human ranking of honour. To follow Christ is to take on, in whatever slight degree, the possibility of a share in his suffering and in his ministry. When Christians start getting proud of their achievements, when they think that they can do great things in their own strength, when they would like the privileges of faith without its responsibilities, they may do well to remember that 'Servants are not greater than their masters'.

Among our Lord's twelve Apostles there were two of the same name of Judas, both chosen to be, as it were, Angels of light; one continuing to be really such, and the other ending most miserably; both, as it were, calling out to us to remind us of our danger; the one by his warning words, the other by his sad example. St. Jude's Epistle is altogether of admonition, and stern, mournful prophecy of evil; but these evils he urges as incentives to us of more earnest care and diligence, beginning and ending with words of encouragement, if we thus live. 'But, ye beloved, building up yourselves on your most holy faith, praying in the Holy Ghost, keep yourselves in the love of God.' This is, as it were, his one lesson of advice for this day.

Isaac Williams

Loving Master, as you have called me to your service, make me worthy of my calling. May I be united with Simon and Jude and all your saints in trust and humility, seeking not my honour but yours alone, expecting no reward but that of having done your will.

All Saints

It is not influence, power or even great virtue that is the mark of sainthood. The grace of God which changes and sanctifies ordinary people is the glory of his Kingdom.

Matthew 5:1–12
'Blessed are the poor in spirit, for theirs is the kingdom of heaven' (v.3).

It is a remarkable series of blessings that begins the discourse generally called the Sermon on the Mount. They go against all the usual expectations of the world. They are conferred on the poor in spirit, those who are not spiritually proud and self-satisfied but seek humbly to follow the will of God; those who show the love of which St Paul writes that it 'does not insist on its own way' (1 Corinthians 13:5). There are blessings also for the meek, those thrust aside in a competitive society; those whose zeal for goodness is stronger than any physical appetite; even those who suffer persecution. It reads like a list of the features that have marked the lives of those whom we call saints, those who are honoured in our worship, and those who have left no memorial on earth, those whose lives may have touched our own with a sense of their goodness. The note of this day is praise and thanksgiving. At the same time, there is a solemn reminder that the ways of God are not our ways. He takes our false values and transforms them into holiness.

We crowd these all up into one day; we mingle together in the brief remembrance of an hour all the choicest deeds, the holiest lives, the noblest labours, the most precious sufferings, which the sun ever saw. Even the least of those Saints were the contemplation of many days – even the names of them, if read in our Service, would outrun many settings and risings of the light – even one passage in the life of one of them were more than sufficient for a long discourse. Martyrs and Confessors, Rulers and Doctors of the Church, devoted Ministers and Religious brethren, kings of the earth and all people, princes and judges of the earth, young men and maidens, old men and children, the first fruits of all ranks, ages, and callings, gathered each in his own time into the paradise of God.

J.H. Newman

Almighty God, in whom the saints have found their support on earth and their joy in heaven, grant to me also your sanctifying grace. Bring strength from my weakness, zeal from my slackness, love from my indifference, so that I may worthily offer my prayer and praise with all your saints.

St Andrew

S t Andrew was zealous in bringing people to Christ. God calls and empowers his faithful witnesses in every age.

Matthew 4:18–22
'Follow me, and I will make you fish for people.' Immediately they left their nets and followed him (vv.19–20).

Andrew was clearly a natural fisherman in more than one sense. The Fourth Gospel tells that he brought his brother Peter to Jesus and later was the intermediary between Philip and some enquirers. We know nothing of him outside the Gospels, though there are legends of his subsequent mission and martyrdom. Jesus calls Andrew in language that he could well understand, and more than once uses the idea of the net as an image of gathering people into the Kingdom. From Galilee to every part of the world, men and women were called to spread the Christian message. Many suffered for the Cross, even to a martyr's death. In our time, missionary work does not suggest the collecting-box and the lantern-slides of scenes in Africa or India. The need for preaching the gospel lies all around us, and every Christian is called to mission in a situation of darkness and ignorance in apparently sophisticated circles. We too can fish for people, and we may not have to cast the net very far.

> All this day, O Lord,
> let me touch as many lives as possible for thee;
> and every life I touch, do thou by thy Spirit quicken,
> whether through the word I speak,
> the prayer I breathe, or the life I live.

> Mary Sumner

Lord, as Andrew heard your call and followed you, keep me always open to know your will for me and ready to perform it. Give me gifts of wisdom, persuasion and tact, to make me more fitted for the mission that is the duty of all Christian people.

St Stephen

Faithful following of Christ has often been at great cost, even to martyrdom. Those who hate him have also hated those who love him and believe in him.

Matthew 10:17–22
'You will be hated by all because of my name. But the one who endures to the end will be saved' (v.22).

As we come to the second day of Christmas, rejoicing in celebration of our redemption, we are given a story of brutal killing. It is a jolt to our devotion, which perhaps has become too smooth after the many carol services and celebrations that have come before Christmas Day. Because a child was born, a faithful follower died violently, the first of many to suffer for his sake. Between the stable and the Cross, Jesus spoke many severe words; he came not to send peace, but a sword (Matthew 10:34). One of our favourite Christmas hymns reminds us of the Babe 'who has redeemed our loss, / From His poor manger to his bitter Cross'. The story of St Stephen does not destroy the rejoicing of the season. The message of joy at Christmas is not only that we have received great blessing but also that human suffering is drawn into the Godhead. The example of blessed Stephen is one of suffering for Christ. It is also of forgiveness and reconciliation; and that is something needed in all our lives, and in the world today as much as in the year of the first Christian martyr.

> Blood must be my body's balmer,
> No other balm will there be given,
> Whilst my soul like a white palmer
> Travels to the land of heaven,
> Over the silver mountains,
> Where spring the nectar fountains;
> And there I'll kiss The bowl of bliss,
> And drink my eternal fill
> On every milken hill.
> My soul will be a-dry before,
> But after it will ne'er thirst more.
>
> Walter Raleigh

Lord Jesus, as I praise you for your glorious Incarnation, I praise you also for the witness of blessed Stephen and all who have suffered for your sake. Their steadfast faith shames my lukewarm faith; their power to forgive shames my failures of love. Give me grace to accept your will for me, to confess my love without fearing contempt and to feel more deeply the wonder of your eternal presence.

St John

The sight of the glory of God was regarded both as a high privilege and also with deep fear. In Jesus Christ the glory is revealed for the joy of all his people.

John 21:20–25
This is the disciple who is testifying to these things and has written them, and we know that his testimony is true (v.24).

The name of John in the New Testament raises many questions among scholars. There is the disciple, the son of Zebedee, brother of James and a favoured but sometimes truculent disciple. The Fourth Gospel, declared to be written by 'the disciple whom Jesus loved', is known by the name of John. There are three letters of John, and the John who recorded the visions in the Book of Revelation. How many Johns are there, and what did they actually write? Today such questions can be laid aside as we honour the Evangelist who wrote the Fourth Gospel. Here important historical details are mingled with images of light, vision and new life that have inspired Christian devotion. Here we have the long discourse of the teaching that Jesus gave to his disciples on the eve of his Passion. Here we see the beauty of holiness, and have a glimpse of the strange borderland where narrative and mystery meet. St John is well celebrated in the Christmas season, when we are rejoicing in the Light of the world, the Word made flesh, to whom he has left his testimony.

> He first hoping and believing
> Did beside the grave adore;
> Latest he, the warfare leaving,
> Landed on the eternal shore;

And his witness we receiving
Own thee Lord for evermore.

John Keble

Lord Jesus Christ, light of the world, Son of God, guide and teacher of human friends, I thank you for the witness of St John the Evangelist. Help me so to read and meditate upon his words that I may draw closer to you day by day and be worthy to proclaim the mystery of faith.

Holy Innocents

All through history, suffering has come to the innocent as much as to those who have done wrong. Only faith in the ultimate triumph of love can support us in this terrible mystery.

Matthew 2:13–18
When Herod saw that he had been tricked by the wise men, he was infuriated, and he sent and killed all the children in and around Bethlehem who were two years old or under (v.16).

Because a child was born, a devout man would be the first of many to die for faith in him. Because a child was born, another man would write of things too deep for human imagining. Because a child was born, many children would die in their innocence. Stephen, John, Holy Innocents – the days after Christmas are filled with matter for devotion. The suffering of the helpless and innocent, most especially that of little children, is one of the hardest challenges to faith. There is no easy answer, and all the Christian can do is to hold fast to a belief that is centred on the Cross, the ultimate symbol of innocence tormented and killed. The children of Bethlehem moved quickly to their eternal blessedness, but that did not dry the tears of their mothers. A sombre note at a time of rejoicing, a salutary reminder that there is no time when someone is not suffering. The Church does well to keep the commemoration at this time. What happened soon after the wonderful birth recalls us to the paradox, the deep mystery of the Incarnation.

Festivals

Farewell dear babe, my heart's too much content,
Farewell sweet babe, the pleasure of mine eye,
Farewell fair flower, that for a space was lent,
Then ta'en away unto Eternity.
Blest babe, why should I once bewail thy fate,
Or sigh thy days so soon were terminate,
Since thou art settled in an everlasting state?
Is by His hand alone that guides nature and fate.

Anne Bradstreet

Loving Father, strengthen my faith and deepen my compassion when I hear of the suffering that I cannot alleviate, the sorrows that are beyond my reach except through prayer. At this season of rejoicing, make me more grateful for all the blessings of my life, and make me more sensitive to the needs of others, those simple and close at hand as well as those great and far away.

Acknowledgements

I am grateful to the following for permission to reproduce copyright material:

Mrs Elaine Bishop for the late Revd Dr John Bishop, *The Ultimate Mystery*, The John Bishop Charitable Trust, 1998.

The Revd Dr Edgar Dowse, *The Resurrection Appearances of Our Lord*, Avon Books, 1996.

The Revd Dr Brian Horne, 'Apprehending Joy: The Imagination', in *Building in Love*, St Mary's, Bourne Street, 1990.

The Very Revd Michael Perham, *The Sorrowful Way*, SPCK, 1998.

Index of Sources

(Poems by well-known poets which appear in many editions are cited by the title or first line. In a few instances, I have not been able to trace detailed references for extracts remembered, or personally transcribed at an earlier time.)

Abbreviations:

ANF   *The Ante-Nicene Fathers*, T & T Clark, 1996
CSEL   *Corpus Scriptorum Ecclesiasticorum Latinorum*, Vienna, 1866
NPNF – 1   *The Nicene and Post-Nicene Fathers*, Series 1, T & T Clark, 1994
NPNF – 2   *The Nicene and Post-Nicene Fathers*, Series 2, T & T Clark, 1991
PPS   Newman, *Parochial and Plain Sermons*, Rivingtons, 1882

Index of Sources

Index of Sources

Index of Sources

Index of Sources

Index of Sources

Index of Sources

Index of Principal Themes

Scripture Index

Scripture Index